FRONT-LINE CUSTOMER SERVICE

15 Keys to Customer Satisfaction

Clay Carr

WILEY

John Wiley & Sons

New York ▪ Chichester ▪ Brisbane ▪ Toronto ▪ Singapore

To Clay and Elizabeth
(My Mother and Father)
and
To the Thousands of Frontline People
Who Do Their Job Expertly
Day After (Often Weary) Day
And Thus Make Life Much Easier for All of Us
This Book Is Gratefully Dedicated

Library of Congress Cataloging in Publication Data

Carr, Clay, 1934–
    Front-line customer service / Clay Carr.
      p. cm.
    Includes bibliographical references.
    ISBN 0-471-51616-3
    1. Customer relations. I. Title. II. Title: Front-line customer service: 15 keys to customer satisfaction.
HF5415.5.C37   1990
658.8'12—dc20   89-27570
                          CIP

Printed in the United States of America

10 9 8 7 6 5 4 3

ACKNOWLEDGMENTS

I'm indebted most of all to the frontline people who've made my life more pleasant by doing their jobs extremely well. A few of them are mentioned in the book; many others aren't.

The book also mentions five exemplary firms: Cooker Restaurant Corporation, Micro Center, The Orvis Company, Ricart Motors, and WordPerfect Corporation. I'm indebted to each one for the information they furnished—and for the dedication to customer satisfaction that distinguishes them.

Regrettably, I'm also indebted to the far-too-many frontline people and their managers who believe that a perfunctory, just tolerable job is satisfactory. They've provided dozens of examples for the book. Their organizations will be grateful to know that all bad examples are anonymous or suitably disguised. Unfortunately, they'll never know either that they lost me as a customer, or why they did.

Back to the bright side. My wife, Gayle, is unfailingly understanding of a husband who has to do his writing in the evenings and on weekends. Her love and companionship make it worthwhile.

Many of the passages in this book have profited from the ideas of Dr. Anthony Putman, President of The Putman Group in Ann Arbor, Michigan. Tony's suggestions have enriched my thoughts in many ways.

John Mahaney, the editor for my first book, has been consistently helpful for this one as well. I'm indebted also to Mike Snell, my literary agent, whose consistently relevant comments helped the work develop into its present form.

We all take our libraries for granted. I'd like to break from that reflex for a moment to thank the public libraries of Columbus, Westerville, and Worthington, Ohio. I'm also grateful for the chance to use the libraries of Franklin University and The Ohio State University.

I head an organization in the Department of Defense, which is trying to shift itself to a market-driven, customer-focused operation. We can do this because the staff is dedicated, talented, and willing to experiment. Working with them is a joy, and I thank every one of them.

Finally, I have to acknowledge the stubborn resistance of the English language to any attempt at nonsexist pronouns. The best solution I've been able to find is to alternate the use of masculine and feminine pronouns. Unless they're referring to specific characters, please understand that "he" and "him," "she" and "her" are names for members of the human race. Thanks.

CLAY CARR

Westerville, Ohio
January 1990

CONTENTS

ABOUT THE BOOK

MOMENTS OF TRUTH

Moment of Truth #1

On the wall behind the counter is a sign that says, "your satisfaction guaranteed." A customer walks up to the counter.

"I need another gallon of wall paint. This one didn't cover with one coat. I think it's the pits to pay $17 for a paint that takes two coats."

"What color did you paint over?"

"A pastel yellow—not even a bright one."

The clerk doesn't reply. He blends the paint then turns the mixer on. While the mixer is going, he takes the customer's money. He rings the sale and hands the customer the change.

The customer sticks the bills in his pocket and picks up the paint. "You know this'll be the last time I'll buy any paint here for a long time."

There's a pause. As the customer turns to go, the clerk says, "Have a nice day."

Moment of Truth #2

The customer walks up to the hotel desk and hands the clerk his key. She prints out the bill, which he looks at.

"I don't think I should pay you full price for the movie last night. There was a black line across my screen I couldn't get off." He pauses, ready to ask her to cut the price in half.

"In that case, I don't think you should pay anything at all. Here, let me take it off your bill."

Two dissatisfied customers—two moments of truth. Ask yourself two questions about them:

1. How do you think the customer reacted to each moment of truth?
2. Which incident would be more apt to happen at your business?

Jan Carlzon coined the phrase "moments of truth" to describe the "golden opportunities to serve the customer." This book focuses on the most critical of the moments of truth: golden opportunities to turn unhappy buyers into loyal customers. You can't control the value of the dollar, the rate of inflation, the cost of advertising, the entry of other competitors into your markets, or hundreds of other factors important to your success. However, you *can* control every aspect of how you deal with dissatisfied customers. Nothing else your firm does—*nothing*—gives you the return on investment produced by dealing successfully with an unhappy buyer.

THE ADVANTAGE OF BEING (OR AT LEAST ACTING) SMALL

The principles in this book apply to any kind of organization—Fortune 500 corporations, "mom-and-pop" stores, hospitals, colleges, professional firms such as clinics and law practices, and even public agencies. Several extremely large firms practice these principles religiously, and a whole chapter addresses how to use the principles in public agencies. Nonetheless, if you manage a small-to-medium-sized business (or a small business unit of a large corporation), rejoice. Their smaller size permits these businesses to be flexible and truly close to their customers. Larger organizations can do this, but they require greater imagination and perseverance.

Another advantage of many small-to-medium-sized firms is that they're often privately held. There are advantages in being a public company, of course, but there are also advantages in being private. As the president of one company said, "Because we're a privately held company, we can afford to provide toll-free services to our users without having to worry about shareholders crying for more money." Though many publicly held companies focus on customers, it probably is easier to do so if you're your own master.

Small-to-medium-sized firms have one other advantage: Most of them are not caught in the obsessive numbers games played by so many giant firms. One of the recurring themes of this book is that you can't focus on the customer and on numbers at the same time. One of them has to take priority over the other. If you're busy planning to make or prevent mergers, takeovers, and leveraged buyouts, you don't have a lot of time and attention left to focus on customers. And if you don't focus on your customers, who will?

FOCUSING ON THE CUSTOMER

What Is a Customer Focus?

"Focusing on the customer," by the way, isn't just a pat phrase. Jan Carlzon turned SAS (Scandinavian Air Systems) Airlines around, spectacularly. His biggest single change there was to ensure that "the *entire* company—from the executive suite to the most remote check-in terminal—was focused on service." Micro Center, an immensely successful personal computer retailer, takes this seriously, too. There, *every* manager deals regularly with customers. And at a Cooker restaurant, the manager checks with the customers at each table to see that they're happy. (If you're not familiar with Micro Center and The Cooker Restaurant Corporation now, you will be by the end of the book. They're both exemplary at dealing with unhappy customers.)

This book shows you how to focus on customers every day. Most important, it shows you how to treat them when they're dissatisfied—not just to "handle" them, but to turn them into your best and most loyal customers. This isn't easy. It isn't something you can do in three quick steps and then go on to something else. It has to be a day-in-day-out concern. But it can be done. In fact, as this book describes, it is done by dozens of highly successful firms of all sizes. From the United Airlines flight attendant who says that her job is to do everything she has "to do to get the person to fly United again" to Flowers by Snellings in

Winchester, Virginia, "where satisfaction is *absolutely guaranteed*," successful firms and their customer-service people practice it passionately.

Despite its title, that this isn't just another book on "customer service," though you'll read those words over and over again. Customer service is something that a firm *does*; customer satisfaction is something that *happens inside the customer*. Good customer service is essential if you're going to have customer satisfaction—but so is good marketing, good sales, good manufacturing, good product service, good human resource management, and so on. In other words, customer service—as important as it is—is only one part of a successful, customer-focused firm.

I believe that focusing first on anything *inside* the firm, even if it's customer service, is a basic mistake. First, you focus *outside* the firm, on the customers. You orient your whole firm around satisfying them.

Why Focus on Satisfying Customers?

Satisfying customers is worthwhile in its own right, and emphasizing service is certainly a fad these days. But the reason I wrote this book has nothing to do with either of those. Instead, it has to do with my views of (a) what should be the basic goal for a company to pursue, and (b) what managers should do to achieve this goal.

In a nutshell, I think the goal of any well-managed firm must be *to increase its value to its market*. In the long run, the company strives to become a value leader in its market—whatever its market is or becomes. In the short run, the company makes itself more valuable to its present customers. Everything else that happens occurs between those two poles.

How do you increase your value to your market? By increasing your value to every customer, every day, at every moment of truth. And how do you do that? *You provide her increasing benefits and/or you provide the benefits at a decreasing cost.* To my mind, that's the name of the game. Any other corporate strategy is, at best, second best.

That's the background for this book. The book assumes that your overriding objective is to increase your value to your customers. While it deals with every aspect of this theme, its primary focus is on how to deal with unhappy customers. The goal in dealing with them isn't simply to correct a problem—it's to restore full value to their original transaction and *create the expectation that future purchases from you will be valuable for them.*

Clearly, the key concept here is *value.* It's discussed at length in Chapter 2, but it's really quite a simple concept:

> *Value* is the benefit that a customer gets from your product or service, minus the cost of purchasing it from you.

Benefit can include utility, excitement, peace of mind, a full stomach—whatever the customer values enough to pay for. *Cost* includes not only the money but also the time, effort, and disruption that a customer has to spend in order to get that satisfaction.

THE STRUCTURE OF THE BOOK

After a brief prologue, Chapter 1 lays the foundation for the book with a review of the basics of customer psychology. Because this book focuses on those "moments of truth" when your frontline people deal with dissatisfied customers, Chapter 1 takes a hard look at how customers respond when they're dissatisfied. Understanding these basics—and their implications for a successful business—is critical.

Chapter 2 is the basis for the rest of the book. It makes clear just what *value* is for a customer, and how important it is for you both to understand it and to produce it. As the end of this chapter says, "You sell value—or you don't sell anything at all."

The next three chapters describe your frontline people: what they have to do, how you should train them, and how you keep them doing it:

> In Chapter 3, you'll look both at what your frontline people have to do and at how you should support them as they do it. They're the heart of your organization: You succeed when they do well; you fail when they don't.

Chapter 4 describes the kind of training your frontline people need to have. Dealing with customers is a demanding job. Dealing with dissatisfied customers is doubly so. The people who do it need high-quality, effective training.

Chapter 5 describes what you need to do to keep your frontline people doing their job. This goes into the nitty-gritty of a customer-focused organization—policy, procedures, and reward systems.

Chapter 6 provides a transition from the first half of the book to the last. It deals with how you get feedback from your customers. If you haven't worked this problem, you probably think the solution is to make comment cards available and do occasional surveys. These help, but they're not sufficient. Chapter 6 explains why and suggests what else to do.

Chapter 7 gets down to the actual process of dealing with unhappy customers. The point here is that it's not enough to give the customers what they thought they were getting in the first place. If you're going to provide them value, you need to do something more. Chapter 7 describes that "more."

Chapter 8 extends the theme from Chapter 7. When a customer is dissatisfied, she expects that dealing with you will be dissatisfying in the future. By solving her problem, you start to change that expectation. However, before you can demonstrate that you can satisfy her, you need to get her back into contact with you. Chapter 8 shows you how to do so.

Chapter 9 deals with the objections you may have to a completely customer-focused organization. The point of the chapter is that any approach other than complete customer satisfaction is less competitive—and thus riskier for your firm. To illustrate this, the chapter presents snapshots of five highly successful firms (scattered from Vermont to Utah) that thrive on a fanatical focus on the customer.

Chapters 3 through 9 present all of the basic principles and skills for focusing on the customer. Chapters 10 and 11 extend the general coverage of these to specific situations:

If you manage a public agency, Chapter 10 is directed to you. It deals with the problems of implementing a strongly customer-focused approach in a public agency. Public organizations have certain problems in being customer focused that private firms don't have. These problems are explored, but the exploration ends with a familiar conclusion: A customer-focused approach is the most successful one in this type of organization, too.

Are you in a private or public organization, but you don't run it? Would you like to make your piece of the action more strongly customer focused? Chapter 11 analyzes the problems you may encounter and suggests ways of overcoming them.

The epilogue brings it all together for you. It summarizes the main points of the book. Then it takes you systematically through what you need to do to establish, improve, and/or maintain a strongly customer-focused organization. It helps you take everything you've gotten from the book and make it work *for you.*

There's a final bonus for you. The appendix takes the meat of the book *from the point of view of frontline personnel* and summarizes it for them. This is only a fraction of the information your frontline people need, but it's what they need to get started in the right direction.

PANACEAS AND TARGETS

Before moving to the prologue, I want to introduce a point that's elaborated and explained in the pages that follow. Dealing successfully with dissatisfied customers is essential to your success; if you don't do it, everything that you do well will suffer. On the other hand, skill in dealing with unhappy customers is no panacea. It won't save you if you execute poorly in other areas. In fact, if you try to paste a strong customer-satisfaction program onto an organization that can't market, sell, manufacture and service well, it will make things worse, not better.

In other words, you can only deal effectively with dissatisfied customers if you do everything else well. You may not believe that now, but you will before you finish reading this book.

The following chapters describe exactly how you can turn unhappy buyers into loyal customers—keeping always in mind that the basic objective of your business is to constantly increase its value to your customers and your market. Here's a preview of the most important ways to increase your value to your customers—the 15 keys:

1. From the point of view of your customers (potential, actual, or former), your only excuse for being in business is to satisfy them.

2. You don't sell products or service or even benefits. You sell value— or you don't sell anything at all!

3. Customers define value in their own terms. If you want to satisfy them, you have to look at your products or services through their eyes—always!

4. If anything happens after the sale to prevent the customer from getting at least the value he expected, he hasn't gotten the value he paid for—and the customer knows it! In short, you've created a dissatisfied customer.

5. Dissatisfied customers aren't problems; they're golden opportunities.

6. The really picky, demanding customers are *platinum* opportunities. Keep satisfying them, and you're in business for life.

7. If you intend to deal successfully with dissatisfied customers, focus on saving the customer, not on saving the sale.

8. Either customer satisfaction and loyalty are primary, or something else is. No compromise is possible.

9. Your frontline people won't treat your customers any better than you treat your frontline people.

10. When a customer provides honest comments, he's doing you a favor—and that's how he looks at it. Give him a reason to do you the favor.

11. To satisfy an unhappy customer, you must add extra value to make up for the value you promised but failed to provide in the first place.

12. Always treat a customer as if he will remain a customer. Never treat him as though this is the last time you'll see him.

13. Always provide a dissatisfied customer a positive reason for dealing with you again.

14. The whole process by which you create and deliver your product or service must support the creation of customer satisfaction and loyalty.

15. Every organization has customers—every one. The organizations that thrive and prosper and *feel good about what they do* are those that consistently satisfy their customers.

Here's a final thought. Captain David Quirk, USN, is a submariner. According to him, there are two kinds of ships: submarines and targets. If we transfer that logic to dry land, it comes out like this:

> There are two kinds of businesses: customer-focused businesses and targets.

This book will show you how to avoid being a target.

PROLOGUE: GOOD NEWS (AND BAD NEWS) FROM THE FRONT

Notice to our customers: We want to provide you with quality goods and unbelievable service at fair prices. Our sales personnel will do whatever is necessary to see that you're satisfied. We don't want you ever to be dissatisfied—but if you ever are, we're going to overwhelm you with what we'll do to make it right. We don't want you to be unhappy in any way; frankly, we can't afford the expense of your dissatisfaction.

Could you honestly post a notice like that for your customers? Why not? Though they don't use exactly these words, hundreds of businesses could make that statement. Unfortunately, thousands couldn't.

What a firm says about itself isn't always an accurate account of how it actually behaves. But here are what several companies, well-known and not, have said.

WORDPERFECT CORPORATION (UTAH):

We want to be the best in the computer industry, not only in the quality of our products, but also in the support of these products.

FRED GATTAS (TENNESSEE):

My greatest worry is your possible complaint that does not come to my personal attention.

L. L. Bean (Maine):

I do not consider the sale a success until the goods are worn out and the customer still satisfied.

(By the way, in my opinion, this is the single greatest description of total quality—and it comes from a flyer sent in 1912!)

Cooker Restaurant:
(From the card in the middle of every table.)

100% Satisfaction Guaranteed. Yes—that is exactly what we mean. Your satisfaction is guaranteed by all of us here at The Cooker. Our goal is high quality food, friendly and efficient service and comfortable and clean surroundings. If you find we haven't reached that goal, please let us know. If we fail to make you happy, then we don't expect you to pay. *It's that simple.* We value you as a customer and a friend, and your *happiness* is our primary goal. Thank you.

Notice the extreme customer focus that these statements reflect. You'll see as you go through the book that this emphasis on customer satisfaction characterizes some of the most successful companies in the country. If you want to be truly competitive (and profitable) in today's environment, you need the same emphasis.

That sounds good, doesn't it? But is it really practical? Do people really do it? Yes—and an example of it happened to me the day before I wrote these lines.

CASE STUDY: What Stellar Customer Service Looks Like

I had picked up my envelope at the National Car Rental desk at Washington, DC's National airport and went outside into the heat and humidity. I was late for an appointment, and the shuttle van didn't get there as quickly as I thought it should. I peered down the street to make sure it wasn't coming then dashed back into the terminal and up to the National desk.

"Is someone really going to pick me up?" I asked—balanced precariously between civility and humidity-induced rage.

"Haven't they picked you up yet?" the woman asked. She reached for the phone, and I dashed back out the door.

A few moments after I got outside, the van pulled up, and I climbed on board. We made a necessary U turn and were headed for the lot when the woman from the counter came running up and stopped the van. When the driver opened the door, she looked inside, saw that I had made it, smiled at me, and waved the van on. Then she darted back inside.

I found out later from the manager that her name was Saba Zegeye, and I wrote to the company about her exceptional focus on customer satisfaction.

Just to make it clear that I intend for this to be a practical book, let me ask you a question: How many Saba Zegeyes do you have working for you? How many do your competitors have? If you don't know the answer to that question, you're in trouble. If you don't think the question is important, you're in *serious* trouble.

WORDS ARE CHEAP

All of the preceding quotations are strong messages about customer satisfaction. I picked them because WordPerfect, Fred Gattas, L. L. Bean, and The Cooker *mean* what they say. Just saying it, though, isn't enough. Your customer satisfaction policies won't mean anything until your frontline people are Saba Zegeyes—willing to do their equivalent of running through the Washington, DC humidity to make sure a customer got on the company shuttle bus.

Just saying the words, even if they're exactly the right words, won't make this happen. Two examples show just how true this is.

CASE STUDY: Making Your Motto Mean Something

Bad Example #1

As I travel over the country, I notice policies, mottos, statements of service. The service statement of one particular chain struck me on a trip over a year ago, and I made a mental note of it. When time came to include it in this book, I wanted to be sure I remembered it correctly. So I called the store where I had seen it. This is how the conversation went:

Phone rings. "Hello."

"Hi. I'm doing a book on customer service and I was particularly impressed by your company's statement of its customer orientation. I wonder if you could tell me the first sentence so I could copy it down."

"Oh, gee—I'm not sure what you mean. I just work here. Let me transfer you to the manager."

(Pause) "Hello, may I help you?"

"Yes. I really like your statement of your customer orientation. Would you tell me the first line of it so I could get it exactly, for a book I'm working on."

"Huh? Oh, yes—just a minute. . . . Here it is." Reads the statement to me.

Would you guess that the company's statement of its policy—as good as it is—is a living document? Or do its customer-service personnel see it as just another piece of paper from the front office?

Bad Example #2

I had chosen the current motto of a regional firm that operates over much of the Midwest and South. In fact, it was even included in the first draft of the preceding list. The motto is posted in several places in each of the company's stores. It was a little long, so I wanted to get a copy of it to save myself from having to write it down. I walked over to the young woman at the customer service counter, and this is what happened:

"I'm writing a book on how to satisfy customers and I'd like to use your current slogan. Could I get a copy of it from you?"

"Gee, I don't know if we have one. Let me look." She walks back into the office and looks through several drawers, then returns. "I'm sorry, I can't find one. Let me see if Bob can help you." (Everything is fine to this point; she gets good marks.)

She pages Bob, the manager on duty. He comes over. I introduce myself and repeat my story.

"No, we don't have any other copies."

"Well, I'd really like to include it in the book."

"We don't have one."

By now, I'm thoroughly exasperated. "Look, isn't it worth a little trouble to get a positive mention for your firm in a book on customer satisfaction?"

"I can't help you. You'll have to take that up with our general office."

If this had been your firm, and your manager on duty had said that, how happy would you have been with him? (It's worth noting, by the way, that the customer-service person did her job. It was the manager who blew it. I find that all too often this is how it happens in the real world. See Chapter 3 for more on this.)

Neither of these incidents was unique—though both were striking. Having a policy is a necessary step, but only a preliminary one. Seeing that the policy is implemented, that it's lived by your frontline people every day—this is what the game is all about. This is why I've written the most practical book I know how to write. I want to make it as easy as possible for you to develop and execute the powerful customer focus that will make you and your business successful.

SOME SITUATIONS TO THINK ABOUT

Because this is a practical book, it might help to begin by describing a few situations involving dissatisfied customers. Read each one, and mentally decide what you'd do to satisfy each customer. Chapter 8 looks at the situations again, to help you evaluate your decision.

THE UNSUITED TRAVELER

You're the manager of Reliable Cleaners and Laundry in Bentonville, an upscale suburb. You took the day off yesterday. When you get into work today at 6:30 A.M., this is the note your assistant manager left you at the end of the day yesterday:

> Mr. Wentz left his suit for same-day cleaning this morning. Said he needed it for a trip he's leaving on tomorrow. Don't know what happened, but we didn't get it cleaned. He was awfully steamed when he came to pick it up at closing. Betty cleaned it last thing before she went home. His phone number is 555-4438. Hope you can do something.

You're the only person in the store; the rest of your staff won't arrive until 7:00 A.M., when you open for the day. You know Mr. Wentz. He's a good customer. He will probably leave for his plane within an hour. What are you going to do?

THE UNSUITABLE ROOM

Suppose that you're the manager of the Hospitality Hotel in a midsized city. The corporate office has sent you a letter the hotel president received from Mark Esterline. He and his wife just took advantage of your weekend special—and this is how Mr. Esterline described the weekend in his letter:

> First, your people showed us to a room that wasn't made up. When we

got that corrected and into a new room, the TV didn't work. We moved into yet another room. This time, the TV did work, but the handle kept falling off the shower.

We had room service for supper. It took almost 45 minutes for the food to get to us, and then we were billed for the wrong meals. The food was cool, but pretty good. When I went to get ice for after-dinner drinks, the ice machine on our floor was empty.

The next morning, I had to do some work, which I left spread out on the desk in the room. So it wouldn't be disturbed, I hung the "Do Not Disturb" sign on the door when we went for breakfast. You guessed it—when we got back, the sign was hanging neatly inside the door and our room had been made up. I had to reorganize all my paperwork.

To top everything off, your valet parking brought us the wrong car when we got ready to leave.

Scribbled across the bottom, in the president's hand, is, "Take care of this immediately and let me know what you did."

What do you do?

THE MANGLED COMPUTER

You're the president of a small company that sells personal computers by mail. You've told your customer-service people to let you know any time a customer has a serious problem. Andy, who handles most of your complaints, has just brought you this note:

Customer called right at 9:00 when we opened. Received her computer yesterday, three days late. Hard drive doesn't work. Two keys on keyboard don't work. Monitor works, but the case is cracked. B drive won't format correctly. I told her we'll fix or replace everything. Anything else you want me to do?

Is there anything else?

THE AIR UNCONDITIONER

You're the manager of the largest heating and air conditioning firm in the city. You're walking by Marguerite, your customer-service representative, who's on the phone to a customer. This is what you hear:

"Oh, yes, Mr. Olsen. Robert fixed your air conditioner on Tuesday. . . ."

"It's still not cooling? That's terrible. We're awfully busy today, but I'll get someone to take care of you as soon as I can and get back to you. Will you be at your work number? . . ."

As Marguerite hangs up, she notices you standing there. "Did you hear that?" You nod. "Susan called in sick today and I've had to split her calls between Robert and Enrique. Everybody has an overload. What do you want me to do about Mr. Olsen?"

What do you want her to do about Mr. Olsen?

Keep these four situations in mind. You'll return to them in Chapter 8.

Just in case you're not convinced that focusing on customer satisfaction is an absolute necessity in the 1990s, here's one last thought. While I was finishing this book, I bought a new car. As the salesman and I waited for the paperwork, he talked about his profession. One of the statements he made was this:

> Five years ago, we twisted their arm, sold them a car, and kicked them out the door. Today, the sales manager makes us kiss the customers' feet.

I probably wouldn't have put it just that way—but that's today's competitive environment. The rest of this book is your training manual for the competition.

1 UNDERSTAND CUSTOMER PSYCHOLOGY

"Murray, what do you say we stay at the Imperial Hotel tonight? It's the closest one to the Fidelity Building."

"You can stay there if you want, but not me! I stayed there last fall when I was in town, and that's the last time they'll ever see me."

"You must have had some experience! What did they say when you told them?"

"Tell them? Hell, I didn't tell them anything! It's not my job to count their mistakes and report to them. If they can't do it right, there's a half-dozen other hotels within two blocks that can."

"I don't blame you. Want to try the Sherman . . . ?"

When people act as citizens, they vote with their ballots.
When people act as customers, they vote with their feet.

THE UNHAPPY TRUTH

This is a book about dealing with dissatisfied customers—and these are the brutal facts about how customers behave when they're unhappy:

Ninety-six percent of all dissatisfied customers won't ever complain to you about the way you treated them.

Ninety percent of them won't be back to buy from you.

Each of the ninety percent will tell at least 9 other people how dissatisfied they are with you.

19

Thirteen percent will tell 20 or more other people how poorly you treated them.

You've probably seen these figures, or ones like them, before. Please take a moment, though, and think about them. Think about what they mean to your business and what it will take to deal successfully with your dissatisfied customers.

First of all, unless you take positive steps, you won't even know when 19 out of 20 of them are dissatisfied. You'll notice that you don't have as many customers, but you won't know that:

- Marybeth Jonas was insulted when one of your customer-service people questioned her honesty, so she started shopping at your competitors up the street.

- Sam Donnelly tried to call in about a problem he was having and got "lost on hold" two times. The third time, your customer-service person interrupted the conversation to handle another call. Sam got disgusted and started ordering what he used to get from you from a mail-order house.

- María Estebán wanted to buy something, but your counter person was in the middle of an interesting conversation with an assistant manager and didn't notice her. So she left—and she hasn't been back.

How many times has this happened in your business? Unless you're already practicing some of the tactics in this book, you don't really know. To make an educated guess, take the complaints you know about and multiply them by 20. Does that start to sound scary?

That's just the tip of the iceberg. The customers you lost because they were dissatisfied with your product or service are just the beginning. Here's what it means if last month you had just 10 unhappy customers:

- One of them (maybe) told you that he or she was dissatisfied.

- Nine others didn't say anything to you, but most of them became *ex-*customers. Eight of the nine, being bashful, only told nine friends apiece how bad you were. The ninth may have told as many as 20 people.

- In other words, 1 person told you she was dissatisfied, 9 other people were just as unhappy—but as many as 101 people now have a poor opinion of your products and/or services.

This is the first fact of life about customers: Most of them feel no obligation at all to tell you when you make them unhappy. Not only do you have to deal with the preferences and idiosyncracies of each different customer, but you can't count on a customer to tell you when you've failed.

(These averages are just that—averages. Different customers behave in different ways. A few factors can help you predict whether a customer will tell you when she's dissatisfied. For instance, a customer is more apt to complain if she knows she will have to deal with you again (because you have a practical monopoly or because her firm requires her to deal with you). She's also more apt to complain if she has the time to complain—which means you won't often hear from the really busy people.)

WHY, WHY, WHY?

Why are your customers treating you this way? Why won't they be the good, honest, responsible people you know they are and just let you know when they're dissatisfied? If you could listen to their internal thoughts, these are some of the answers you'd get.

WHY I WON'T TELL YOU I'M DISSATISFIED

- You don't care about me.
- You make it hard for me to tell you I'm dissatisfied (which proves you don't care about me!).
- Why should I do your work (correcting your mistakes) for you?
- You don't even deserve my comments!

Sounds harsh, doesn't it? Here's a closer look at each statement and what's behind each one.

You Don't Care

Most people make the day-in-day-out assumption that other people treat them as they do because they intend to treat them that way. This is even more true for the people and companies that do business with you. If a customer is dissatisfied with your product or service, his first reaction is that you just don't care about satisfying him.

In fact, you may care passionately. Your staff may care passionately. But unless something happens to communicate that, directly and clearly, to customers, they won't believe it. They'll simply believe that what they got is what you intended for them to get:

> The line was busy the first three times Armand Westin called in to report a problem with the new deluxe model you sold him. On the fourth call, the phone rang three times, then a janitor answered it. This was good, because she knew that you didn't want it to ring more than three times. She didn't know what a deluxe model was, though, and she put the phone down while she went to look for someone who did. Another worker saw the phone lying there and thought someone had been careless. Without checking to see if there was anyone on the line, she hung it back up. By then, Armand was fed up and decided to call the manufacturer directly. No one intended to be unconcerned about him—but try to tell him that!

This illustrates one of the major themes in this book:

> You must find ways, constantly and effectively, to communicate to your customers that you intend for them to be satisfied. You must persuade them that you *want* to correct any dissatisfaction.

(Words by themselves won't convince them. Think again, though, about the slogan in Fred Gattas's stores: "My greatest worry is your possible complaint that does not come to my personal attention." You know how your customers will act when they think you don't care about them. How differently would they act if they really believed you felt the way Fred Gattas says he does?)

If you stop and think for a moment, can't you remember a few (all too few!) instances where someone communicated to you that he or she really *cared* about your satisfaction as a customer? Can you remember how you felt? That's how you want your customers to feel.

Remember, your customers believe that the way your firm treats them is the way you intend to treat them. They react accordingly.

You Make It Hard

Often, firms take some very specific steps to reinforce the idea that they don't care about their customers' satisfaction. Here are a few:

- They don't make it clear where or how to file a complaint.

    If it's the corner store, you file it with the clerk—unless the clerk is the problem. Then what? ("Excuse me, but I need your boss's phone number so I can tell her you're atrociously rude.")

    Or suppose it's a hotel bed that wobbles because a caster is missing; do you call Housekeeping, Maintenance, the Front Desk or the Hotel Operator? Is there any indication that anyone cares? If you call one of them, and it's the wrong one, what happens? ("I'm sorry, we don't do that. You'll have to call Security.")

- They don't make it easy to file a complaint or to get satisfaction.

    The complaint forms are in the corner of the Customer Service desk, they take five minutes to fill out, and they don't provide you a pencil.

    The Customer Service Representative clearly thinks you're out of your gourd to complain about *that*. ("Madam, in five years, we've *never* had a complaint about this product!")

    You fill out the form and take it to the clerk, who smiles and tells you someone will get back with you immediately. Two months go by, and you still haven't heard.

Now, you'd never do anything like this, would you? Perhaps not, but consider this: In one study, over two thirds of the executives thought they did a good job handling complaints—but only 50 percent of the customers felt that way. For every 100 customers, that's 17 you thought you satisfied but didn't. (You might want to review the statistics at the start of this chapter to help you put into perspective the impact of those 17 dissatisfied customers.) The following case studies show the difference between empty, hollow words and sincere communication that you care about customers.

CASE STUDY: Showing Customers You Care

How to Go Through the Motions:

On the poster was a picture of the general manager, but none of the staff of the store. Under the picture, it said,

> At Hot Diggity Food Stores, Quality Customer Service is taken seriously. My staff and I are committed to meeting this goal.
> If you are not satisfied with the service you receive, please tell me about it.

(Then, in much smaller print:)

> Suggestions, comments, thoughts: Tell me, I truly want to know how to serve you better.

(This was followed by a phone number—a local number, not an 800 number.)

Now, picture yourself as a customer who's just had an argument with the store manager. Do you ask to use her phone? Or do you go outside and pay 25 cents for the privilege of contacting the manager? What if it's after the company's business hours?

What do you do? In all probability, you just walk away, complain to your friends, and find another convenience store.

Did the poster help? No. In fact, it may have made you even angrier—because it stated all the nice words but did nothing to make it easier for you to get your complaint resolved.

(**Note:** Unless it specifically says otherwise, all case studies are factually accurate. When the case is a positive example, real names are generally used. When the case is negative, as here, all names have been changed to protect the guilty.)

How to Do It Right, # 1

Acme TV is a major discount merchandiser that's concerned about customer service. While the company mentions service and satisfaction, its primary competitive weapon is price.

Tom Edelman went into one of Acme's stores to buy a VCR (videocassette recorder). He found one he wanted and was idly looking at a combination TV/computer monitor. He remarked that he was interested in it but wasn't sure it would work.

"We have a three-day return policy. You can bring it back if you don't like it."

Tom was about to open his mouth to say that he didn't really want to go through the hassle of returning it, but the salesman continued, "I'm the department manager, and if you don't like it, I *want* you to bring it back.

The difference between "if you don't like it, you can bring it back" and "if you don't like it I *want* you to bring it back" is the difference between *saying* that you care about customers and *showing* that you do.

How to Do It Right, # 2

When I started this book, I bought a new, faster printer. For reasons I didn't understand, my WordPerfect word processor wasn't working as it should with it. So I called WordPerfect customer service, at their 800 number.

The young lady I talked to was very helpful and took almost 15 minutes to help me with my problem. But that's just the start of her help.

We talked for several minutes, until she fully understood my problem. Then she said "I think their [the printer company's] customer service is still open." I expected her to be helpful and assist me in finding their customer service number.

But she didn't. She said "If you don't mind holding for a minute, I'll call them and see if I can find out some more from them."

Wow!

Even that wasn't all. She solved my basic problem, and I was getting ready to thank her and hang up. Then she said "For my own peace of mind, I want to send you our latest printer driver for your printer. Can I have your name and address?"

This wasn't an exception. I've seen some of the letters the WordPerfect Corporation gets. What would happen in your company if a customer called and took 15 minutes of your customer-service rep's time—to solve a problem the customer had created? WordPerfect's customer service person would probably have told him that she was delighted she could help.

That may help explain why WordPerfect continues to be the number one high-end word processor for personal computers.

Why Should I Do Your Work?

Surprising as it sounds, your customers don't feel a burning urge to help you improve your service to them. They buy, you sell. They do the comparing, the paying, the using. You do the providing. Just as it's their responsibility to see that their checks don't bounce, it's your responsibility to provide satisfactory products and services the first time.

The fact that you have a form they can fill out, or even that you ask them for comments, doesn't change this. First, you fail to satisfy them— then you add insult to injury by asking them to tell you how and why you failed. From their point of view, as Robbie the Robot used to say, "that does not compute."

Chapter 6 deals with the difficulty of getting useful feedback and with some of the ways you can improve the situation. For now, just remember that giving you feedback is not at the top of most of your customers' to-do lists for today.

You Don't Deserve My Comments!

This one is the real killer. "If you treated me badly," the customer thinks, "you don't deserve any comments from me. In fact, you probably don't deserve to stay in business. Go ahead, do a lousy job, and go out of business—it serves you right!"

Of course, this begins with the idea that you don't care about how customers are treated. If you can persuade your customers that you do care, and then you make it easy for them to complain, most of them won't react this way. Unless you do accomplish this, though, you may get this hostile a reaction.

Why? Why would anyone have such a terribly mistaken idea about someone as conscientious and sincere as you? There are as many answers to this as there are people, but here are two of them you may not have thought of: satisfaction and dissatisfaction.

SATISFACTION AND DISSATISFACTION

You're not just selling your customers products—you're selling them *satisfaction*. When they're *dis*satisfied, they're not just generally un-happy. They're reacting to a situation where you deprived them of the specific satisfaction your product or service was supposed to give them.

That might not be a rational reaction, but it is an emotional one—and a real one.

Why is the reaction so strong?

- The individual may have a specific problem he expected your product or service to cure. The problem may have been acne, crabgrass, an unreliable car, the threat of a civil suit, or hunger. He came to you because what you offered seemed to be the solution. If it wasn't the solution, he's wasted time and money—and he's still got the problem!

- Often, just the wasted time and effort are enough to thoroughly aggravate the individual. Most of us these days feel rushed and harried, and it doesn't do much for our peace of mind if we just wasted precious minutes or hours on something that didn't work. (This is another reason not to bother giving you comments on the poor product or service: You've already wasted enough of my time!)

- All too many products and services are *oversold* to consumers: They promise emotional satisfactions far beyond what they can deliver. Deodorant soaps and shampoos promise popularity; automobiles and clothes promise social acceptability; diet and exercise books promise attractiveness. In fact, in any "hot" market, many of the offerings will be oversold as a competitive strategy. If you happen to sell these offerings, your customers will begin with expectations that can't be satisfied. When the customer's goal is popularity, acceptability, attractiveness, and so on—it doesn't take much to produce fervent dissatisfaction. Guess who'll be the primary target of the fervor?

- Dissatisfaction is also influenced by the price of the product or service. The more expensive the product or service, the higher the dissatisfaction if it doesn't deliver. This is hardly surprising. Any of us will get more worked up over a defective washing machine or security system than we will over a stale loaf of bread or a pair of shoes that's not comfortable. (Remember, though, this refers to the strength of the emotional reaction—not whether the customer will return. A stale loaf of bread or an uncomfortable pair of shoes can easily cost you a customer; he just may not be quite as upset with you.)

- The demographics of your customers are also important. People with high incomes, good educations, and high-status jobs feel more in control of their lives. They expect to take care of themselves. If you can't satisfy them, you may lose them as customers, but they won't spend a lot of emotion on you. If they're further down the income/education/job pyramid, though, they don't feel as much in control. They expect you to take care of them. When you don't, when your product fails, your service isn't adequate, or your complaint procedure is demeaning—they'll probably have a strong emotional reaction. From their point of view, you've betrayed their trust.

- People aren't always conscious of what's important to them. This is especially true of oversold products, by design. It's also true of products and services in general. You may infuriate a customer because what you provided didn't meet a need that he never mentioned and that you never thought of. (More on that in Chapter 2.)

WHY BOTHER?

If dissatisfied customers are noncommunicative, emotional, uncooperative, ready to walk away from you—why bother? Why spend time, effort, and money trying to deal with them? Why not just keep looking for new customers to replace the ones you lose? If there weren't any good answers to that question, there'd be no need for this book. There are good answers, and these are the principal ones:

WHY SWEAT DISSATISFIED CUSTOMERS?

- New customers are very expensive.
- Current customers are very valuable.
- Satisfied customers are very forgiving.
- Customers respond more strongly to the way you treat them than to anything else.

New Customers Cost—Bundles!

First of all, new customers are expensive. The best current estimates are that it costs *five* to *six* times as much to get a new customer as it does to keep one you already have.

That multiplier of 500 to 600% ought to provide a powerful incentive. You can afford to spend a lot of care and concern finding and dealing effectively with unhappy customers when the alternative is that expensive. As you go through this book and read about what it takes to deal with dissatisfied customers, you may react with "That's too expensive!" No matter how expensive it sounds, though, keep this alternative cost—500 to 600%—in mind. (Costs are dealt with again in Chapter 9.)

The Real Value of the Customers You Have

It costs more to get a new customer than to keep an existing one—but just what is one of your customers worth to you? These questions might help you answer that question:

- If you sell cars, how many will a satisfied customer in her twenties probably purchase from you over the next 30 years?

- If you're a dentist, how many times will a satisfied patient and her family be back to see you in the next two or three decades?

- If you sell custom software, how many times will just one product bought by just one customer need updating and upgrading over the next 10 years?

- How many pairs of shoes will you sell to a young executive before he retires?

In other words, the value of a customer is seldom one, or even a few, purchases. Loyal customers come back for months, years, decades. Some firms who understand and practice the principles in this book are selling to customers in the third and fourth generations of some families.

When it seems that something the book suggests for dealing with a dissatisfied customer is awfully expensive, stop and calculate the value of that customer over time. Then make your decision about what's too expensive.

Repentance and Forgiveness

As valuable as a present customer may be, why spend money if he's dissatisfied? The answer to that one, happily, is simple. When your customer sees you responding to his dissatisfaction with concern and skill, you keep him as a customer. Here are some specifics:

- For every 10 dissatisfied customers whose complaint you resolve satisfactorily, 7 will do business with you again. (If you use the ideas in this book, you raise that proportion significantly.)
- For every 10 dissatisfied customers whose complaint you discover and resolve *on the spot*, at least 9 will continue to do business with you.
- Just as important, if you satisfactorily resolve the complaint, the customer will tell 5 people about how you handled it. That's the kind of word-of-mouth advertising you want!

Now you begin to see the tremendous payoff you get when you find and resolve customer complaints quickly. You can figure how great the payoff is for yourself, but here's a start. Every time you identify a dissatisfied customer and resolve that complaint, you:

- Save a customer whose future purchases will average about 10 times the amount of the purchase that dissatisfied her (though this varies widely from one type of business to another).
- Save 5–6 times the cost of keeping the customer (which you would have spent in getting a new customer).
- Prevent somewhere between 9 and 20 people from hearing how poor your product and/or service are.
- Get free word-of-mouth advertising to 5 other people about how effectively you resolved the complaint.

I defy you to find another expenditure outside the design/R&D (research and development) area that will yield this level of return. But that's not the end of it. Another set of statistics spotlights even more clearly how great your opportunity is. Those statistics relate to why customers stop buying a firm's products or services.

Treating Your Customers Well

In a study several years ago, researchers looked at the reasons why customers stopped dealing with a firm. If you're an "average" firm, this is why customers will leave you:

- Less than 10 percent of them will leave for reasons unrelated to your business (such as moving out of the area, going out of business themselves).

- Less than 10 percent will leave because they prefer the product or service of one of your competitors.

- Less than 15 percent will leave because they're dissatisfied with the specific product or service that you offer.

- More than 65 percent will leave because they don't like the way they were treated by the owner, the manager, or some employee of the company.

People become dissatisfied for many reasons—but the main reason they will leave you is the one that you have the most control over: the quality of treatment they get from your business. Not only is it critical to deal well with dissatisfied customers, but it's also a high-payoff activity. That fact suggests the first of the critical keys to customer satisfaction in this book:

Key #1: From the point of view of your customers (potential, actual, or former), your only excuse for being in business is to satisfy them.

This doesn't say that sound marketing, product design and delivery, sales, cost control, and a host of other facets of running your business aren't important. Of course they are. But they only pay off if their consistent result is customer satisfaction. This book returns to that key again and again.

CHECK POINTS

Most of the following chapters end with a short section labeled "Check Points." It has a simple purpose—to help you apply the ideas and skills in the chapter to your own business. You may find it worth your time to look at each statement and ask yourself carefully how true it is of you and your firm.

1. When I make decisions about how to deal with dissatisfied customers, I keep in mind the large number of actual or potential customers just one dissatisfied customer can influence.

2. I care about my customers and their satisfaction—which is why I make it easy for them to tell me they're dissatisfied.

3. I understand the basic reasons why customers get dissatisfied with my products or services.

4. I give priority to keeping the customers I have before trying to get new customers.

5. I understand my customers' willingness to forgive me when I act promptly to resolve their dissatisfactions—so I do just that.

6. I and my frontline people understand that the way we treat our customers is the single most important reason why they will either remain loyal customers or leave us for a competitor.

7. I and my frontline people understand that from my customers' point of view, my firm exists only to satisfy them.

2 SELL VALUE

Salespeople sell benefits,
manufacturers produce quality,
but firms provide value—
or else.

A QUICK LOOK AT THE OBVIOUS

You're in business (or you'd like to be), and you'd like to stay in business. You have (or want) customers, and you want to keep them. You've identified your market, developed a good product or service, organized your sales force or distribution channels, and you're ready to go. You're reading this because you want to cover all of the bases; you want to deal effectively with your customers, especially that small fraction of them who find your product or service less than perfect.

Before you start, though, let me ask a question:

> Do you know exactly what you're providing to your
> customers?

How silly—of course you know what you're providing! Indulge me for a moment, though. Assume that it's worth spending some time on this question.

Actually, it's an important question—perhaps the most important one for your business's success. Not understanding just what you're providing your customers is one of the sure ways for your company to fall on its marketing sword. You may already understand what you're providing to your customers (I genuinely hope that you do). To make sure that you do, this chapter takes a brief look at the fundamental economics of buying and selling. It won't take long, and it's the basis for everything else in the book.

ROSALIND JONES BUYS A LOAF OF BREAD

On her way home from work, Rosalind Jones stops off at the Handi Dandi convenience store. She picks up a loaf of bread, pays Laetitia Willers (the store manager) for it, and drives off. Every day, in a variety of ways, this basic transaction is repeated millions of times.

But just what is the basic transaction? Superficially, Rosalind exchanged her $1.25 for a loaf of Healthgrain bread. This simple action, though, is just the tip of the iceberg. Rosalind decided to do what she did instead of

- Buying a different brand of bread, or
- Buying a larger or smaller loaf, or
- Buying rolls or biscuits or bagels, or
- Buying prepared sandwiches, or
- Shopping at a different store, or
- Picking up fast food, or
- Buying a microwaveable dinner, or
- Going straight home, or
- So on . . .

Rosalind wanted something and made a choice to get it. So did Laetitia. She (or higher management) chose to

- Carry that brand of bread, and
- Price it at that price, and
- Maintain that level of stock, and
- Remain open at hours Rosalind could shop, and
- Be effective enough to stay in business, and
- So on . . .

That simple transaction, buying a loaf of bread, represented the intersection of many, many choices that Rosalind and Laetitia individually made. It was a very specific kind of intersection: The purchase occurred because Rosalind wanted the bread more than she did that $1.25 and Handi Dandi wanted the $1.25 more than it did the loaf of Healthgrain bread. The exchange provided each party with more value than each had before the transaction.

Stop for a moment and make sure you grasped that last sentence. Each party to the transaction left with greater value than each put into it. That's why sales and purchases occur: Each participant walks away with *more* than he or she had before it occurred. Rosalind Jones walked away from the store with a loaf of bread that gave her more value than the money she paid for it. And Laetitia and the Handi Dandi chain valued the $1.25 more than it did the loaf of bread it exchanged for it.

This is basic economic theory (though the economists tend to call what people get from transactions "utility"). It's not just for college classes, though. The exchange of value is what customers do every time they purchase something—and they know it. They may not put it in just these words, but they know it. Getting value for their transactions is what the game is all about for them.

Of course, you have to get value from your transactions as a seller if you're going to stay in business. (The technical economic term for not getting sufficient value from your transactions is *going broke.*) This book, and particularly Chapter 9, shows that the best way to get value for your firm is to give value to customers. The present chapter, though, is concerned with *what* your customers value. If you want to have successful customers, this is the critical key you must remember:

Key #2: You don't sell products or service or even benefits. You sell value—or you don't sell anything at all!

BENEFIT: THE FIRST COMPONENT OF VALUE

You sell value—but just what does that mean? *Value* isn't the same thing as *benefit*, but benefit is part of value. So, every aspiring salesperson is taught to "sell the benefit." Over my monitor as I write this is a permanent reminder of why I'm writing: "What's the benefit?"

What is a benefit? In the broadest terms, a *benefit* is something a customer gets from a product or service that she wants and didn't have before. Here are some examples:

- For Rosalind Jones, the benefit of the loaf of bread was the ability to make soup and sandwiches for supper and then get out of the kitchen as quickly as possible.

- Her son Byron is saving for a car; the benefit he's looking for is the ability to attract and date popular girls.

- Walter, her husband, wants a trolling motor for his boat; his benefit will be the ability to fish some private lakes that don't allow boats with motors larger than trolling motors.

- Her daughter Sarah has just bought the latest tape by Michael Jackson to get the benefit of the feelings that come from listening to it and from discussing it with her friends.

"Benefit" Is Internal

The first thing you have to understand about a benefit is that you can't touch, taste, see, smell, or hear it. The benefit is something that exists only inside the mind of the customer. Look at the Jones family:

- The benefit of the loaf of bread that was primary for Rosalind is only a minor benefit to the others; having it in the kitchen is handy if they happen to be hungry.

- The benefit of Byron's car to Rosalind and Walter is that they can stop chauffeuring him everywhere. Sarah doesn't see a benefit because she knows that Byron won't take her anywhere.

- Rosalind doesn't see any benefit at all in Walter having another motor for his boat; the kids don't care whether he has one.

- Because none of the rest of the family like Michael Jackson, Sarah's new tape has no benefit for them. In fact, because they'll have to put up with her playing it over and over, it's a definite negative.

What a variety! It's not necessary, though, to look at different products to see the difference in benefits people are seeking. For example, Rosalind bought the loaf of bread to make her evening chores easier. A few other people bought a loaf of the same bread that afternoon, seeking different benefits:

- Marie Sanginiti bought it because it was a high-fiber bread that she could eat as part of her diet.
- Nate Templeton bought it for his camping trip because he'd heard that it would stay fresh longer.
- Elaine Berman bought it because her kids think it tastes good in sandwiches.
- Bill Withers bought it because it's the brand he's been buying for the past 20 years.

This argument could be carried even further by looking at how the benefit of the loaf of bread might be different for Rosalind (or any of the others) from one time to another. This means that the benefit of any product or service is personal not only to the individual but also to the individual's situation at a particular moment.

If you think about it, you may wonder how enough people agree on any product or service to make it worth selling. It certainly should give you a new perspective on what marketing people go through trying to identify the need for a new product.

To repeat, the benefit of any product or service is what the buyer thinks it is—and that's something that's completely personal to her. Advertising may create the image of a similar benefit in the minds of thousands of people (a BMW is the car to drive if you've "arrived," for instance). When the time comes to make the buying decision, though, that general benefit will be translated into the situation of that specific buyer—or it won't be a benefit.

Where Quality Fits into the Picture

A number of writers, Tom Peters in the forefront, have stressed that *quality* is a major determinant of value. Yet this chapter hasn't mentioned quality up to this point. Why? Is it suddenly unimportant?

Not at all. If you want to compete in today's world, you have to offer high-quality products and services. Studies have shown consistently that firms with a reputation for quality have much higher than average profit margins. If you want to see what a reputation for poor quality can do to an organization, you need look no further than the market-share bloodbath taken by American automobile manufacturers in the early 1980s.

Having acknowledged quality's importance, note that quality isn't the whole of benefit—not by a long shot:

> The quality of Japanese cars is generally understood to be topflight, and the quality of American cars is improving dramatically. This is true if you look at quality as absence of defects and reliability. As soon as you broaden the definition to include *repairability*, though, the picture changes significantly. Today's cars, Japanese or American, are significantly more difficult and expensive to repair than those of a decade ago. The manufacturing processes used today do prevent defects and enhance reliability—but they often increase the expense of repair. It's not unreasonable to suppose that, within the next five years, repairability may become a major benefit for which car buyers look.

By all means, plan on producing and delivering high-quality products and services. Every level in your firm should expect to follow the first commandment of quality: Do it right the first time. But don't confuse quality with benefit. If your product or service has a benefit for your customer, high quality will enhance that benefit. If the benefit isn't there, no amount of quality will create it.

Quality is important. Benefit is important. Just don't confuse the two.

THE THREE KINDS OF BENEFIT

Just in case you don't think that the idea of a benefit is slippery and confused enough already, look at another level of complexity that it has. When you set out to provide a benefit to a customer, there are three distinct levels of benefit you can provide (or not provide).

THE THREE KINDS OF BENEFIT

- The *expected benefits*: what your customer knows he's looking for and can tell you about.
- The *assumed benefits*: what your customer expects to get from the purchase that she's not aware of at the moment.
- The *bonus benefits*: what your customer doesn't realize is available from the purchase, but which you can provide.

Each of these is worth a closer look.

Expected Benefits

The expected benefits a customer is looking for are the easiest to handle. She knows what they are, and she can tell you what they are. In the preceding examples of the Jones family, each family member was aware of the expected benefits:

- Rosalind could tell Laetitia she wanted the bread so she could get supper prepared and over quickly.
- Byron and the car salesman both knew he wanted the car to be competitive for dates, though neither might specifically say so.
- Walter could describe exactly the trolling motor that would meet the requirements of the lakes he wanted to fish.
- At the music store, Sarah could tell the clerk in great detail how good it would feel to listen to Michael Jackson and to be able to discuss the tape with her friends.

When I ask you what you're looking for in a car or home or a sandwich or a hotel room, and you tell me—that's the expected benefit. Even if I don't ask you or you don't tell me, you still know what it is, and you still expect it. That benefit is important, and if what I have to offer doesn't provide you that benefit, there won't be a transaction.

Assumed Benefits

The expected benefits are just the beginning, though. You may not be aware of them, but you also have a set of assumed benefits you're looking for. These are benefits that you don't think about or ask the salesperson about, but that you take for granted in the product or service. Here are some of the Jones's:

- Rosalind assumed that the bread would be fresh, that it would stay fresh for at least several days, that it was completely baked, that the ingredients were all harmless, and so on, . . .

- Byron assumed that the car would continue to run, that it wouldn't have a strange smell in the upholstery, that it wouldn't explode when he started it, that the bumpers weren't just glued on, . . .

- Walter assumed that he wouldn't have to get the motor repaired every week during the fishing season, that the propeller wouldn't fall off, that it wouldn't electrocute him, that it wouldn't freeze up when it got hot, ...

- Sarah assumed that the tape wasn't torn, that it wouldn't foul up her tape player, that there weren't advertisements on the tape, that it was Michael Jackson and not an impersonator singing, ...

All of them assumed that they could count on these benefits, so they didn't need to ask about them. In fact, they'd probably have been insulted if the clerk had assured them that they would get the assumed benefits. If one of the benefits hadn't been there, though—if the bread got stale the next day, for instance—the value of the purchase would have dropped sharply.

There's another, completely different level of assumed benefits. These are largely created by advertising and are the emotional benefits promised from the purchase. While they may be completely out of awareness when the purchase is made, their impact can be dramatic. Here are some examples (and, mercifully, they don't concern the Joneses):

- If you buy a European luxury car to get the assumed benefit of status, and your friends accuse you of ostentation, you may end up quite dissatisfied with the purchase.

- If you buy a preparation to gradually dye the gray out of your hair to appear younger, but no one notices, you'll feel cheated.

- If you bought rolls to demonstrate how much you love your family, and they gripe because you didn't have biscuits, you probably won't buy the rolls again.

The list could go on and on. It's standard practice for many advertisers to imply that their products will create popularity, happiness, desirability, and so on. These become assumed benefits of the products. When they're not delivered, the customer feels shortchanged. The fact that neither they nor you were aware that these benefits were important makes no difference at all.

Bonus Benefits

The final benefits, *bonus benefits*, are the benefits the customer would like to have but doesn't know you can give her. When you do, she's pleasantly surprised, and the value of the transaction goes up. That's the fun part of running a business:

- When the customer buys a sporty sedan and she finds that its short turning ratio makes it much easier to park

- When he buys a pair of comfortable shoes and finds that they hold a shine longer than he expected

- When she flies on your airline and finds the food is really quite good

- Or when he buys a computer to do his taxes and finds that the game you gave him (for his kids, of course) is a ball of fun.

There are almost always some bonus benefits because it's impossible to talk about all of the potential benefits of a purchase. To make the sale, you want as many benefits to be expected as possible. For customer satisfaction after the sale, though, a few bonus benefits are marvelous.

Because bonus benefits don't play an important part in dealing with customer dissatisfaction, they aren't described further. However, both expected and assumed benefits are mentioned later in this book time and time again. They play a critical role in customer satisfaction.

VALUE

Now that the groundwork is laid, it's time to tackle the idea of *value*. *Value* is the benefit a customer gets from a purchase in return for what she gives up to get it. Put just a little more exactly,

> *Value* is the benefit of a product or service to a customer minus the cost of getting the benefit.

Value is a very practical concept. Though it's educational to talk of benefits, they're abstract. What counts in the marketplace is the benefit compared to the cost—the value.

- Anita saw an advertisement last week for a sports version of the Bentley sedan. Tooling down the road and up to work in one of those would be a real kick for her. She'd love it. Will she buy it? Theoretically, she could. Between her life savings and her income, she has enough to make the payments for at least a year or two. But she won't buy it, of course—because its cost in terms of her limited income drastically outweighs its benefit to her.

- Marty paid $10 for a note holder that attaches to his windshield with a suction cup. The darned thing is made of plastic and couldn't have cost $1 to make. But Marty is a columnist, and he often gets his best ideas while he's driving. The note holder gives him a way to capture them. Overpriced as it may seem to you and me, for Marty, its benefit outweighed its cost.

- When I began to write this book, I bought a new printer for my personal computer. Its only advantages over my older one are that it prints faster and that I don't have to take out the sprocket-fed paper to put in individual sheets. Not very much difference, is it? The difference was enough, though, to make the $500 for the printer a good value for me.

Every day, each of us makes judgments about the value of different goods and services to us. Based on these judgments, we purchase some and pass up others. And that's exactly what your customers do: They buy from you when the value you offer is high enough, and they don't buy when it's not.

Service Merchandise, a major retailer, understands this concept. Their slogan is:

No one offers more value at any price.

COST

The Many Kinds of Costs

It's tempting to think of the cost of an item as the number of dollars that changes hands. This is the most visible part of it, but hardly all of it. This is what *cost* really is:

Cost is the sum total of the time, effort, and money that the customer has to put forth to get the benefit.

This is critically important! All too many firms—particularly new and small ones—concentrate only on the money cost. The more savvy ones at least expand this to include location. Actually, cost is much more complex. Here are just a few of the costs of your offerings to your customers:

- The time and frustration it takes to park at your store.
- The irritation of having to go find one of your clerks for assistance.
- The difficulty of getting service for a durable product you sold.

- The delay while waiting for your service (whether you're a doctor or a service station).

- The time spent trying to get through to your order line or support line on the phone.

- The other expenses that this purchase will cause (such as the increased insurance costs for a sports car).

These and dozens of other costs like them are part of the cost of your goods or services to your customers—who add those costs to the money cost, to arrive at the total cost of what you want to sell them. Some buyers will pay for the convenience of shopping close to home; others will take the time to shop at a more distant store with lower dollar costs. Some will patronize you because your sales associates are appropriately refined; others want to deal with friendly "down-home" folks.

The "We're Cheapest" Trap

This isn't a book about what you should sell or how you should differentiate your offering from that of other firms. Read other books for that. If you take seriously what was just said about cost, though, you might draw this conclusion:

> For most firms, attempting to succeed by being the lowest-cost provider is the *least* effective way to differentiate themselves (and to stay in business).

There are obvious exceptions to this. In every city, there are a small group of firms who invite business primarily because they're the low-cost offerer and succeed at it. There's always a much larger group who try to do business this way and fail, because:

- Lowest dollar cost isn't the same thing as lowest overall cost. Lowest dollar cost can be overwhelmed by the cost to the customer of poor service, limited selection, poor location, and so on.

- Consistently making money as the low-cost provider is a demanding art. It requires not only knowing how to do it, but also knowing how to organize an entire business around doing it.

- Customer loyalty based on price alone is fleeting. As soon as someone else can beat your price, you've lost the customers who came to you because of price.

- Finally, if price is your main competitive weapon, it's a weak barrier to new firms. *Anyone* can open a business on the basis that their prices are lower. They don't even need to succeed to kill your business; as long as enough of them try, they can fragment the market so that no one can survive.

When to Offer Low Prices

So, do you forget about having low prices? NO! Price is a constant influence in the buying decision for almost every customer. Other things being roughly equal, you and I will buy based on price. Your task is to keep your prices as low as you can—and to keep other things from ever being equal. It's the "other things," particularly your treatment of customers—particularly dissatisfied customers—that will make you a success. Or a failure.

There's another entirely different function of low costs: They open up new markets. In this case, you aren't the low-cost provider of an established product or service to an established market; instead, you make the product or service available to individuals who couldn't/ wouldn't buy it before. For instance, Jan Carlzon is most often mentioned because of the level of service that his airline, SAS, provides. He earned his crack at the presidency of SAS, however, by his success at turning around Linjeflyg—Sweden's domestic airline. Significant cuts in fares were absolutely critical in his success there.

THE POINT OF IT ALL

All the ingredients are finally in the pot. Customers buy so they can obtain expected *benefits*. To get these benefits, they incur various *costs*.

The benefits minus the costs represent the *value* of the product or service you offer. When a customer makes a purchase, she's decided that this is a worthwhile value—that its benefit exceeds its cost. You might disagree; her husband or boss or kids might disagree. That's irrelevant. She's placed a value on what you offer, and she's acted on that value.

This sounds simple, doesn't it? Nonetheless, it's critically important. The customer's perception of value is the balance point of the sale—and it's personal to the customer. Which leads directly to

---

Key #3: Customers define value in their own terms. If you want to satisfy them, you have to look at your products or services through their eyes—always!

"But wait," as the TV pitchman says, "there's more!" When a customer makes a purchase, he's not buying value directly. As Harvard University marketing guru Ted Levitt says, "individuals buy expectations, not products." Even more specifically, they buy *expectations of value*. They don't find out until later whether their expectations were correct. If the purchase is frozen yogurt in a cone, they find out quickly. If it's a state-of-the-art computer, it will be weeks, months, perhaps even years before they find out.

Why is it important to say that a customer is purchasing an expectation? It's simple: The *actual* value of the product or service may turn out to be greater or less than the customer's expectations. If it's greater, both you and the customer are lucky. If it's less, you both lose.

At the moment of the sale, the customer expects to receive a benefit greater than the cost. And if you want to deal successfully with dissatisfied customers, you must understand this:

> If anything happens after the sale that unexpectedly adds to the cost or decreases the benefit, the value decreases and you have a dissatisfied customer.

ROSALIND JONES GETS DISSATISFIED

Changes in Value, Costs, and Benefits

It's worth looking closely at this and how it shows up in the situation with Rosalind and her loaf of bread. Rosalind arrives home with her loaf of bread and enters the kitchen. What happens to the value of the loaf when she takes it out of the bag and discovers that the wrapper has a cut in it and most of the slices are stale?

She debates a few seconds about going to the local supermarket to get another loaf. This is their busy time, though, and she'll spend at least as much time there as it will take her to drive back to Handi Dandi. Besides, it's Handi Dandi's responsibility to replace the loaf. She dumps the loaf back in the bag, snatches up the bag, and strides to her car. Six minutes later, she's standing across from the manager of the Handi Dandi, showing her the cut wrapper.

Neither the manager of the Handi Dandi, Laetitia Willers, nor Rosalind knows the other's name, but Laetitia recognizes Rosalind as a frequent customer. She apologizes profusely for the problem and immediately gets her a new loaf. After making a point of checking the wrapper, she bags it, hands it to Rosalind, and apologizes again. Rosalind thanks her and leaves. After another six-minute drive, Rosalind is home and ready to fix soup and sandwiches.

Everything is okay and Rosalind is satisfied, right? WRONG! The benefit from the loaf has changed. She bought it to save time fixing supper, and she's lost almost 20 minutes replacing the original loaf. On the other side of the equation, the cost of the loaf has risen sharply. She'd expected to pay $1.25 and a couple of minutes of her time. Instead, she paid:

- The $1.25 and a couple of minutes of time, *and*
- The time it took to drive back to Handi Dandi, *and*
- The hassle of waiting for Laetitia to wait on her, explaining the situation, and getting the replacement loaf, *and*
- The time it took to drive back home.

From Rosalind's point of view, that loaf cost markedly more than $1.25. The loaf was worth $1.25. It wasn't worth $1.25 plus the extra driving and extra hassle. In other words,

> Because something happened after the sale that decreased the value of the purchase, Rosalind got less value and is now a dissatisfied customer.

Expecting Dissatisfaction

Will Rosalind start going to a different store? Probably not. For one thing, Laetitia's prompt, apologetic response took some of the edge from her dissatisfaction. For another, Rosalind probably believes that this disappointment was an exception and probably won't happen again. However,

- If Rosalind bought a car from Supreme Motors, and the seat had an obvious tear that took a day in the shop to fix after she got the car, she might not buy another car from Supreme Motors, or
- If she bought a suit from Contemporary Clothiers and one pocket was torn halfway off, and she had to argue with the clerk to have it fixed, she probably would be willing to drive another few miles to try another store, or
- If this was the third defective purchase she'd made from Handi Dandi this week, she might try out the new Zip-In Market on Walnut Street.

When a customer is dissatisfied, something extremely important happens:

> Because she has been dissatisfied this time, she now has an expectation that she'll be dissatisfied next time.

Because Rosalind has dealt with Handi Dandi for a long time, the one loaf of bread isn't enough to get her to change stores yet. She'll certainly check the bread she buys there, though, and probably the rest of her purchases as well. She hasn't dealt with Supreme Motors before, though, and the one incident may create enough of an expectation of dissatisfaction that she never returns.

Why so strong a reaction? The answer is really quite simple: Rosalind's expectation that she will be dissatisfied next time lowers the value of the firm's products or services to her. The value of Handi Dandi's products is lowered only slightly because she has purchased other products from them that have been satisfactory. The value of the automobile from Supreme is lowered far more; the dissatisfying experience is the only experience she has with the firm.

The effect of frequent contacts versus rare contacts is considered again in Chapter 9. For now, just keep firmly in mind that a dissatisfying experience not only reflects a drop in value of the current purchase, but also the expectation that future purchases will be less valuable. Whenever you deal with a dissatisfied customer, you have to deal with *both* the present dissatisfaction and the expectation of future dissatisfaction.

BUT IT WASN'T MY FAULT . . . !

Keep another point in mind: It really doesn't matter much to Rosalind whether Handi Dandi (or Supreme or Contemporary) caused the problem. The problem (the drop in value) occurred. If the company didn't cause it, it didn't prevent it, either.

It may seem grossly unfair to you that you get blamed for a mistake that was your supplier's fault. Your frontline people will often feel that way when a dissatisfied customer yells at them. It doesn't matter. It doesn't change the facts. Either a customer gets the expected value or he's dissatisfied—period.

The moral of this is that explanations alone aren't enough. The value isn't restored when you say,

> "I'm sorry it happened, but we weren't responsible" and
>
> "It's just something we can't control" and
>
> "What she told you was wrong" and
>
> "50 cents won't buy you a cup of coffee in most good restaurants."

In the words of one entrepreneur, "I discovered that customers didn't *care* how it happened. They wanted things right or they wouldn't be back."

Does this mean that you don't attempt to explain what went wrong and why? Not at all. As long as you understand that explanations by themselves won't satisfy customers, you can use explanations effectively. These are some of the goals a good explanation can achieve:

- It can help assure a customer that what produced the dissatisfaction wasn't your lack of concern.

- It can reassure her that you know what caused the dissatisfaction and so can prevent it from happening again (particularly if you make it clear that you *will* prevent it from happening).

- It can show her that you're taking responsibility for her satisfaction even though you didn't directly cause the dissatisfaction.

You can see how important each of these goals is. So use explanations of what went wrong to help; just don't count on them to restore the value of the transaction.

LAETITIA'S STAKE IN THE ACTION

By the way, Rosalind wasn't the only person affected by the defective loaf of bread. Take a quick look at the impact of the transaction on Laetitia.

Laetitia Willers's store has targets both for sales and for profits each month. Her performance numbers go into the district office, where she's compared with every other store manager. At the end of each quarter, she gets—or doesn't get—a bonus based on her performance. Underlying this is the corporate policy that managers who don't meet minimum sales and profit targets are replaced.

The loaf of bread she just sold represents a small contribution to sales and, more importantly, to profit. When Rosalind Jones returns 15 minutes later, points to a cut in the wrapper, and asks for a new loaf of bread, that has an impact on profit, too. Laetitia takes care of Rosalind's immediate problem by replacing the loaf. But now Laetitia has a problem.

She has to get Healthgrain to take the loaf back. This is one more bother, and it's been happening all too often with Healthgrain's loaves. She makes a mental note to start counting the number of returned loaves. She knows that she has to replace the loaves if she wants to keep the business of Mrs. Jones and the rest of her customers—but she can't afford to be constantly replacing loaves for them.

Laetitia is looking at Healthgrain in just the same way that Rosalind is looking at Handi Dandi. When she has to deal with a defective loaf, she applies the same standard of value as any other customer would. Ralph, Healthgrain's route man, may replace the loaf that has the bad wrapper without any question. Laetitia still had to put forth extra effort just to get what she thought she had bought in the first place: a saleable loaf of bread. Healthgrain has caused her the same problem that she's caused Rosalind. In fact, Healthgrain has caused her to have the problem with Rosalind in the first place.

In short, the value of Healthgrain's loaves is dropping sharply for Laetitia. She's dissatisfied with Healthgrain and already on her way to being an ex-customer of theirs.

WRAPPING IT UP

Here's a quick summary of the key points in this chapter:

- *Benefit* is the full range of satisfactions that a customer gets from a purchase. Ultimately, what's a benefit and what's not is personal to the customer.

- *Cost* is the sum total of time, effort, and money spent to obtain the benefit.

- *Value* is the benefit derived from a purchase minus the cost of getting the purchase. This formula is the basis of

---

Key #2: You don't sell products or service or even benefits. You sell value—or you don't sell anything at all!

It's also the basis of

> **Key #3**: Customers define value in their own terms. If you want to satisfy them, you have to look at your products or services through their eyes—always!

- When something happens after the sale, which raises the costs of the product or service, it takes away some of the value. The result is a dissatisfied customer. Stated formally, this is

> **Key #4**: If anything happens after the sale to prevent the customer from getting at least the value he expected, he hasn't gotten the value he paid for—and the customer knows it! In short, you've created a dissatisfied customer.

The rest of the book is about the importance of these keys, especially Key #4, to your success.

CHECK POINTS

1. I can quickly name five of the major benefits my customers get from dealing with me.
2. My frontline people could answer this question even more quickly than I can.
3. My frontline people understand clearly what it means to provide benefits and value. They never think of themselves as just delivering products or services.
4. Not counting money, I can quickly name five of the major *costs* that my customers have to pay to do business with me.

5. All of my workers—not just those who deal directly with custom-ers—understand how they can add to the benefit *or* to the cost of my customers' purchases.

6. I can even tell you the value that my accounting department adds to my customers (and so can they).

7. My frontline people understand the ways in which what happens after the sale is critical to customer satisfaction.

8. I clearly understand and capitalize on the value I offer my customers that my competitors can't. So do my frontline people.

3

SEE WHAT YOUR FRONTLINE PEOPLE HAVE TO DO

"Helping a customer will always take priority over any other task."
(Eckerd Drug Stores)

"We're paid to do everything we have to do to get a person to fly United again." (Carla—a United Airlines flight attendant)

At least on paper, Eckerd Drug Stores understands what the primary job of their frontline people is. So does Carla. Here are some other examples of people who understand—and people who don't.

CASE STUDY: Helping a Customer Comes First

Walter Ellis was checking out of the Marriott Courtyard Hotel in Andover, Massachusetts. As he walked over to the counter, the assistant manager was explaining something to the other person behind the counter with her. As Walter got to the counter, he heard her saying "Now I need to explain to you about . . ."

Let's back up from the scene for a minute and speculate on what might happen next. Does this sound like your experience?

- At least 50 percent of the time, the assistant manager would have continued what she was working on until she was finished. Then she would have turned her attention to Walter. In the meantime, he would have stood there, more or less resignedly.

- Perhaps another 25 percent of the time, she would have looked up, smiled or otherwise acknowledged Walter's presence, and continued until she was done. At least she'd have communicated that she knew Walter was there.

- No more than 24 percent of the time, she would have looked up, said something like "I'll be with you in a moment, sir," and finished what she was doing as quickly as possible. Then she would have waited on Walter. That's a clear improvement over the first two responses.

Wait a minute—that's only 99 percent. Yes. This assistant manager didn't do any of these. She interrupted herself in midsentence and turned to wait on Walter. Presumably, she went back to telling her associate what she needed to later; while Walter was there, he had her undivided attention.

Perhaps a short, simple incident that happened to Elena Limon is closer to the experience of most of us. She was at the head of the "6 Items, Cash Only" line at her supermarket.

"Excuse me just a moment," the checker said. "I need to get some change." She pulled two large bills from the cash register and walked the few feet to the customer service office.

The customer-service person on duty was on the phone, and she continued her conversation while the checker waited. When she finished the call, about a minute later, she took the money from the checker and gave her the small bills she wanted.

The checker returned, apologized to Elena, and checked her out.

This was a small thing. The delay was no more than a minute and a half. In the express check-out lane, though, a minute and a half matters.

More important, it didn't have to happen. If the customer-service person had understood her job, the delay would have been less than a third as long.

Of course, anything can be taken to extremes. Just as Werner Schmidt was checking out of his hotel, the desk clerk took a phone call. To deal with Werner, he put the caller on hold. A small problem developed, and completing the checkout took several minutes. When Werner left, the caller was still on hold.

The priorities of a customer-service person should always be clear. Balancing these priorities in the actual situation, though, takes skill.

The hotel's assistant manager was part of that small minority of customer service personnel who really understand that helping a customer should always take priority over any other task. In other words, she is one of that small minority who understand completely and exactly what her job is.

WHERE YOU START

Jan Carlzon, the dynamic head of SAS airlines, has popularized the term "front line" for people who deal directly with customers. He's right. Everything you've planned, every product or service you've developed, every bit of marketing you've done—the success of it all depends on the competence of your customer-contact personnel.

It starts with your sales personnel, as they deal with potential customers over the counter, out on the road, over the phone. No matter how expert and concerned they are, they can't atone for a poor product—at least not for long. If they're overbearing, deceptive, or uncaring, though, all the product planning and development in the world won't save the situation for you.

Your service personnel are also part of the front line. They may train customers, install and explain your products, repair them, or order and install the spare parts your customers need. They can't make or break you as quickly as your salespeople, but over time, their treatment of customers will build up or tear down the value you're trying to provide.

This book focuses especially on how frontline people deal with unhappy customers. This includes the people in your Complaint Department, if you have one. Don't think for a moment, though, that it's only for them. Never! Everyone who deals with customers will have to deal with dissatisfied customers at some time. None of them will produce greater benefit for you, though, than those who most often come into contact with unhappy customers. They have the opportunity to produce the most immediate positive effect on your customers. That's why you're targeting them.

Many of the skills that your frontline people need in order to deal with unhappy customers are the skills every customer-contact person needs when they deal with customers in general. Everything in the book can be used by everyone who deals with dissatisfied customers. Whatever job your frontline people do, they'll do it better if they under-

stand what customers want and how to deal with them when they don't
get it.

WHAT YOUR FRONT LINE REALLY IS

What image does the term *front line* conjure up for you? The down
linemen on a football team? The sopranos and altos in the front row of
a chorus? Perhaps the front seats in a theater?

The front line may be all of these, but its basic meaning comes from
the military. The *front line* is the first echelon of troops—those who have
to fight well and successfully if the army is to achieve its objective. Every
military commander worth his salt knows that these troops are the heart
of his army. The battle rises and falls by them.

That's just how important your front line is to you. Your customer-
contact people are the heart of your attempt to satisfy your customers.
You need to regard them with the same respect and give them the same
support that a successful commander gives his front line.

Just calling them the "front line," though, sounds rather impersonal
and distant. There's nothing impersonal about your front line. It's
made up of *people*—the people who are going to make your company
succeed, or hasten its failure. Use their full name: frontline people.

There's one other idea to look at quickly. Every commander has his
frontline troops. Whenever possible, he also has his reserves. These are
the troops held back from the front line—ready to enter the battle at the
last minute to stave off defeat or ensure victory. You might want to think
of your customer-service people who deal with dissatisfied customers as
your reserves.

Every moment of truth, every customer contact, is important. The
moment of truth when a dissatisfied customer contacts you is one of the
most critical. Often, it's your last chance to keep that customer; one
more mistake, and the customer is gone. Your people who deal with the
customer really are your "reserves"; if they fail, your battle is lost.

Even a good metaphor can be overused, but here's a last thought:
When your frontline people are dealing with a dissatisfied customer,
you've committed your reserves. Like a battlefield commander, you win

or lose with their performance. Unless you're very, very lucky, you don't get another chance.

BUYING BREATHING ROOM

It might help to pause for a moment and put this into perspective. The point has already been made that no amount of talent, commitment, and expertise in your frontline people will make up for poor market research, sloppy product design, low product or service quality, or any other failure in the chain that leads from business plan to loyal customer. The subtitle of this book is *not* "How to Substitute Frontline Sizzle for Total Organizational Competence."

Having said that, this is also true:

> Effective frontline people will make customers more tolerant and more patient with your product or service defects—if your customers believe that your frontline people truly represent the intention of your company.

Effective frontline people are an extremely important asset to any company. For instance, they were a critical factor in the Japanese penetration of the American new car market. They were an even more critical factor in the defense of hundreds of American car dealers against this penetration. Because they rendered superior service at the local level, customers were willing to stick with their products while the automobile companies changed their organizations and manufacturing methods.

For the moment, just keep in mind that—at least in the short run—your frontline people can give you breathing space with your customers when other parts of your organization are having to fall back and regroup.

WHAT YOUR FRONTLINE PEOPLE NEED TO DO

Your frontline people need to deal with unhappy buyers so effectively that they become and remain loyal customers. That kind of expertise doesn't come out of thin air. It requires training (see Chapter 4) and support (see Chapter 5). It begins, though, with a clear understanding—by you and by them—of what your frontline people must do.

The job of your frontline people is to:

- Create a successful transaction with the customer, by
- Relating personally to him

    To solve his immediate problem and

    Increase the value he expects from his future transactions with you.

- By using common sense and a practical understanding of company policy.
- So well that the process is satisfying to your frontline people as well as their customers.

Your frontline people should also perform one other essential function:

- They should be a basic source of your firm's market intelligence.

Does this sound like a very long list? It is—but the ability to do everything on the list effectively should be part of the skills of every frontline person in your organization. Your sales force should be good at it, your technical support people should be good at it, your repairers should be good at it, your counter clerks should be good at it—every frontline person should be good at it.

What's more, the frontline people who deal consistently with unhappy buyers should be absolutely brilliant at it. It won't be easy. No matter how strenuous or difficult it may be, though, when your frontline people deal with unhappy customers, they should excel at every item in the list. Here's a more detailed look at each of the items.

Creating a Successful Transaction

These items describe what your frontline people need to do to create this successful transaction. They also describe what a successful transaction is. If your people follow this process, the transaction will be as successful as possible.

Relating Personally to the Customer

Personalizing the contact is the heart of a successful transaction. You may have thought of this mainly in regard to your sales force. Indeed, one of their high priorities should be establishing a long-term personal relationship with their customers. (For instance, Nordstrom's expects each sales associate to be a "personal shopper" for his or her customers.) That's a good start, but it's not enough. *Every* customer contact must be personalized.

The previous chapter looked at the economic concept of *value*. Customers buy value, which is made up of many elements. For almost everyone, almost all of the time, *being treated as a person* creates value. The reverse is also true: Being treated perfunctorily or impersonally almost always decreases value.

The moral is clear. Treating customers as valued persons is an intrinsic part of every successful transaction. It's a critically important part of every moment of truth with unhappy customers. It's difficult— often extremely difficult. It can be emotionally draining for the people who have to do it. But it must be done, and done well.

How do you do it? In essence, relating personally to a customer involves three steps.

> ### TO RELATE PERSONALLY TO A CUSTOMER, A FRONTLINE PERSON MUST
>
> - Recognize the customer as a person.
> - Focus on the customer.
> - End the contact gracefully.

Recognize the Customer as a Person

How does a frontline person do this? By:

- Establishing eye contact with the customer.
- Clearly attending to the customer.

- Smiling, shaking hands, looking concerned—making whatever facial expression or gesture is appropriate to the moment.

In most circumstances, this recognition takes only a few seconds. Its purpose is to acknowledge the customer and establish contact.

Some firms use a standard opening, such as "I'm _____, how may I help you?" Clearly, they believe that this works for them. Whether you use a standard opening or not, the critical point is that the contact must be sincere, not canned.

As the standardized quote suggests, your frontline people should normally introduce themselves by name. This is particularly important when they're dealing with someone on the phone; unless there's a compelling reason otherwise, they ought always to begin by introducing themselves. Remember that a phone is intrinsically impersonal—you need a little added personalization (such as the individual's name) to counteract this right from the beginning.

I had an excellent illustration of the importance of using a name two weeks ago. I attended a conference at a resort in Utah. The service, as one would expect there, was excellent. I was standing in the lobby as the desk clerk handed the room keys to a guest and said,

"This is your room. If there's anything not right about it, call me."

That was good, of course. Think for a moment how much better it would have been if she'd said,

"This is your room. I'm Dana—and if there's anything not right about the room, please call me and I'll take care of it."

A small difference—but small differences add up to competitive advantage.

Focus on the Customer

The sincerest compliment one person can give to another is undivided attention. Treating a customer as a person means paying this undivided attention. A frontline person should take each of these steps:

- *Forget any other concern while dealing with this customer.* If another concern is so absolutely pressing that it can't be put aside, the frontline person should quickly explain the situation, excuse himself, take care of the concern, and then return to paying undivided attention to the customer. (An example of such a pressing concern might be the need for a frontline person to coach a surgeon through emergency brain surgery.)

- *See the customer's problem through the customer's eyes.* The basic meaning of "the customer is always right" is that the customer gets to define the problem. However familiar the problem may sound to a frontline person, to the customer, it's unique and needs to be responded to that way. Whatever else may happen, your frontline person hasn't personalized the transaction until the customer sees that the frontline person is trying to deal with the problem just as the customer sees it.

- *Help the customer to focus on solving the present problem.* Many times, customers get hung up on what *happened* to them. They may have been offended, hurt, insulted. These feelings, and their wish that the incident would go away, are very real. Real as they may be, they aren't the problem. By definition, a problem is a situation for which there is a solution—and changing the past isn't ever a possible solution. In other words, it's very important for your frontline person to direct the customer's attention to what you can do for the customer *now,* and keep it there.

- *Listen for as long as necessary to understand the problem*—and to convince the customer that the problem is understood. This requires active listening, which involves questions, appropriate responses and prompts, and whatever it takes to communicate to the customer that she's truly being heard.

- *Clearly attempt to resolve the problem.* Please note that this may differ from resolving the problem. It's not enough to be working on the problem; your frontline people need to communicate that they are doing so. One easy way to do this is for the frontline person to tell the customer exactly what's being done.

End the Contact Gracefully

A psychologist would call this "achieving closure." It's simple, but it's important. A frontline person must take the following steps:

- Check to see that the problem is solved or, at the least, that they've agreed on a way to solve it.
- As far as possible, check to see that the customer feels good about the contact and about the solution to his problem.
- Assure the customer that the frontline person is still available if there is any further problem.
- End with an appropriate phrase and/or gesture—such as "have a good day" or a short handshake.
- Make a final eye contact during the closing statement.

The three-step process isn't limited to dealing with dissatisfied customers, of course. With appropriate variations, every frontline person should follow this sequence when dealing with a customer. And while it's written with a bias toward face-to-face contact, it's just as applicable to telephone contacts and even to correspondence.

There's nothing new about all of this. The firms that excel in their moments of truth have always personalized these contacts. As our society becomes more and more automated, however, personalization becomes even more critical. People are deeply offended when they're treated impersonally, as a *thing* (aren't you?). Conversely, each of us responds positively when someone reaches out and recognizes us as a *person.*

CASE STUDY: Reach Out And Touch . . . ?

AT&T has been pushing their version of personalization—"Reach out and touch someone"—for several years now. It's designed to get people to see the telephone not as an impersonal communication device but as a supportive tool for warm human contact.

There's an interesting twist on this. When you make a long-distance call on AT&T, operators are trained to "Thank you for using AT&T." If the call is a placed on a credit card, and no human intervenes, you still get the cheery "Thank you" from a recording.

That may sound a little dumb, but at least it's pleasant if still impersonal. Contrast this with the message of one of the numerous phone companies whose purpose in life is to connect hotels and motels to the long-distance nets and bill you for the expense. This company—which will remain mercifully anonymous—has their own recorded message. After you've dialed your number, a recorded voice comes on to say "Thank you for using _____." The message is a recording of a real, live human being, but it's delivered in a flat, mechanical, completely bored tone of voice.

This kind of incompetence in a moment of truth raises two questions:

- Because the recording only has to be done once, why can't the company produce a version that at least *sounds* like a friendly human being?
- How many things like this is your company doing because the people making the decisions aren't focusing on the customer?

Solve the Customer's Immediate Problem

If your frontline person doesn't focus on solving the customer's immediate problem, everything else he does will be simple manipulation. It will also be unsuccessful.

When a dissatisfied customer contacts your firm—in person, by phone, or by letter—that customer has a specific problem that must be resolved. It's up to you to resolve it satisfactorily. Half of what you need to do has been covered: respond personally, let the customer define the problem, make sure the problem is understood, and then be clear about how you're working to solve it.

What follows is the other half: pure problem solving. While there are a hundred variations, these are the three basic steps to effective problem solving:

1. *Define the problem.* Your frontline person has already done that, by letting the customer define it.
2. *Identify the alternative solutions.* This is the heart of problem solving. There's abundant evidence that the people most successful at solving problems are those who can generate many, many practical alternatives. Training your people to look for alternatives should be a key part of your overall training program.
3. *Select the right solution.* In many cases, you can involve the customer in identifying alternative solutions. Whenever possible, your frontline people should involve her in selecting the best solution. If there's only one realistic alternative, they should check to see that

she will accept it as the solution. If there's more than one, they should offer her a choice.

Increase the Value He Expects from Future Transactions with You

Effectively solving your customer's problem does more than just remove his present dissatisfaction. It also increases the value that the customer expects in *future* transactions with you.

The previous chapter showed that a customer who's disappointed in your product or service develops an expectation that future purchases from you will have less value. After one or a few dissatisfactions, the customer concludes that you just can't provide the value he needs. He takes his business elsewhere.

Happily, the reverse is also true. Every time a customer has an experience that confirms the value of the purchase—*and the value of the total transaction with you*—his expectations rise that you will provide him value in the future. While your frontline people should concentrate on the individual's current problem, they should also be aware of this aspect of the transaction. Chapter 1 showed that the value of a customer is many, many times the value of any individual transaction. Your frontline people need to understand this. Even more, they must keep it clearly in mind each time they deal with a dissatisfied customer.

This aspect of transactions with unhappy buyers is so important that all of Chapter 8 is focused on doing it successfully.

Using Common Sense to Satisfy Customers and to Feel Satisfied

> By using common sense and a practical understanding of company policy, so well that the process is satisfying to your frontline people as well as their customers.

These two characteristics are a matched set: If frontline people use common sense and a clear sense of policy to satisfy customers, what they do will be satisfying to them. It generally won't be satisfying unless they do.

In other words, your frontline people really can find their job satisfying. (If you don't believe this, watch someone who understands customer service and who takes pride in it deal with an angry customer and turn him around.) They really can use their own common sense and practicality to satisfy their customers (and yours).

Providing Market Intelligence

The reason that providing intelligence is listed last is simple. When your frontline person is dealing with an unhappy customer, her primary job is to solve the customer's problem. She needs to concentrate fully on it. If she's trying to analyze what the customer is saying, or trying to use the process to learn about the customer instead of solving the customer's problem, she'll short-change this primary job.

After the problem is solved, though, your frontline person should take just a moment to think through what the customer's problem was. If there was a unique aspect about it, she should jot it down—preferably on a form designed for just that purpose.

There's even a way to make this part of the overall successful transaction. I would never suggest this for a beginning or merely an average customer-contact person, but in the hands of a practiced and skillful one, it can work. Let the person tell the customer just what she's doing, that the firm wants to know when its products or services fall short and why. In this circumstance, asking a follow-up question or two can be appropriate.

Why not have the customer fill out the form? Chapter 6 discusses this at much greater length, but here's a short answer. Don't have the customer do it unless one of the following is true:

- The volume of people your frontline people have to deal with makes it impractical for them to take the extra time to fill out the form. (If this occurs constantly, you may not have enough people to do the job properly.)
- The customer has specialized knowledge of the product or service

(such as a special computer card, or a sophisticated make-up system) that your frontline person doesn't have and can't capture effectively. When the reason for this need is this clear, the customer generally won't mind.

Remember, though—no matter who fills out the card, it shouldn't happen until *after* the customer's problem has been solved.

Frontline people can't replace a strategic marketing plan—but no marketing plan can ever replace them, either. Your firm needs the intelligence that can only come from the people who deal with customers day after day—and not just those who deal with dissatisfied customers. *Every* moment of truth between a frontline person and a customer is an opportunity for your firm to learn more about the customer's wants and expectations. One contact may not produce earthshaking news (though it might), but dozens and hundreds of them can. Every frontline person should understand this and should act on it.

It takes training to do this well (and the next chapter covers this). It also takes a system that makes it easy for frontline people to tell you what they know. Most of all, it takes an atmosphere that makes it clear to frontline people that their input is wanted and will be used. (This book concentrates on frontline people who deal with dissatisfied customers. If you want an example of how one firm uses its *sales force* with dramatic success for market intelligence, look up the article on Ballard Medical Products in the April 1988 issue of *Inc.*)

As mentioned, the next two chapters look at the training, the support systems, and the reward structure you must provide if this is to happen. Right now, though, look at another requirement for this level of performance: delegating real authority and responsibility to your frontline people.

EMPOWERING YOUR FRONTLINE PEOPLE

The current buzzword for effective delegating is "empowering"—and your job is to empower your frontline people to handle moments of truth with great independence and a strong sense of personal responsibility.

Often—probably usually—this doesn't happen. Here's a quick picture of an all-too-typical organization:

Budget Fashions operates half a dozen retail outlets in a three-city area. The central office does the purchasing for all of the stores, which use a standard layout to display merchandise. The company policy and procedures manual contains detailed instructions concerning returns, refunds, and exchanges. All sales and customer-service personnel are hired through local employment agencies. Store managers are expected to interview applicants, but because they're only minimum-wage clerks, the interviews are typically cursory. Clerks receive a one-hour video training and orientation session; after that, they're expected to learn and follow the customer-service procedures manual. If a situation isn't covered in the manual, or if a customer wants an exception, the situation has to be referred to the manager (which means that clerks often tell a customer "no," only to have the manager overrule them and say "yes"). Clerks who exceed their authority and authorize a return or a replacement in error are counseled against it because returns come out of the store's profit.

What do you think the chances are that the frontline people in this organization satisfy customers by using common sense and a practical understanding of company policy, or that they find it satisfying? Somewhere around zero to zip? (Fortunately, your company is nothing like this, is it?)

Why don't Budget Fashions' frontline people live up to our expectations? Well, perhaps the firm has a tight labor market. Perhaps they're afraid their clientele will try to take advantage of them. Perhaps they're afraid they can't properly control their clerks. Perhaps everyone is just too busy.

The fact of the matter is that these are nonreasons. Any one of them might have some influence, but you can't tell. Budget Fashions' hiring, training, and reward procedures guarantee that their frontline people won't use common sense or get satisfaction from their work. First and foremost, though, their frontline people are ineffective because that's how the business is organized.

How should they be organized? Here's how:

> Your frontline people should understand that *they* are the ones who will bring success to their moments of truth—and everyone else should understand that their first job is to *support* the frontline people as they do it.

Why Empower Them?

Does that sound like a little too much? A little risky? Perhaps like something an academic without real-world experience (which I'm not) might say? Well, here's what several very different people have to say about it.

Jan Carlzon produced one of the most dramatic turnarounds in the airline industry. One of his key changes was to give responsibility and authority to his frontline personnel. As he says,

> By giving more responsibility to the frontline personnel, we are letting them provide the service that they had wanted to provide all along but couldn't because of an inflexible hierarchical structure.

Shoshana Zuboff has studied the impact of automation intensively over the past few years. When she evaluated the impact of an automated system on a London-based appliance/TV rental organization, this is what she found:

> It became clear that the shops had an important role to play in providing service and developing new businesses. Corporate management's job would be to see that they had *both the information and the authority* they needed to do that . . .
>
> What happened was that the nature of the shop employee's job changed. It went from being a low-skill, low-wage, high-turnover job to being a managerial job with different career implications and requiring a good deal of business knowledge, training, imagination, and the intellectual skills to deal with abstract, electronically based information . . .
>
> Six years ago there were 13 levels of management and probably a hundred people in corporate headquarters. . . . Now, there are 3 or 4 levels of management . . ."

Kaoru Ishikawa is one of Japan's leading proponents of "Total Quality Control" (or "Total Quality Management"). This is part of his advice to managers:

> The fundamental principle of successful management is to allow subordinates to make full use of their ability.
>
> The term humanity implies autonomy and spontaneity. People are different from animals or machines. They have their own wills, and do

things voluntarily without being told to by others. They use their heads and are always thinking. Management based on humanity is a system of management that lets the unlimited potential of human beings blossom.

. . . Top managers and middle managers must be bold enough to delegate as much authority as possible. That is the way to establish respect for humanity as your management philosophy. It is a management system in which all employees participate, from the top down and from the bottom up, and humanity is fully respected.

Americans are used to thinking of the Japanese and quality control in terms of fit, finish, durability, and other physical characteristics. That's only part of the story. One of the basic goals of "Total Quality Control" is, in the words of Dr. Ishikawa's translator, to make it possible "for the product design and manufacturing division to follow the changing tastes and attitudes of customers efficiently and accurately so that products can be manufactured to meet customer preference consistently." In other words, the goal of "Total Quality Control" is customer satisfaction.

By the way, lest you think that these ideas just work in Japan, here's what *Business Week* said about the impact of Japanese management and manufacturing methods on American auto manufacturers:

Companies that had nearly given up on American workers are finding that giving them decision-making power can be a powerful motivator.

(Remember that the "American workers" in the quote are *production workers*—who're certainly no more qualified to make decisions than frontline people.)

According to Daniel Finkelman, companies that consistently provide high levels of customer satisfaction

give their employees the responsibility and authority to deliver a higher level of satisfaction. Decision-making processes are simplified. Tangled and complex approval processes for expenditures are replaced by the discretion of responsible employees. This means that employees at—or very near—the point of customer contact can make the decisions that make a difference.

The Orvis Company is a mail-order company specializing in sporting goods. Their customer-service representatives have the authority to resolve issues with dissatisfied customers however they can. This includes issuing gift certificates to make up for customers' "trials and tribulations" and sending letters directly to customers to resolve any outstanding problems.

Finally, the WordPerfect Company puts it simply and succinctly:

> We try not to limit the customer support operators on what they can and cannot do to satisfy a customer; we trust our employees and their judgement.

I have no interest in telling you how to run your business. I can tell you this: Unless and until your frontline people are given the opportunity to develop their competence, you're wasting not only money but also customer goodwill. Does that sound extreme? I'm going to give you some reasons why it's not. Don't just read them abstractly. Think about how they apply to *your* business.

From the Customer's Point of View

I want you to envision that *you* are the dissatisfied customer. Put yourself in a situation where a product or service has really disappointed you. Perhaps your new mower won't start, or the chair in your hotel room is broken, or the new program for your personal computer keeps freezing your keyboard. Whatever turns you off—imagine that it's happened, and you've just walked up to a customer-service person. The person listens for a few moments and then says one of the following:

- "Gosh, that really is bad—but the person you need to talk to isn't here right now. If you don't mind waiting a few minutes, I'm sure he'll be back soon . . ."
- "I've never heard about that before. If you'll wait just a moment, I'll go get our supervisor and . . ."
- "I think we can help you with that. Just a minute while I check here to see just what I can do . . ."
- "Oh, that's too bad, but we don't handle that over here. If you'll just go back that corridor and take the first door on the left . . ."

- "It's a real shame, and you're not the only one who's complained about that. It's actually easy to fix, but the only person who knows how is off until a week from Wednesday . . ."

Were the customer service people rude? No. Did they not care? No. Did they try to get rid of you? No. Did they solve your problem. No. What they did was *delay* the solution. And in every case they delayed it because, for one reason or another, they didn't have the knowledge or the authority to solve it for you then and there.

Did that frustrate you and dissatisfy you even further? You bet it did. In fact, you may have felt—as I have dozens of times—that the organization is using its frontline people to *keep from* having to deal with your complaint. Once you communicate that to your customers, you can start planning your going-out-of-business sale.

Impact on Your Bottom Line

Even that's not all. Step back and look at the examples strictly from the point of view of business costs for a moment. Each moment of truth required a minimum of *two* of your frontline people to resolve. In the last one, the second person needed wasn't available, so the problem couldn't be resolved until later.

In other words, when your frontline people don't have authority all but the most common customer dissatisfactions require two or more people to solve. That's a great full-employment program, but are you sure you're profitable enough to fund it?

Impact on the Players

A final note. When frontline people lack authority and independence, *everyone* starts out unhappy.

- The customer is unhappy because she knows she'll have to spend more time than she wants.

- The frontline person is unhappy because he knows that he probably won't be allowed to solve the problem.

- The supervisor is unhappy because she knows she'll keep getting interrupted to handle customers because she just can't get good help which means she won't get her work done and . . .

- And you're unhappy because nobody's doing what you need to have done very well.

There's enough unhappiness in having a dissatisfied customer. You can do without this extra layer of it.

The Importance of Hands-On Managing

Many writers have stressed empowering your front line. Companies that are good at satisfying their customers do it. I've found that these companies also have another characteristic: Their managers stay in close contact with what's happening on the front line.

Micro Center expects their managers to be right in there dealing with customers. The Cooker's managers are expected to check on the satisfaction of every customer. The president of Ricart Motors talks with specific salespersons about specific customers every day.

I wasn't expecting this at first; at least I wasn't expecting it so strongly. When I stopped to think about it, though, the logic was clear. It's easy to talk about supporting the front line. If you let yourself get tied up in an office, buried under paperwork, infatuated with great ideas— it's easy to lose touch with what really happens out there. By insulating yourself in this way, you lose most of the good ideas that your frontline people could give you. And you lose your feel for how your policies are *really* being applied on the front line.

If you and your managers want to support your frontline people, you have to know what's happening on the front line. You can get this knowledge in only one place in the world: on the front line itself. You have to actually be there, seeing how customers are responding, talking with your frontline people.

This is an important theme, and it's touched on again later.

The Next Two Chapters

All right, you're convinced. Frontline people need to have the authority and the support to do their job effectively. Now, how do you provide it? The next two chapters are filled with practical ideas for selecting, training, supporting, and rewarding frontline people. None of these ideas are terribly sophisticated or exotic, but neither are they quick-and-dirty fixes. They require time, attention, and effort. Take them seriously, practice them, and you'll have frontline people who won't have to put your customers through the hoops shown in some of the preceding examples.

Before addressing these ideas, there's one more topic to consider.

WHAT YOUR FRONTLINE PEOPLE NEED TO OVERCOME

Why not just hire good people and "turn them loose"? That is part of how you solve the problem. If you don't *train, support,* and *reward* them carefully, though, you won't get the responsiveness to customers that you need. This chapter ends with a look at the reasons for this.

AS A FRONTLINE PERSON, I MAY NOT RESPOND WELL TO DISSATISFIED CUSTOMERS BECAUSE

- I didn't cause the problem, so I shouldn't have to deal with it.
- The situation is uncomfortable, so I want to get rid of the customer as quickly as possible.
- The customer is wrong, or unfair, or trying to take advantage of me, or acting in some other unjustified way.
- The customer is rude and doesn't deserve polite treatment.
- The customer's negative emotions are contagious, and I automatically begin to act the same way he's acting.
- I don't know what to do, so I react defensively.

There are more reasons, but these will do for a start. Here's a quick look at each of them.

It's Not My Problem

The gut fact about frontline people who deal with dissatisfied customers is that most of the time they didn't cause the problem they have to solve. An unhappy person shows up in front of them—perhaps yelling at them or accusing them of all sorts of devious behavior—all for something they had nothing to do with.

If the frontline person doesn't feel a sense of solidarity ("we") with the rest of the firm, these are some of the things that can happen:

- He puts the customer on hold—literally or figuratively—and goes to find the offending party to deal with the problem.

- He sympathizes with the customer about the poor-quality service the XYZ section is putting out.

- He gets fed up with being yelled at for the fifth time in one morning and quits.

Even when he doesn't react so strongly, he doesn't like the situation. As Denise, an experienced flight attendant with a major airline, put it: "Sometimes we feel like we have to do everyone's job."

You're probably already familiar with the problem that this presents. If you're not, don't underestimate it. Most of us have a deep sense of what is and is not fair bred into us—and being yelled at for someone else's mistakes is clearly on the "not fair" side of the ledger.

That's why it's particularly important for your frontline people to feel that they're a significant part of the organization—and to feel supported by it. If they're going to overcome this basic reaction in the way you need them to, the payoff for doing it has to be clear and reliable.

It's an Uncomfortable Situation

Most people get very uncomfortable when face-to-face with another person who's unhappy—and almost as uncomfortable if they're on the other end of the telephone with one. Even when you know intellectually that the person isn't unhappy with you, you may react as though the person were. Because it's uncomfortable, you want to settle the situation and get out of it as quickly as possible. You may be tempted to do things such as:

- Pacify the customer at all costs.
- Get someone else to deal with him as quickly as possible.
- Yell back, so he'll shut up and be polite.
- Or one of a dozen other responses whose goal is to bring the unpleasantness to an end as quickly as possible.

Needless to say, this isn't a very productive strategy. To avoid this, make it easier for the frontline person to handle the problem in other ways. It's easier for a frontline person to put up with the discomfort if he's confident he can handle it—and that you will back him up. This is another reason why effective training and support are so important.

The Customer Is Unfair

Even when you can deal with problems that others have caused, you may react strongly to a customer who's being unfair to you. She may want an unreasonable solution, perhaps even to get you to replace something she didn't get from you. So what do you do?

- You may commit a basic customer-service sin: You argue with her.
- You may start trying either to find holes in her story or to find subtle ways that you can cast doubt on it.
- You may become determined to give her the absolute minimum that your policies require.

Some customers really are unfair, and that fact really has to be handled (in Chapter 7). Effective frontline performance is based on discipline, though—discipline that says you try to satisfy the customer. If you can't, it's a failure, not a success. Frontline people have to *believe* this if they're to deal effectively with all the unfair customers they'll encounter.

The Customer Is Rude

This is almost like the preceding one, except that it's the customer's behavior and not what he wants that causes the problem. If you're not careful, his behavior may push you to

- "Bring him up short," to show him he can't treat you that way.
- Be rude back, until he becomes more reasonable.
- Just walk out on him.

Actually, there are times when the third alternative is the only feasible one. Not many times, but some. Except in those times, frontline people need to understand that rude people generally believe that it's the only way they can get satisfaction. Then it becomes a challenge to prove them wrong—at least where your firm is concerned.

The Customer's Negativity Is Contagious

When a customer who's extremely upset and negative confronts you, the negativity can spread almost as though it were an infection. You intend to "keep your cool"—but the next thing you know, your voice is rising and your knuckles are turning white.

If you react this way, you probably know how difficult it is to avoid the reaction. It's hard for frontline people as well. Experience helps somewhat. Confidence in being able to handle the problem helps even more.

I Don't Know What to Do, So I Get Defensive

This is one of the most common of all human reactions. An individual who knows that he can cope can afford to be patient and understanding.

One who's afraid of what may happen next or feels that his ego's on the line can't. It just feels better to go on the attack.

Experience and confidence are the best cures.

MAKING THE CUSTOMER THE PROBLEM

All of these reactions are inadequate, but it's important to understand just why. Superficially, it's wrong to be rude or get angry or "put a customer in his place." More important, the responses share one common characteristic, and it's the bottom line:

> When a frontline person reacts negatively to a customer, she communicates not that the customer *has* a problem but that he *is* the problem.

This is absolutely critical. No effective customer-contact person ever lets the customer feel that he is the problem. Instead, the frontline person accepts the customer's problem as her own, and solves it. Does this sound like so many words? Evidently Federal Express doesn't think so. This is what one of their customers says:

> In an age when most attempts at customer service raise my blood pressure, the mere sighting of a Federal Express truck calms me down. The drivers treat my problems as *their* problems.

Fortunately, one solution helps with each problem. In each of these situations, the response is worse to the extent that the frontline person lacks skill at dealing with unhappy customers. This, of course, is why you need an effective training program.

This last comment is a natural lead-in to the next chapter, which describes the training you must provide if your front line is to make you successful. Before turning to the next chapter, here are three more critical keys. It's important for you to understand them; it's far more important for everyone on your front line to understand and practice them:

> **Key #5**: Dissatisfied customers aren't problems, they're golden opportunities.

> **Key #6**: The really picky, demanding customers are *platinum* opportunities. Keep satisfying them, and you're in business for life.

The next key should be obvious to you, from the emphasis on both the value of a customer in Chapter 1 and the customer's future expectations in Chapters 2 and 3: Here it is:

> **Key #7**: If you intend to deal successfully with dissatisfied customers, focus on saving the customer, not on saving the sale.

CHECK POINTS

1. My company's frontline people know that helping a customer always comes first, and they practice it.

2. All of the people in my company understand that anyone who deals with a customer is part of our front line and thus is critical to the success of our organization.

3. Our frontline people know that they must create successful (personalized) transactions with our customers, and they consistently do so.

4. Our frontline people are truly expert at solving customers' problems for them.

5. Our firm is organized to take full advantage of intelligence from frontline people about product or service shortcomings.

6. Our frontline people derive great satisfaction from dealing with our customers.

7. Every manager in the organization knows that her first responsibility is to support the front line. She also knows that she must stay in close touch with both customers and frontline people.

8. Our frontline people have both the authority and the skill to solve almost every problem with which a customer presents them. Very, very few problems ever get "bucked up the line" for solution.

9. We understand the common negative reactions that frontline people have to overcome, and we work with them, when necessary, to overcome them.

4 TRAIN THEM TO DO IT

WANTED: Customer Service Representatives. Must deal with angry and otherwise upset customers for eight long hours each day. Will be primary company representative, charged with solving all the customers' problems and sending them away happy. Will be responsible for the success of the business. No experience required and no training is given. Pays minimum wage, with modest raises if you can last that long. A particularly attractive position for those who like dead-end jobs.

Of course, no one would run an ad like this. However, hundreds—no, unfortunately, thousands—of firms try to deal with customers and their dissatisfactions in just this way. Therein lies your opportunity.

The previous chapter described what your frontline people need to do if you're to succeed. The next chapter explains how to reward them and otherwise keep them doing it. This chapter deals with the key to it all—effective training.

WHAT EFFECTIVE TRAINING REQUIRES, #1

Now you're expecting me to tell you how do to effective training, right? Wrong. This section isn't about training at all. It's about the things you have to do if you want the training you provide to do you—and your frontline people—any good at all.

Here's a quick example of the impact of training:

"Carol, we're delighted to have you join us. Our personnel department has a two-day course for new customer-service employees, and their next session starts on Monday. That'll give you a week to get used to your job."

So, Carol goes down to the customer-service desk. This is a sample of what happens during the next three hours:

- "Oh, oh, here comes that witch with the two yowly kids. Carol, you get to handle her this time. Just remember that when she starts yelling at you, it's time to call Mrs. Joseph to take care of it."

- "Carol, we're giving too many refunds this month; it's making the store look bad. If a customer absolutely insists on it, give him a refund—but try and get him to take a store credit if you possibly can."

- "Look, Carol, you seem to be a nice kid, so take a little advice. You just can't spend that long with one customer and her problem, no matter how much you think she needs help. You've got to deal with the customers and get them out of here. You know our quota is a customer every two minutes."

She sees the same kinds of actions and attitudes for the rest of the week. Now, what do you suppose her reaction is when she's sitting in the new employee class and a smiling, freshly scrubbed lady begins by saying "The most important thing for you all to remember is that around here the customer comes first"?

In other words,

> Actual life in your company is the real trainer. The way other frontline people and their supervisors act, the kind of performance that gets rewarded, the day-to-day attitudes workers have toward each other and toward customers—these are what your people will learn and practice.

If your firm is honestly focused on the customer, just working there will train each new worker to be focused on the customer. Formal training, important as it is, just makes the process easier and faster. If your focus is somewhere else, though, every dime you spend trying to change it by training alone will probably be wasted.

A Reminder, Again

An important part of all this is effective support to the customer in a variety of ways. When your frontline people deal with unhappy buyers, it shouldn't be because the rest of your organization doesn't know how to do its job. They should be backed up by an organization that does the following:

- It sells the customer the right product in the first place and creates realistic expectations about its benefits.

- It makes sure that the customer knows how to install and use the product correctly, instead of leaving him on his own.

- It has the necessary replacement parts in stock or quickly available, particularly if the product has just been recently released.

- It has enough phone lines so that the customer-service person who picks up the phone doesn't encounter 15 busy signals worth of frustration.

- It otherwise avoids creating unnecessary (and exasperating) work for its customer-service people.

CASE STUDY: "So Simple a Child . . ."

Eddie Willis bought a waterbed and had it more-or-less neatly spread out around his room, ready to assemble. He was trying to decipher the directions that came with the bed. As well as he could tell, they were prepared by someone practicing what he had learned in his first month of English as a Second Language.

He finally gave up and called the store for help. The clerk tried to explain what to do over the phone; if you've ever tried to do this, you know how truly challenging it is. When he saw Eddie wasn't getting it, he suggested that Eddie come in to the store to let him show him how.

"But that's a five-mile drive," Eddie said, "and I'm right in the middle of putting it together."

"I'm sorry," the clerk said (with no conviction behind his words at all)— "I'm the only one here and there's nothing I can do to help you if you can't come in here."

Look at the situation the clerk was put in. Suppose he had really wanted to help Eddie, that he was the kind of frontline person we're talking about in this book. What alternatives did he have? Keep trying on the phone, frustrating as that was for both Eddie and him? Close the store for an hour, or call in a manager so he could come help Eddie?

The fact is that he didn't have a worthwhile solution available to him. Because his firm delivered a product with ambiguous instructions, it created a situation where customer satisfaction was impossible.

Like everything else in the process of creating customer satisfaction, by the way, good instructions are important but not enough. At the same time that Willie was wrestling with his waterbed, Rachael Lindsay bought a sprinkler for her front yard. The instructions were absolute models of what good instruction should be: clear, humorous, complete. When she finished, she really understood that product and the dedication of the company behind it. Unfortunately, the sprinkler died before the dandelions did . . .

WHAT EFFECTIVE TRAINING REQUIRES, #2

Ah, here's the discussion about training your frontline people, right?

Sorry. You'll get there—but first you have to look at something else that effective training requires: selection of the right people.

Skills, Motivation, and Affinity

Training can't realistically prepare a person to function responsively in an organization that doesn't function that way. Neither can it realistically prepare a person to function responsively who isn't cut out for that kind of work.

The performance of each individual—you and I included—is a product of three related but very different factors:

1. Skills—which training can provide.
2. Motivation.
3. Affinities—the kinds of things that each person finds interesting and enjoyable.

When the person is in the right job, these three work in harmony. Because she enjoys the work, she's motivated to be good at it, and she develops the skills she needs. Because she's good at it, she's motivated to do it. And the better she gets at it, the more she enjoys it.

This works in reverse, too. If he dislikes it, he's usually not motivated to learn to do it well. Because he doesn't do it well, he isn't well motivated, and he doesn't enjoy it. These negatives feed on one another, and it's extremely difficult for training to break up that pattern.

In other words, the interaction of skills, motivation, and affinities can produce a rising spiral of competent performance or a vicious cycle of deteriorating performance. There's nothing absolute about it; individuals continually go into lines of work they don't initially like, and some of them end up both enjoying it and excelling at it. There are also many who go into lines of work they don't initially like and end up miserable on their job for the rest of their working life.

Creating Friendliness

The moral of all this? If you want people who can be trained to be effective customer-contact people, you need to start by selecting individuals who will enjoy relating personally to people and want to become skilled at it. This is particularly true of the people who will deal with unhappy customers; it takes a special kind of person to enjoy that job and to tolerate the tension.

Two points in the previous chapter make this particularly important. First, your frontline people must relate to customers, no matter how unhappy, as valued persons. They must *not* hide behind the impersonal facade that many so often adopt when they must deal with unhappy people. This is hard enough for anyone; it's impossibly hard, though, for someone who doesn't enjoy interacting with people.

The second point is closely related. Remember the discussion at the end of the previous chapter, that when people are face-to-face with other unhappy people they often react to the *people* as the problems. And you don't want your frontline people treating customers as though they were the problem—ever. If you're to avoid this, you need to pick the kind of frontline person who will keep her cool and do her best to satisfy the customer.

What kind of person will do this? Above all else, you're looking for someone who likes other people and enjoys dealing with them. Firms such as Nordstrom's and Marriott call this characteristic, "friendliness." WordPerfect wants customer support employees who "like working with people." Micro Center looks for individuals who know how to treat guests well in their home—believing that they'll treat the company's guests (customers) equally well.

In more formal terms, this might be called the ability to "meet and deal," or "high interpersonal skills." Personally, I would describe this most important characteristic as a highly developed ability to empathize with others. Regardless of what you call it, a strong people orientation is the basis for success in dealing with dissatisfied customers.

There are many other characteristics you'll probably want. You can find them in other books on excellent service, in trade magazines and other publications dealing with your kind of business, and in your experience and that of others like yourself whom you talk with and trust. No other characteristic, though, can replace this basic liking for people.

Some Practical Tips

Selection is much too complex an issue to be discussed in the space available here. You might find these few more hints useful, though:

- Hire people who understand your customers. They don't have to be from the same cultural or ethnic background as your customers, but they need to understand how your customers feel and think and act. Your frontline people need to understand what your customers expect, and how they react when they don't get it. They may need to understand, for instance, that individuals who are loud and hostile may not be more dissatisfied (or more difficult to satisfy) than those who are very quiet and apologetic.

- The other side of this particular coin is that you need to beware of your own stereotypes. Unfortunately, many of the books on selections these days make something of a fetish of the personal side of selection. They emphasize "fitting in" and extensive interviewing and other very subjective criteria.

On the one hand, all of these are important. Your workers must fit your company's culture, and you do need to trust your own instincts. Picking employees is more than just a matter of tests and checklists. On the other hand, everyone has stereotypes about what really "good" workers are like. Some of these are accurate, some are distorted, and some are just plain wrong. The problem is, you're not a good judge of which of your own stereotypes are which.

All of this means that you need to use formal methods, too. There is a point in formal, validated tests, references, and the other paraphernalia of selection. It will probably be worthwhile for you to talk with a personnel consultant, or at least to read a book on selection by a professional.

- Here's the last and most important point: Don't ever make a selection on the basis of an interview alone. Virtually every one of us believes he can "read" people in an interview—but the evidence that we can't reliably do it is overwhelming. Some of the worst selections I have seen (and made) were based primarily on an interview.

In short, good selections use a mixture of methods and all of the information available from any source, leavened with common sense.

WHAT EFFECTIVE TRAINING REQUIRES, #3

Now it's time to talk about training, right?

Yes, but not training frontline people. It won't do you any good to train them if the organization doesn't practice what you preach; it won't do you any good to train them if they're not suited to the job; and it won't do you any good to train them unless their supervisors understand that their role is to support them.

If all your frontline people report directly to you, you can skip this. But if you have even one supervisor between you and the people who deal with unhappy customers, that supervisor needs to be trained. If you have several layers of supervision between you and the front line, *all* of them need to be trained.

The previous chapter described the kind of organization effective frontline people need. This organization requires a very specific kind of supervisor, one quite different from the traditional idea of a "boss." Here is what Jan Carlzon and Shoshana Zuboff have to say about the new role of supervisors:

- According to Carlzon, the primary reason for the authority of middle managers is "translating the overall strategies into practical guidelines that the front line can follow and then mobilizing the necessary resources for the front line to achieve its objectives."
- Zuboff, speaking of the kind of organization she believes will be most effective over the next decade, refers to the "need to shift our managers' roles. In our new organizations, they won't be the guardians of the information. Instead, we have to show managers that we really need them to be the educators—to create, manage, sustain, and nurture the environment in which learning and value creation can occur."

Without training, it's unlikely that your supervisors will see their role this way. Both Carlzon and Zuboff point out in their books the problems that arose when supervisors, who didn't understand what was needed in the new environment, fought the new role.

In fact, one of the biggest obstacles to most of the changes designed to empower workers—whether through Quality Circles, job enrichment, service quality, or whatever—is middle management. What appears to workers and top management as a powerful program for increasing effectiveness often feels to middle managers like the loss of their authority. If that's all they see, if they can't visualize a payoff for themselves—your whole program will founder and probably fail. At best, it will succeed despite the efforts of some of your most experienced people (your middle managers).

It needn't be this way. To change it, though, you need to see that your supervisors and middle managers understand their new roles. They need to understand how important their experience and support are to the success of a customer-focused firm.

Just what does this mean? Here are some specifics:

- Tom Peters refers continually in his books to managers and executives as "cheerleaders." There's no monopoly on this at the top of the organization. Your supervisors and middle managers can become cheerleaders for your frontline people. This means encouraging and emotionally supporting them. It also means keeping higher management aware of how important their frontline people are.

- Shoshana Zuboff refers (in the passage quoted on page **90**) to the need for managers to "create, manage, sustain, and nurture" an environment in which *learning* can occur. First-line and middle managers are absolutely essential to this. They need to create a climate in which honest mistakes are accepted as learning opportunities, in which employees are guided to use their native intelligence in dealing with customers. Thus they become educators and mentors, using their experience and knowledge of the firm to leverage performance by the people they manage.

- Two of the most critical skills for a supervisor have always been the ability to *develop trust* in her work group, and the ability to *delegate* successfully. These remain critical skills in a management team whose primary job is to support the front line. Because your good managers already have them, they provide a natural base on which to create the additional skills a truly customer-focused organization requires.

You cannot do this through training alone. The most critical element is your personal example—your willingness to make customer service and your frontline people a continuing priority. You must also create a reward structure for your managers and supervisors that pays off when they do what you want, and not otherwise. Finally, you need to be *their* cheerleader and mentor, encouraging and explaining what needs to be done—and celebrating with them when they do it well.

Nonetheless, training can help. You should already have systematic training for new supervisors and planned development for managers, just as a part of normal operations. This should already emphasize customer support and maximum responsibility on the front line—or at least be compatible with it. That makes it easy to add the proper modules needed to anchor the approach in your management team.

What if your training hasn't been directed that way? What if it has been more "traditional," concentrating on the authority of supervisors and the duty of employees to follow orders? Worse—what if you haven't had any systematic training at all, so that the organization's management style has just grown up on its own?

If so, you have a much more serious problem. You're going to have to do *re*training, which is always harder than initial training. You'll get some ideas in the following discussion about retraining of frontline people. You'll need to get more ideas from your training department, if you have one, or from a good training consultant. Whatever you do, prepare yourself to be patient, understanding and *firm*. This is where you get to be a leader, cheerleader, and educator! You can do it if it's what you really care about.

WHAT EFFECTIVE TRAINING REQUIRES, #4

Is it finally time to talk about training your frontline workers? Well, almost. There is one last preliminary. And it's going to be short. That doesn't mean that it's unimportant. It's not. It also doesn't mean that most managers already do it. Many of them don't. What I'm speaking of here is effective training of your *customers*.

That's already been covered, hasn't it? Part of it has—the part that deals with how to use your products or services. That's not all there is, though. It's not even the most important part. The core meaning of training customers is an excellent prelude to our discussion of training frontline people. Here's the essence of it:

> The real training is what happens consistently in day-to-day relationships.

This is just as true for customers as for the people in your firm. Every moment of truth with a customer is a minitraining session. What gets trained? Many things, but most of all the customer's *expectations*. Your frontline people need to train customers to expect the following:

• They will receive reliable, courteous, and effective responses to their problems. (When customers expect this, they don't have to "raise hell" to get satisfaction when they have a complaint. Think what a payoff this is for you and for your frontline people.)

- You really do intend to provide them the value they pay for, no matter what. (Many customers will just assume that you don't really intend to be excellent here, and they will accept a variety of problems and malfunctions that you'd fix in a minute if you knew about them.)

- There are some situations that you cannot remedy—if there really are. (For instance, they may need to know that the warranty is voided if they open the case, that they still pay if they cancel an appointment less than 24 hours in advance, and so on. The time for a customer to find this out—and gripe about it, if necessary—is *before* the transaction occurs.)

You can easily think of other ways that customers need to be trained. You don't have to tell your frontline people that this is what they're doing, certainly not when they're just starting. If they do what they need to do, though, the training will occur.

EFFECTIVE TRAINING

Ahah—this section is really about how you train your frontline people effectively.

Please remember the point that's been made before: Real training is what happens consistently in day-to-day relationships. Formal training well done can prepare workers for this and help them adapt to it more quickly and more effectively. It can't substitute for it; if the work situation isn't what it ought to be, training by itself isn't enough to correct it.

Is formal training unimportant, then? Jan Carlzon said that "frontline employees must be trained properly so they become empowered to respond to customers' unique needs with speed and courtesy." Did he mean it? Well, one of the first things he did to create the turnaround at SAS was to train 12,000+ *existing* staff.

Carlzon also points out that frontline training has another benefit: It shows that you're willing to put attention and resources into dealing with customers.

Does this seem like a lot of training? Look at what Mazda does for their *production* workers at their first American plant:

> Unlike many traditional plants where an applicant is "hired on a Friday and is on the job the following Monday," Mazda people, in most cases, are hired 10 to 12 weeks before they are placed on the assembly line.
>
> New hires receive three weeks of "soft training" in which they learn the basics of teamwork and Mazda philosophy. Then they are assigned to an area such as the body shop and they get seven weeks of classroom and hands-on training in welding . . .
>
> The cost of training the 3,500 workers is expected to be more than $40 million . . .
>
> At Mazda, "just-in-time" applies not only to materials but also to training, which is given precisely when needed.

Just in case your math is rusty, that training costs more than $11,500 *per worker*. Remember—these are production workers. You certainly don't think they need more skills than your frontline people, do you?

The Skills They Need

If we're agreed that you need to train your customer-contact people carefully, just what training do they need? You already know that they need to do the following:

- Create a successful transaction with the customer, by
- Relating personally to him

    To solve his immediate problem and

    Increase the expected value of his future transactions with you.

- By using common sense and a practical understanding of company policy.
- So well that the process is satisfying to your frontline people as well as their customers.
- And they should be a basic source of your firm's market intelligence.

The heart of this involves these skills:

- Being able to relate to an unhappy customer as a valued person, and to maintain the relationship until the customer is satisfied.
- Identifying and solving the problem that the customer brings to them.
- Using common sense and a practical understanding of company policy.

Please note that all of these are "hands-on" skills. It's not enough for your frontline people to know about them, or even to believe deeply that they're right. Above all else, they must know *how to do them.* This hands-on know-how is where so many training programs fall short.

An Example of Effective Training

What's your image of a training session? The instructor, lecturing from carefully prepared notes, probably using slides or transparencies? Sticking in a video- or audiotape or two, and perhaps a few workbook exercises or small-group discussions? Testing the students at the end to see that they've picked up the main ideas?

I hope this isn't your image, because this *is not* the way to teach skills, particularly the skills that frontline people need. To learn these skills, your workers need:

- To see what customer service looks like when it's done by an expert.
- To practice doing it that way, in realistic circumstances, but where mistakes are treated as helpful learning opportunities.

If training for your first-line people doesn't contain these two components, it won't be effective training.

Please understand, I don't mean that lecture and discussion aren't valuable. They are—but only when used to support the hands-on learning. Lecture can communicate the firm's policy, expectations, and support. Discussion can help first-line people get a clearer idea of their roles, and perhaps help them voice their insecurities and fears. However, these simply aren't enough. Employees have to *see* good customer service done, and then they must practice it themselves.

Here's how one session in a good training course might go:

- The instructor presents the firm's policies on satisfying customers. Each trainee is given a copy, plasticized, in a convenient size.

- The instructor leads the group in a discussion of the policies. He asks for their suggestions about where the problems will come and writes them on a blackboard or flip chart.

- He breaks the group into several small groups and asks each group to take a (different) problem from the list. Their job is to look at the problem and come up with as many ways as possible to solve it.

- The small groups meet back together and report to each other on their solutions. When each group reports, the other groups react and make suggestions.

- Then the instructor shows a portion of a videotape. The video shows three versions of an individual dealing with a situation similar to one raised by the group. In the first version, the individual handles it badly. The group briefly discusses why it was poorly done.

- Then the second version is shown, in which the problem is handled satisfactorily. Again, the group discusses the situation and how it was an improvement.

- Finally, the third version, which demonstrates excellent handling of a customer problem, is shown. The group discusses this, identifying why it was exceptional and how the example could be generalized to the problems that they identified.

- Then a student volunteer is selected to play the unhappy customer and another to be the customer-service person. They role-play the situation, with the customer-service person applying the approach used in the "excellent" video.

This is only one example. A complete course would use this movement from learning policy to observing effective practitioners to personal practice over and over again. As the course went along, the examples would get more and more difficult.

How long should the training course be? That varies with the job, the time and funds available, and the capabilities that the customer-service people bring with them into the firm. In some circumstances, a half-day could get them started satisfactorily. In others, a three- or four-day course might be just barely long enough.

The important point isn't the length of the course, or even its exact structure. You start by identifying the skills your frontline people need. Then you identify the training required to develop these skills. Finally, you need to see that the training actually helps to develop skills instead of just talking about interesting (even important) ideas or policies or procedures.

"Job Aids"

Often, many hours of training can be saved by developing job aids. A *job aid* is any device that a worker can refer to for help in getting the job done. The device could be as simple as a checklist or as complex as a small expert system. Job aids include such helps as:

- The checklist pilots use before taking off.
- A form to fill out when taking information on a new client.
- A pop-up help screen in a computer program.
- A chart that compares and distinguishes the features in a line of similar products.

Well-done job aids both reduce the training time required and help workers maintain a higher level of service. If you have a training department, you should ensure that they understand job aids and how to create them. You'll also find that frontline people will develop job aids of their own; discovering them and making them available to others is a high-payoff activity.

Problem Solving

If you intend for your frontline people to solve customer problems, they need to understand how to do so. This means they need to learn an effective problem-solving method that they can apply on the spot. The previous chapter outlined the gist of the problem-solving process. Here's a slightly different version of it, which summarizes a number of the themes discussed so far. This is what you should tell your frontline people:

- Begin by listening carefully to the customer—to identify what she believes the problem is. *Don't assume!* If you don't hear what she thinks her problem is, you can't solve it. Then you'll both be frustrated. You'll also both waste time unnecessarily.

- Unless there's a specific reason why not, ask the customer what she believes a satisfactory solution would be. Even though you understand how she sees her problem, the two of you may not see the same solution.

- If the solution she suggests is practical, will solve her problem, and is something your policy would clearly authorize—do what she wants.

- If it's not practical, try to negotiate a solution. Work with her to come up with a solution that you can support and that will satisfy her. If several alternative solutions are possible, give her a choice.

- If the customer's proposed solution won't really solve her problem, suggest another one—even if it takes longer and costs more. You don't want her to be "nice" just to please you and walk away with something that won't really satisfy her.

- Remember that a satisfactory solution not only takes care of the immediate problem but also increases the customer's expectations of the value of future dealings with you.

SOME TRAINING SPECIFICS

You'll want to tailor any training program for frontline people to your specific circumstances. A few basic practices and skills, though, are universal:

- Acknowledge the customer.

- Don't argue with the customer.
- Develop and use interpersonal skills.

Acknowledge the Customer

This basic practice has already been mentioned, but it's worth repeating quickly.

If the transaction is face to face, your frontline person should speak to the customer as soon as he approaches. The assistant manager at Marriott Courtyard (at the start of the previous chapter) was an excellent example. This simple act communicates that you think the customer is important—even if you (the frontline person) can't deal with him for a minute. If the minute drags on, your person should reassure him that you know he's there and will respond to him as soon as you can. Remember that if what your person's doing isn't dealing with a customer, she should drop it and take care of the customer.

What if the moment of truth occurs over the phone? Here, one of the worst things you can do is to lose the customer on hold. I'm amazed at how many so-called up-to-date phone systems let you do this. The good ones bring the call back up every 30 or 60 seconds; this is the kind you should have. If you don't, make sure you constantly stay aware of any customer on hold. If you can't take care of him yet, still pick the line back up every minute or so to reassure him he's not been forgotten.

Another question concerns automated answering and routing devices. You know the ones I mean—when the phone rings, they come on and instruct the caller which button to push to get to the person he needs.

These systems are a tremendous time and money saver, but they aren't necessarily "user-friendly." I've encountered some that were so frustrating that by the time I got to the customer-service person I had a whole new layer of anger over my original complaint. Even the best ones, though, are less customer friendly than a human operator.

Guess what the message in that is. If you're not completely sure about the effect of yours, have a few friends call into it, and then get their reactions.

Don't Argue with the Customer

Chapter 3 dealt this, but it's time to look at it again—because it's so important. It's really quite simple: Never argue with the customer. Period. As John Guaspari has said, "Once the supplier of goods or services puts itself into a contentious position with its customers, the game is lost."

No one with experience in customer service would disagree with this. However, that doesn't mean that it's easy to implement. When a customer comes in, upset, making "unfair" accusations (particularly when it's something the customer-service person had nothing to do with)—well, the natural reaction is to argue, to show the customer that *he's* the one in the wrong. Natural or not, though, it's the wrong reaction.

Training must deal with this reaction, and explain how non-productive it is. It's not enough, though, to *tell* frontline people that they shouldn't get angry with customers. They might know it intellectually, and even believe it strongly—but that's seldom enough to overcome as strong a natural reaction—which means that just talking about it isn't enough.

For this, your frontline people need practical training such as observing *exemplars* (very skillful people), through role-playing or through some similar form of hands-on training. Nothing short of this can assure you that your customer-service people will really practice what's been preached to them.

CASE STUDY: What Arguing Does

The scene was a busy airport terminal.

"But, sir, we called that flight several times."

"*I* didn't hear it. I was sitting right here and I never heard it called once."

"Sir, we did so call it. I can't understand why you didn't hear it. Everyone else heard it . . ."

That conversation continued not just for a minute or two, but for several minutes. Not only that, but another counter person—presumably wanting to help out her associate—added her own comments on how wrong the customer was.

Look at what was happening. The customer wanted to get somewhere and missed his flight. He was upset and probably wanted someone to blame for what happened to him. By arguing with him, the counter personnel were keeping his attention focused on what had happened to him—not on what they might do to resolve his problem.

This is a basic rule of problem solving:

> All solutions for problems lie in the present and the future. No solutions lie in the past.

In other words, by keeping the customer's attention focused on the past situation, these frontline people were *preventing* themselves from solving his problem.

Good frontline people let the customer "blow off steam." Over and over, effective customer-contact people have told me that many customers need to vent their anger at what happened to them. They understand this, and they let the customers vent. They don't return the anger—and as soon as the customer has "cooled down," they direct themselves to solving his problem.

After I finished the first draft of this chapter, I encountered a superb example of what a good frontline person does.

> I stopped at a McDonald's to minister to my favorite addiction: Diet Coke. I got my supersize drink (it really is an addiction!) and took a sip before I left. It didn't taste as I'd expected it to taste. I'm particularly sensitive on this point because the "Diet" doesn't always register on people.
>
> The individual who had waited on me was busy, so I told another server that I'd gotten the wrong kind of cola. She immediately began to fill a new cup with Diet Coke.
>
> My original server came back and asked what she was doing. When she found out, she said, "No—I fixed him a Diet Coke. I heard what he said."
>
> The other server finished filling the cup and gave it to me. Up to this point, everything had been unexceptional. Then the first server turned to me and said, "I'm sorry, Sir. I hope you have a good day."
>
> She *knew* she was right and I was wrong. When I tasted the cola carefully, *I* realized she was right. But she understood what customer service means.

Develop and Use the OLAF Skills

There were kings and saints named "Olaf," but the OLAF skills have nothing to do with them. OLAF is an acronym for Observe-Listen-Ask-

Feel. This book has shown repeatedly how crucial it is to listen to the customer. Listening can be expanded to include to these four, closely related skills.

1. *Observe* the customer. If your frontline people learn basic observation skills, they'll know a lot about a customer before he comes face-to-face with them. Remember "body language"? Good observational skills help frontline people to understand customers and to shorten the time it takes to respond effectively to them.

2. *Listen* to the customer. Successful listening requires definite, specific skills. It requires the frontline people to remain calm and objective and to focus on the customer's problem—not on their own responses. Skills training in listening belongs in every frontline training program, but particularly for those who deal with unhappy customers.

   (Marilyn has been a flight attendant with American Air Lines for 10 years. When I asked her what was most important in dealing with unhappy passengers, she didn't hesitate a moment. "The best thing is to listen to them." In the next five minutes, she repeated this sentiment at least a half-dozen times.)

3. *Ask* the customer for more information. This helps you understand the customer, but it does something more. It communicates that you *want* to understand her. Asking questions is a real art. For instance, a basic guideline is to ask open-ended questions ("What went wrong with the product?") instead of ones that can be answered with a simple "Yes" or "No" ("Was it the amplifier that caused the problem?").

4. *Feel* the customer's situation. This is what's called "intuition"—and it's difficult to define, much less to learn. Perhaps the most you can do is to encourage your frontline people to use their feeling for customers and develop their self-confidence in doing so. A carefully developed intuition will often get to the core of a problem much faster than just thinking about it will.

This, of course, just scratches the surface. The biggest problem in intelligent training of your frontline people is knowing just what training to select and when there's been enough of it.

FOLLOW-ON TRAINING

Businesses tend of think of training as something that happens when an individual first goes into a job. Certainly that's important, for all the reasons already covered. However, three other situations call for *re*training in one form or another. These aren't dealt with in detail, but here's a quick summary of them.

- *Refresher training.* Even in the best circumstances, jobs and policies and procedures get old and routine. What may have been a sharp edge dulls. Your frontline people need to be reminded every so often of the performance you expect. They may even need to practice some of their skills that have gotten rusty. No matter how well things seem to be going, you should provide regular, short update sessions. They help keep your people sharp, and they underscore your commitment to customer satisfaction.

- *Update training.* No matter how well trained your frontline people are, situations change—and that requires you to retrain them. This may be a simple update, a two- or three-hour briefing on changed products or policies. Or it may involve days or even weeks of intense workshops to adapt to a major change in markets or product or service line.

- *Corrective training.* This is the training you have to do because your people aren't performing correctly. They may have slacked off from an originally effective level of performance. They may have been doing it wrong from the beginning. Or you may be making dramatic changes in the way you deal with customers. This gets particularly difficult if your people believe that the way they were doing it was "right" or "fair"—and the new way isn't.

Refresher training is relatively easy and straightforward, especially if you don't wait too long between sessions. The other two are more difficult. It's much harder to train people to do something in a way that's different from the way they're accustomed to than to train them to do it that way initially. When they're used to doing it a particular way, they not only have to learn how to do it the new way—they have to *unlearn* the old way.

"Unlearning" is difficult. When people really learn how to do something, it becomes second nature to them. They do it well without thinking about it. Even if they want to change, the new way requires thought and attention; it's just plain harder and more stressful. If they don't particularly want to change, the problem is compounded.

Here's a final thought on follow-on training. If you have to do it, prepare carefully, be patient, and persist. It can be done; it just can't be done quickly or easily.

CHECK POINTS

1. The best source of training for my new frontline people is my experienced frontline people—because the experienced people are so good at what they do.
2. My firm uses selection methods designed to select people for frontline jobs who have the basic skills, motivation, and affinity for the work.
3. We select people for frontline positions only if they like people and enjoy dealing with them.
4. The supervisors of our frontline people are trained to support them, and they're comfortable with this role. None of them are threatened by the independence and responsibility we expect from our frontline people.
5. We consciously train our customers in what to expect from us.
6. Our training concentrates on developing the skills our frontline people need, not just giving them ideas.
7. We make maximum use of job aids to reduce the training time required for frontline people.
8. Our frontline people see their job as solving problems for customers, and they're trained in effective problem-solving methods.
9. All of our frontline people receive training in the OLAF skills.

5 KEEP THEM DOING IT

"Miss, that room you just sent me to is a mess! It hasn't been cleaned, it stinks—I can't believe you'd do that to someone!"

"I'm very sorry. Let me find you a different one and . . ."

"You ought to be sorry! I'm just not used to people treating me this way. Are you so incompetent that you don't even know when a room is ready?!"

"I'm afraid we had some bad information on our computer. Here, I think this room will . . ."

"Miss, I don't care about computers—I just want you to do a half-decent job of taking care of your customers. It's disgraceful that you can't even do a simple thing like . . ."

"Excuse me. I'm Howard Estes, the manager, and I think I'm the one you need to be talking to. I'm afraid our new computer system isn't working as it should just yet. But let's forget that and get you into a really nice, clean room now . . ."

BAD EXAMPLES

You've got a clear idea of what your customer service people need to do. You know how to select and train them to do it. That's not enough. This chapter is about the other steps you have to take if you want the system to work. Because so many firms don't take these steps, or take them poorly, it might help to start with some bad examples. As you read each example, decide for yourself what's wrong in the situation.

EXAMPLE #1:

Customer: Sir, you sold me a defective product, and I want to return it!

Employee: Let's see. It looks all right to me.

Customer: Well, it doesn't work all right.

Employee: There are some scratches here—like someone knocked it off a table or something.

Customer: Well, I didn't do it!

Employee: Now, now, Madam, let's not get excited. We just can't be too careful about people these days, you know.

Customer: I *don't* know, and I don't care. I want my money back.

Employee: I'll see if I can help you. Do you have the sales slip?

Customer: Yes, I . . . No, I left it at home. But you can see your sticker right here—and you haven't been carrying this but a week.

Employee: I'm sorry, Madam—there's not a thing I can do. Company policy is no refunds without a sales slip. I have to follow that, and I just can't help you.

Customer: I can't believe this! I've been shopping here for years, but this is the last time you'll see me!

Employee: I'm very sorry, madam. I wish I could have helped you. Have a good day.

That was an easy one: The employee violated every rule in Chapter 4. He needs training, attitude adjustment, or a new job. Sometimes, though, it's not so easy to identify the cause of poor performance by customer support people. Look at these examples:

EXAMPLE #2:

Customer: The office chairs I ordered from you are too large. I want to trade them back in for a new set—and don't worry, I'll handle the delivery and pickup myself. It won't cost you anything.

Employee: That sounds all right—I think that we can do it. What chairs do you want to replace them with?

Customer: The ones I have are Model J44. I think the ones I need are these—Model J32.

Employee: Oh, my—these are $23 less apiece. We don't give refunds, and I'd have to give you a refund of part of the price. I need to talk to my supervisor for a minute, if you'll excuse me . . .

(Five minutes pass)

> Sir, I'm terribly sorry but neither my supervisor nor the
> assistant manager know what we should do. Please let me have
> your phone number, and I'll call you just as soon as I can get
> in touch with the manager. . .

What happened this time? Actually, there were two shortcomings.
First, the employee wasn't supported by clear, effective *policy and
procedure.* Neither she nor two levels of management knew what to do in
the situation, nor could any of them make a decision on their own. This
points to the second problem: No one had the authority to resolve the
problem when the policy wasn't clear. Because of this, the customer—
who had what he saw as a perfectly reasonable proposal—is going to be
inconvenienced further.

EXAMPLE #3:

Employee: (Picks up phone) Hello, may I help you?

Customer: Miss, this is absolutely atrocious. I ordered five dozen filet
mignons for my party tonight, and you sent me *five.*

Employee: That's terrible, and I don't know how it could have happened.
Please hold on just a minute . . . I'm afraid I have even more
bad news for you. We only have 2 dozen filets in stock.

Customer: What?! Miss, are you brain-dead? I told you that the party is
tonight. I need you to take care of your mistake, NOW!

Employee: I'm trying. . .

Customer: Who cares if you're trying! I don't need some simpering idiot
to tell me you're trying. I want to speak with someone who can
do something!

Employee: Ma'am, I want to see what we . . .

Customer: Do I have to make a federal case out of this?! I have a simple
request—just give me what I ordered from you. But, no, you
can't solve the problem. I've got a dinner party in less than two
hours and . . ."

Here, the company is failing to *protect* the employee against abuse.
Many companies who'd fire an abusive employee on the spot still expect
customer-service people to take any and all abuse that customers heap
on them. An employee who has to put up with this kind of abuse for long
is going to be completely demoralized—and will quite probably become someone else's employee.

EXAMPLE #4:

Customer: Sir, I just can't use the last hundred lights I ordered and I need to return them to you.

Employee: Is there anything wrong with them?

Customer: No—they're just more than I need. And your policy says that you want your customers to be satisfied. Are you not going to take them back?

Employee: Please excuse me, sir, while I check on something . . .

(The employee leaves and goes to talk to the manager of Customer Service)

Employee: Ms. Janos, I have a customer out there who wants to return 100 lights. Should I let him?

Manager: Ow! We really need to let him bring them back—but we're already 10 percent over on returns. If I take any more, it'll wreck my quota on that—and my bonus with it. I'll tell you what—if you can talk him into trading them for something, or get out of taking them back some other way, I'll see there's an extra $10 in your check this week. . . .

This may be the most common way that firms fail at customer satisfaction. The policy says that the customer will be satisfied—but the actual *reward* system places cost before satisfaction. No policy—and certainly not a customer satisfaction policy that appears to cost money—will succeed if the people who administer it are rewarded for controlling costs instead.

Good objectives, good selection policies, good training—all of these are important. They're not enough. If you want frontline people who'll reliably convert dissatisfied customers into loyal ones, you must do more.

HOW TO GET EFFECTIVE FRONTLINE PERFORMANCE

- Develop, support, and enforce clear, effective policies, and develop effective procedures for implementing those policies.
- Protect your frontline people against abuse.
- Implement and stick to a reward system that is completely consistent with your customer-satisfaction policies.

Here these are, in more detail.

CLEAR, EFFECTIVE POLICIES

The Need for Policies

The first step you take is developing and clearly stating your policy for dealing with dissatisfied customers. The "Good News" in the Prologue had examples of policies; if you don't remember them, you might want to turn back quickly and look at pages 11 and 12.

Here are some other potential policies:

- "We will do whatever it takes to satisfy a customer."

- "We cannot give refunds—but we will gladly give you an exchange for an item of equal or greater value or a store credit for the amount of your purchase."

- "All sales of marked down items are final."

- "If any car we sell you fails to run at any time during the basic warranty period, call us. We will pick up your car and loan you a replacement while it is being repaired."

- "No personal item that has been removed from its package can be returned."

- "If any product you buy from us is defective, call our 800 number. We will ship you a replacement and, as soon as we receive the original product, we'll refund 5 percent of the purchase price for your trouble."

Each one of these is a relatively clear policy. (Whether any one of them would be good or bad for your business is a completely different question.) Each one communicates to the customer what your company will do to satisfy her. Each one is more than just a pious statement or a fuzzy restriction.

Is each one enough by itself? Probably not. This is why:

- Do you really mean you will do "whatever it takes" to satisfy a customer? If you do, you do—whether your customer is reasonable or not. If you don't—well, exactly what do you mean?

- You don't give refunds. What if a customer returns a defective electronic keyboard that she needs for a concert this weekend—and you can't get a replacement for a week? What do you do then?

- OK, so all sales of marked down items are final. Does that include marked down items that prove to be defective? All of them, or only some?

- You will pick up any car that fails to run during the warranty period and provide a loaner. What if the car fails to run because the owner left the lights on and ran the battery down? (That's not as easy a question as it might seem.)

- You won't accept the return of any personal items. What about items that can only be discovered to be defective when they're put on? Or items where the package is marked with the wrong size, and the customer can't tell until she opens the package?

- If a customer calls you about a defective product, you'll ship her a good one and ultimately refund 5 percent of the purchase price. Suppose you find that she's returning good items for replacement and 5 percent? Suppose another customer continually returns products, always with some minor flaw?

The point is, of course, that even the best policy isn't enough by itself. Policies have to be implemented through effective procedures— which promote and support common sense and initiative. Effective procedures are discussed in the next main section, but the whole topic of policies requires one more look before we leave it. If they're going to be effective, all policies need to be *clear* and *supported.* Policies for satisfying customers also need to *primary.*

Policies Should Be Clear

Even the clearest-seeming policy statement may have different meanings for different people. That's not hard to see in the case of a policy such as "we will do whatever it takes to satisfy a customer." It really could have a wide range of meanings.

There can also be ambiguity in much simpler statements. For instance, say your policy is to accept returned merchandise for credit within 30 days. Suppose the merchandise includes written material that the customer has marked up? Or the customer has already registered the product in his name?

These are all questions that can be answered—but they need to be answered up front, not when you're standing toe-to-toe with an unhappy customer. Here are two examples:

- One of the policies on page 109 stated that no personal items could be returned if they were opened. It wouldn't be hard to modify it to say "We will be happy to exchange or refund defective personal items or those that have not been opened, but we cannot provide refunds or exchanges for personal items under any other conditions." This is not only a more positive statement, but a clearer one. (Depending on the firm's experience, it might not be complete enough.)

- Another example promised that "If any car we sell you fails to run at any time during the warranty period, call us. We will pick up your car and loan you a replacement while it is being repaired." It would be much clearer if it said "fails to run *because of a defect . . .*" (That would leave many questions to be answered, but not as many as the original policy.)

In other words, if policies are going to be effective, they must be clear. No matter how clear you believe they are, someone else may read them very differently. Give any proposed policy statement to several other individuals, preferably ones with very different jobs and outlooks. If possible, also give it to a variety of customers and ask them how they read it. You can't ever get complete clarity, but this will get you much closer to it.

Policies Should Be Supported

Once you establish a customer satisfaction policy, it needs to be supported—without qualm, without modification, and without reservation. Look at your policies. Can you support them that fully? If your answer is "no," you'd better change your policies.

Organizations don't need to have great numbers of policies. The ones they do have should be ones they will support—not "sort of support" or "usually support," but *support*, period. You should support them, your supervisors should support them, and you should expect your frontline people to support them.

This creates a tremendous obligation on you to create *practical* policies. The road to that well-known resort with no thermostats is littered with policies that sounded great in the executive suite but were disasters on the front line. At a minimum, *no* policy should ever be implemented until the people who have to live by it have examined it and commented freely on it.

Whether to make an exception to policy is a serious question, which is discussed in Chapter 7. For the present, assume that policies are meant to be applied as written—and therefore must be ones that can be supported day in and day out.

(There's no better way to demonstrate support for customer satisfaction policies, by the way, than to build your compensation policy on them. That's discussed a little later in this chapter.)

Customer-Satisfaction Policies Should Be Primary

In the real world, it's almost impossible to have policies that don't conflict with one another at times. Manufacturing policies conflict with warranties, human resource development policies conflict with compensation policies, customer-satisfaction policies conflict with cost control policies. Effective firms recognize and deal with the conflicts and then modify the policies so that they're more compatible.

Regardless, here is an iron rule:

> No other policy takes precedence over customer satisfaction.

Well, here's where the rubber meets the road. Either you're in business to satisfy your customers, or you're in business for some other, less competitive reason.

If you haven't made your mind up on this matter, it's time to stop and think hard. If your firm is truly customer-focused, *nothing* can take precedence over satisfying the customer. If something else does take precedence, you're not really customer focused. Which will it be? (If you don't think its practical to be *this* customer focused, at least finish the book. You may find that you change your mind by then.)

If you want customer-satisfaction policies to be primary, you must implement them through effective procedures.

SIMPLE, EFFECTIVE PROCEDURES

Policies tell your people what the goal is. *Procedures* provide them with the way to get there.

Your first reaction may be that procedures are bureaucratic. After all, who hasn't gotten tangled up in red tape in some government agency or educational system because of endless procedures? "There's no reason for it, it's just procedure" is a standard joke—created by someone who was all too familiar with rigid, senseless procedures.

What's really at stake here isn't whether to have procedures. An organization without procedures is in chaos. The question is whether the procedures will be few, simple, and customer focused, or interminable, complex, and bureaucratic.

What Makes a Good Procedure?

Enough generalizing—look at this procedure:

When the Customer Service Department finds a trend in customer complaints, it will send a memorandum describing the complaints and the apparent problem to the department(s) involved. A copy of the memorandum will be sent to the Vice-President (VP) for Operations.

Any department that receives one of these memorandums will reply to the Customer Service Department within 10 work days. The department will explain the situation and the steps taken to remedy it. A copy of this document will also go to the VP for Operations.

If the Customer Service Department does not believe that the customer's concerns have been adequately handled, someone in that department will inform the VP for Operations, who will resolve the matter.

This procedure is simple; it doesn't even require a form. It's also effective—because it puts the Customer Service Department right in the middle of the decision-making process that produces (or fails to produce) customer satisfaction. It helps make clear to the rest of the organization that customer satisfaction *is* primary. It explicitly supports a strong customer-satisfaction policy.

Here's another critical procedure:

> All associates will take any reasonable steps to see that customers do not leave dissatisfied. If this can be done by refund, exchange or other action permitted by policy, the associate whom the customer contacts will solve the problem on the spot.
>
> If the associate cannot satisfy the customer, or if the steps to do so are apparently too expensive or go beyond store policy, the associate will contact his or her supervisor. If necessary, the situation will be elevated to the store manager.
>
> *No* associate or manager below the store manager level has the authority to refuse any customer request for satisfaction.

That certainly makes the company's intention clear! (By the way, it's not enough by itself. It should be accompanied by a clear policy stating that associates *will not* be penalized for errors of judgment in taking care of a customer. What happens if the firm doesn't have such a policy, and associates and supervisors get criticized for "exceeding their authority" to satisfy a customer? Associates will buck more and more decisions up to their supervisors, who will buck more and more decisions up to the store manager, who won't have time to run the store.)

Again, this procedure supports the firm's policy without becoming overly complicated.

Other procedures are also necessary, spelling out exactly what actions are required to support customer-service policies. This suggests a critical point about procedures: To the maximum extent possible, they should *support* the judgment of customer-support people, not *supplant* it.

The Other Kind of Procedures

The kind of procedure that most irritates customers—including you and me—is the one that tries to freeze human judgment into a set of cookbook rules. In the hands of a true bureaucrat, the simple procedure just described might be transformed into this:

> Associates will take appropriate steps to ensure that customers do not leave dissatisfied. The following are "appropriate steps":
>
> - If the customer presents a dated sales receipt no more than 30 days old, and if the merchandise is in its original condition and in the original packaging, make an exchange (preferred), or issue a refund or store credit. However, if the payment was made initially by check and it has been fewer than 10 work days since the transaction, the associate will fill out Form 1033b and inform the customer that the refund will be made by check from the central office.
> - If the customer presents a valid sales receipt (as above) and the original item is not in stock and will not be available within 5 days, replace a defective item with another similar item, as long as the price difference is no more than 5 percent.
> - If the customer presents a valid sales receipt (as above) and presents an article for refund, credit or exchange as defective merchandise, and the problem could reasonably have been caused by customer misuse, the associate will tactfully question the customer concerning the alleged defect and . . .

This approach is the kind that was memorialized in the description of the between-the-world-wars Army as "a system designed by geniuses to be operated by idiots." This kind of system breaks down quickly in combat, just as it does in customer service.

Note that the problem isn't the specific requirements as such; depending on the situation, they may be effective or misguided. The problem is that there are just too many variables, too many ways that customers can be dissatisfied, for this cookbook approach to work. Combined with a rigid control policy that insists that everyone abide by the procedures or else, it results in the constant elevation of problems to higher and higher levels of management. While the problems are elevating, customer irritation is elevating even faster.

When a firm's customer-service people are well selected and well trained, they should be given broad freedom to satisfy customers. Some will invariably make mistakes; they should be praised for their commitment to customer satisfaction, and then counseled on how to do it more effectively in the future. They should be developed as far as possible, so that they can make more and more sophisticated decisions that will satisfy customers. Not only does this make the job intrinsically more interesting, but also the more customers an individual can satisfy, the more satisfied he or she is going to feel about the job.

The Impact of a Limited Talent Pool

There's a potential problem here, a serious one. In many places, good candidates for frontline positions are becoming harder and harder to find—and more and more expensive to keep. As businesses dip increasingly into the shallow end of the talent pool to find workers, those whom they find will require more and more training and guidance. It may not be possible to bring them along as rapidly, or to give them as much freedom. If this happens, the firm's policies on delegation to frontline people will have to be adjusted to deal with these realities.

If possible, you should prevent this. There are any number of steps you can take, but here are three of the most important ones:

- *Spend more time and money searching for good people.* It's often effective to ask your best frontline people to talk to their friends about working for you. Some firms pay a bonus to workers who recommend individuals that are eventually hired. Whatever you do, put time and effort into finding the best possible people to begin with. An hour effectively invested here will save many, many hours and dollars later on.

- *Provide more training and job aids.* Your training needs to be more complete, but not all of your new hires will need all of the training. You'll need to break the training into modules and then develop a way to identify who should get what training. Tailor the training to the actual people you can hire, not some abstract idea of what you want. This is also fertile ground for job aids. They save training time and make it possible to develop competent performance more quickly. Use them whenever possible. Do careful follow-up and evaluation on both training and job aids, to make sure they're accomplishing what you intend.

- *Pay your best workers in gold bars.* Well, maybe not quite that drastic (though it's how one successful executive explained his compensation plan). The pay differential between a mediocre frontline person and an excellent one should be significant. Fifty or 100 percent isn't necessarily out of line. (If it seems extreme, calculate what it costs you to hire and train a replacement for a really good employee—then look at the cost again.)

A quick note of caution, though. It's easy to establish stereotypes of "good" customer-contact people, and then conclude that those who don't fit the stereotypes are less reliable or harder to train. This is precarious, particularly if those stereotypes are based on racial, sexual, or ethnic characteristics. If you want them to be effective, use selection and training practices that concentrate on the individual—and don't just treat him as an instance of a stereotype.

There's a final point to make before leaving *procedures*. Take a look at this:

> Associates will attempt to satisfy customers with a store credit or exchange. Only if the customer is disruptive and takes the time of the staff unduly will a cash refund be given.

You won't see this procedure written many places, but it's practiced over and over. It's not necessary a bad procedure in itself, but it has a very specific problem. It encourages customers to hold out for a refund. It *rewards* precisely the kind of customer behavior you want to avoid.

Is there an easy to answer to this problem? Probably not. There may be times when getting an irate customer off the floor is the best thing to do, no matter what it costs. Just remember, though, that whenever you offer a benefit *because* a customer is being obnoxious, you reward that behavior and simultaneously penalize your conscientious customers. Do you really want to follow this kind of strategy?

PROTECTION FROM ABUSE

The message of this section is brief: *Protect your customer-contact people from abuse, period.*

It's amazing how often this simple necessity is overlooked. Companies become so dedicated to pleasing customers (right!) that they expect their customer-contact people to put up with anything from a customer, no matter how irrational or abusive (wrong!). If you were a frontline person, what would a policy like this do to you? If you're like most of us, you'd turn into a patsy or, more likely, an ex-employee.

It's unfortunate, but a few folks enjoy saving up their hostility and then unloading it on someone who can't strike back. Every so often one of them will walk up (or phone in) to one of your frontline people and fire a broadside. That's when a manager (or a specially trained employee) needs to intervene—fast!

How do you do this?

- The employee could break off contact with the customer and go get someone. This isn't usually a good strategy because it leaves the customer alone and fuming—and that's something to be avoided whenever possible. If that's the only recourse employees have, though, they should be free to take it.

- An improvement is a watchful supervisor or senior representative. When customer-service people are collected in one spot, this individual can normally tell when one of them is in trouble. Then he can move quickly and quietly into the situation. The employee is protected, the customer isn't kept waiting—and the prompt action by the manager may help to calm the customer.

- A better alternative is a quick-response signaling system. Give the employee a button to press, which alerts the manager, or an equivalent device. Make it clear that when the button is pressed, someone will show up immediately. Then, when the signal is given, the manager should respond to it immediately.

When a system like this is effective, it has a very important side benefit. When they know that help is instantly available, most of your frontline people will "hang in there" with the customer for much longer. This is a tremendous training device, one that helps individual employees increase their skills on their own. It also saves the time of the supervisor. The system is worth having for this reason alone.

Deciding when and how to protect your people is often a gray area. You want to protect your customer-contact people, but you don't want to over-protect them. Just as you want to screen them from abuse, you want them to develop the skills to deal with progressively more difficult customers. The more expert they become, the more self-confidence they'll have, which helps them become more expert, which helps them develop more self-confidence, which . . .

There's no snap answer to this problem. Selections that bring resilient employees on board and a training program that builds strong skills help. A "panic button" that an employee can use to summon assistance at any time helps (by giving them the confidence to keep dealing with the customer).

When all's said and done, though, the sensitivity and sensibility of the supervisor are critical. He has to know the people, encourage them, counsel them and support them—which is another way of saying that the selection and training program for managers and supervisors is at least as critical as that for employees.

(One way for your supervisors to get up-to-date information on effective management is to read *The New Manager's Survival Manual*, published by John Wiley & Sons, which I also wrote.)

REWARDS, REWARDS, REWARDS

Do any of these situations sound familiar?

> "Tony, I want you to know how happy we are with how you handle customers. I really wish I could increase your bonus because of it. You know, though, our bonuses are based strictly on quarterly profits, and this quarter has been low. Keep up the good work, though."

> "Maria, letting that man talk you into paying half of his repair costs was completely out of line! I know we want to keep customers satisfied, and I know I wasn't here at the moment, but we can't go around doing foolish things like that. If it happens again, I'm going to have to write you up for it."

"Tomás, we all appreciate how you've strengthened our Customer Service Department these past few months. That's the good news. The bad news is that you're costing the company money we can't afford to spend. I don't care how you do it, but you've got to cut returns by 25 percent in the next quarter. Oh, yes—you've got to slow down on sending memorandums on product problems to other departments, too. They're so busy trying to answer you that they don't have time to get their jobs done."

It's all too easy for a company to state a policy and then reward very different behavior. Specifically, when it comes to customer satisfaction, it's very easy to voice strong support for the program but give out the "attaboys" and the bonuses to the people who control costs. If you're tempted to do this, just remember that people do what pays off for them. If you pay lip service to customer satisfaction and give your dollars to the people who cut costs, both costs and customer satisfaction will end up cut.

A Variety of Rewards

Of course, it's not simply the dollars. People work for many different rewards, such as:

- *Simple, on-the-spot praise and thanks* from their supervisor or manager for a job well done. A manager should never miss the opportunity to publicly thank a frontline person who's just dealt superbly with a customer—*never.*

- *More tangible forms of recognition,* such as a white hat pin awarded for dealing with a particularly difficult customer or a free dinner for two for 5 favorable letters in a month. (I'm generally opposed to "employee of the month" or " "Customer Service Rep of the quarter" awards. Any recognition that is scarce tends to create tremendous ill feelings among the "losers." This also tempts managers to rotate the recognition rather than use it as it was designed to be used. Award programs that provide quick, meaningful recognition whenever and wherever excellence occurs are normally far superior.)

- *Recognition for teamwork.* If your customer support people have to work together—and they often do—develop a simple form of recognition that they can give each other for being helpful. This directly balances out individual effort with attention to team accomplishment. It could be something as simple as a small "thank-you" sticker or pin. When someone accumulates X number of these in a week or month, it should earn the person something a little more substantial (such as a free lunch). One word of warning: Awards for cooperation probably won't work if your frontline people are broken into strong cliques. If that's the case, start with individual awards until you've built an overall team feeling.

- *More independence.* For many (but not all!) individuals, being able to work and make decisions independently is tremendously rewarding. Provide this reward for those who want it. Set up a series of check points. When a frontline person passes a check point, increase her freedom to deal with customers. For instance, a person might go from (1) approving only exchanges or credits to (2) approving refunds to (3) adding value to the transaction (see Chapter 7) to (4) . . . Make a big deal of each step—and see that the first two or three steps are reached quickly.

- *Money.* If a frontline person does a particularly good job at turning a dissatisfied customer into a loyal one, give him or her money on the spot. That's right: on the spot. Walk out there, call the others together if it's practical, and put actual U.S. dollars into the person's hand. It doesn't have to be much; the more often you do it, the less it needs to be.

  Why not a check, through the established recognition system? Two reasons. First, cold cash in the hand still sings in a way that a check won't. Second, most recognition programs take days or weeks—or months!—to pay off. If superior customer service is going to be recognized effectively, it needs to be done right then, right there. If your formal recognition system can do this, by all means use it. If not, improvise! What about withholding taxes? Have the manager send a voucher to payroll, and let them do the legerdemain to make what you put into the employee's hand the take-home part of the award.)

  Try it—you'll like it!

You can keep adding to the list. If the ones listed don't suggest others to you, there are dozens of good books out there to help you find them.

And Now: Serious Money

Having said all this, I come back to money—and talk about *serious* money. People do work for and respond to thanks and buttons and more independence and dollars in their hands. On the other hand, these rewards, as much as they may help, don't pay the bills. Serious money does. In many firms, money is the basic way that people keep score: I know how well I'm doing by the size of my paycheck. This means that if the compensation system isn't consistent with the other reward systems, the other reward systems will take a back seat.

Let me put this just a little more precisely. If your compensation system is based on seniority, cost-of-living, or other nonperformance factors, you may be able to get really good response to customers with small rewards. If you pay for performance, though, and you want your people to produce customer satisfaction—then that's the performance you'd better pay for.

You need to take this seriously, if you aren't already. It's easy to say "Oh, our people will do what's right for customers, no matter what," or "They know they ought to take care of customers first"—and then pay them for something else. It's easy to say, and it's a losing hand. If you want customer satisfaction and loyalty, *pay* for customer satisfaction and loyalty. If it's what's primary, then it's what you pay for first.

How do you create a compensation system that does this? There aren't any pat answers because there are too many kinds of compensation systems out there. Here are some basics for you to consider:

• Make customer satisfaction part of *everyone's* pay. Oh, all right, maybe you can't do it for the night-shift janitor. But it should be part of the compensation plan of everyone who influences customer satisfaction: designers, salespeople, line managers, manufacturing personnel, customer service reps, and so on. If customer satisfaction is what your firm is all about, then everyone should be focused on it no matter what his immediate job duties are.

- Do you pay a bonus based on profitability? Here's a relatively simple way to modify it to include customer satisfaction. Do routine surveys of customer satisfaction (explained in more detail in Chapter 6). Create a formula that combines the results of the surveys with the profitability measure you use to compute bonuses. For instance, you might deduct a fixed percentage of the bonus for each half-percent customer satisfaction falls below a predetermined level. It can also work the other way: increase the bonus by a fixed amount for each half-percent customer satisfaction exceeds the minimum. (The combination is valid. If customer satisfaction is down, the long-term trend of profitability will be down. And vice versa. If you want a way to combine long-term trends and results with short-term ones, this is a candidate.)

- Here's another thought, one that can be combined with either of the preceding ones or with any other compensation plan based on customer satisfaction. Be sure the check makes it clear what the impact of customer satisfaction (or dissatisfaction) on pay was. A little note like "Your check is $250 less this quarter because customer satisfaction dropped ½ percent" is a real attention-getter.

. . . For Curing Customer Dissatisfaction

All of the methods just discussed pay for customer satisfaction, and properly so. But the compensation system needs to have an item that deals specifically with resolving customer *dissatisfaction*. You may not have many customer-contact people, but every one of them should have an item in his performance plan that rewards for dealing skillfully with unhappy customers. How? That's hard to say because I don't know your compensation system. Here are a few short suggestions:

- Put cash into the hands of customer-contact people for doing their jobs particularly well. You can formalize this into part of your compensation plan (but don't lose the "right there, right then" impact of it). If you're willing to put out 10–25 percent over salary in this kind of payment, it'll work.

- Many companies use systems where customers can award tokens to employees that have been particularly helpful to them. If that works for you, give the tokens a meaningful dollar value.

- What about your salespeople, whether they work in-house, on routes, or in territories? They're often the ones who find out first about customer dissatisfaction. I don't know an easy answer to this one. I do know that if you make it easy for your customers to contact you about problems, and if you regularly survey them, you can find where the problems are—and perhaps where your stars at resolving these problems are, too. Your sales force has at least as great a stake as anyone else in identifying and dealing with the problem—and those who're good at this need to be recognized for their contribution.

EVERYBODY GETS A TURN

Those are the basics for taking care of your frontline people: give them good, sound policies and procedures, protect them, and reward them. There's one other favor you can do them—by understanding the situation they're in and the contribution they make.

How do you do this? One way, practiced by most of the exemplary firms mentioned in the book, is hands-on management. See that managers at all levels are out there on the floor, interacting both with frontline people and with customers. If you have to make a rule that says "one hour a day on the floor" or "talk with 10 customers a day," do it!

I'd like to suggest something else for you to consider. Arrange your firm's work so that everyone gets a turn at dealing with dissatisfied customers. That's right: *everyone.* Have customer-service supervisors do it regularly—but have higher management do it, too. Even the CEO could profit from a few hours listening to what customers—unhappy customers—have to say about the company's products or services.

Why do this? Why take people who are paid to manage and have them spend their time on lower-level customer-service jobs? Here are some of the reasons:

- If you're still looking at your front line as "lower-level jobs," you're missing a basic message of this book. The front line is where the action is. No one is ever underemployed who's working there.

- Things change. When managers put some time in on the front line, they keep their picture of what's happening up to date. They make better management decisions. They support their frontline people better.

- Also, the higher up a person moves in management, the more he loses touch with the details of what happens on the front line. Two or three levels up, frontline problems can seem simple—and invite simplistic solutions. The policies and procedures developed there can become rigid and unnecessarily confining. The only effective cure for this is for each manager to keep in close touch with frontline action. And there's no better way to do this than to deal with a few dissatisfied customers.

Still sound like a waste of time? One more time: what's the basic policy of your firm?

MEASURING WHAT THEY DO

You have your frontline people selected, trained, and in place. You're going to reward them appropriately for their contribution to your firm. How are you going to tell just how valuable that contribution is? For many people, that's the question of how you measure what they do.

Let me warn you right now that I have no easy answer to this question. I'm not sure I have any answer at all. Measuring performance in jobs that require successful transactions among people is extraordinarily difficult. Many writers say that you can *always* measure something meaningful in a job. Perhaps that's true, but a look at some of the issues may help you look at it more realistically.

The Basic Rule

This is the basic rule of all performance measurement:

You will always get (at least the semblance of) what you measure.

The rule suggests two statements. First, people will produce what you measure. If the people who deal with dissatisfied customers are measured and rated on the number of customers they "handle" in an hour, they will handle a lot of customers. The quality of each transaction may drop, slightly or markedly, but the required number of customers will be handled. If they're measured on the percentage of "satisfied" customers on a survey, they will do their best to produce that percentage of satisfied customers.

There may be a catch in the figures they produce, though. The second statement suggested by the rule is that it's hard to tell whether you're getting what you think you're getting. There's no evidence that creativity is concentrated at the top of organizations; in fact, the reverse may well be true. When workers are affected by a measurement that they believe is unfair or misguided or—worst of all—keeps them from doing a good job, they will try to find ways to produce the figures without changing what they do.

Here's a quick example. Because you're trying to control service costs, you establish a quota for your customer-contact people of X number of transactions per day. Say that the quota is 5 percent higher than they're doing now. Lo and behold, by the second month, they're performing at this level.

Are you getting more of the same quality of transaction. Probably not. Each customer may be getting just a little less attention. Or something else may have happened. Before, no one counted customer contacts that weren't really complaints ("What's the phone number for your sales department?"). Now, these have been miraculously transformed into complaints, so that your people can tell you they handle 5 percent more complaints per day.

That idea may offend you. If it does, it may mean that you've been away too long from where the work of the world gets done. If your employees in any department believe that your measurements are unfair or get in the way of their doing their job well, they'll do their best to find a way around them. Count on it!

Quantity Drives Out Quality

A second rule is almost as basic as the first:

> When your measures emphasize quantity, quantity
> goes up—and quality goes down.

In the absence of other factors, workers will meet a requirement for increased quantity by trying to spend less time on each individual item or transaction. If you pack boxes for shipment, and your performance is measured by the number of boxes you pack, you'll try to look good by skimping just a little on each box.

That's bad enough with boxes; think what its consequences are when the "product" is successful transactions with customers. Remember that a successful *personal* transaction has its own rhythm: recognizing the other as a person, focusing on him, and then ending the contact gracefully. If a frontline person tries to hurry any phase of the contact, the success of the contact as a whole may suffer.

(There are alternatives to this. With effective training, your frontline people can learn how to conduct customer transactions quickly and efficiently *and* to do them well. Even better, if you have a trusting relationship with them, *they* can probably suggest ways to expedite transactions without lowering their quality.)

Automatic Measurement

What do you do about these problems? One solution is not to measure—but it's not a very good solution. Another approach is to automate the data collection. This doesn't mean having people punch information on what they've done into your computer system. That just gives you a different way to store data that's still *collected* in the same old way.

Truly automated data collection produces data as a by-product of operations. Many phone systems produce a list at the end of each month of the number of calls made, their destinations and their length. Data entry systems can count the number of keystrokes entered by each worker and how many of them had to be redone.

In these circumstances, the data collected is more reliable—because it's collected without human intervention. That's a definite plus, and having a few systems like this around can keep workers "honest" who might otherwise try to cheat on the system. Another plus is that workers don't have to worry with tracking and entering the data manually.

No matter how reliable, though, automated data collection normally has two shortcomings. First, the data is usually quantitative. The phone system tells you how many calls and how long each was; it doesn't tell you how successful the outcome of each call was. If you're trying to reduce the number of calls made, it won't tell you whether the right calls were the ones eliminated.

Second, automating data collection never improves the *quality* of the data. If it was the wrong data when it was collected manually, it will be the wrong data when it's collected automatically. If it measured the wrong results manually, it will still measure the wrong results when the computer does it. But now, because computer systems are usually rigid, it's a lot harder to change either what you're measuring or how you're measuring it.

Realistic Measurement

There's another solution. The problem is that it's not very sophisticated or exciting, and it doesn't require the latest technology. It's altogether too simple. It's this:

> If you really believe in supporting your frontline people, why aren't *they* helping to set the standards and decide what to measure?

This may sound dangerous, a little like letting the fox decide what the security in the hen-house should be. Certainly, it has risks. Please understand, though, that I'm not proposing just to turn the whole problem over to them. I'm talking about involving them in the process and ensuring that the results you measure are ones they believe are important.

Just as the first two rules make valid measurement difficult, a third rule makes it easier. It's not as universal as the first two, but it's true most of the time:

> People who're good at what they do generally want to
> be measured at how well they're doing it.

As I said, it's not as certain as the other two, but it's true often enough to base business decisions on it. After all, how many good quarterbacks would want everyone to stop measuring their completion percentage?

If your frontline people are really good, and if you really are supporting them, they almost certainly will work with you to develop effective measurements. This *does* need to be a dialogue. People who do a job see all of the complexities and ramifications of what they do. They can—honestly—find flaws in any measurement scheme. They often need someone who can help them identify the measurements that will be good enough to be usable, though not truly flawless.

Recall that managers in an effective organization function as educators who create an environment in which maximum learning can occur. Useful measurement illustrates that function. An effective manager doesn't impose measurements on her frontline people, but neither does she dump the project on them and then react to whatever they come up with. Instead, she (a) identifies the part of the problem that they can most effectively work to solve, (b) frames it clearly so that they understand what's wanted, (c) serves as a consultant to them as they work the problem, and (d) intelligently discusses their results with them. With luck, she develops a consensus on what should be done. If that can't be done, she takes all of the information she has and makes a decision. The *worst* thing that can happen is that she will make a better decision than she would have without the help of her employees.

Here's a final thought on measurement and customer satisfaction. It's comes from Jan Carlzon:

> In a customer-driven company, measurements are derived from how
> well they are focusing their energy on the areas that are vital to the
> paying customers.

Here's a brief summary of this chapter in two different but equally important keys:

Key #8: Either customer satisfaction and loyalty are primary, or something else is. No compromise is possible.

Key #9: Your frontline people won't treat your customers any better than you treat your frontline people.

CHECK POINTS

1. My firm's customer-satisfaction policies are clear and effective. I know because I discuss them with our frontline people periodically.

2. Every employee in the firm knows that *nothing* is more important than customer satisfaction.

3. We have a tested system to protect frontline people from abuse without taking the challenge out of their job.

4. We have numerous small rewards and recognitions for frontline people who satisfy customers well, and we change them frequently to keep them interesting.

5. Customer satisfaction is built into the compensation plan of every employee in the firm. (No? Then what percentage of employees *don't* have it as a factor? Why?)

6. Customer satisfaction is a major part of the compensation of every frontline person in the firm. For employees who deal regularly with dissatisfied customers, it is *the* factor that most affects their income.

7. We measure at least some aspects of customer satisfaction—and the measurements never subordinate quality to quantity.

6 GET (AND USE) CUSTOMER FEEDBACK

"Berneice, I just don't understand people. Whenever anyone eats here, there's a feedback card right in the middle of their table. All they have to do is take a minute to fill it out and either drop it in the box by the door or mail it. We're giving them a chance to tell us what they think and not 1 in 20 of them takes advantage of it."

"That's just how it is, Tom. You try to be kind to people, do them a favor and give them a chance to express their opinion, and what happens? They don't pay attention. I guess they really don't care . . ."

A SHORT PAUSE

Before dealing with customer feedback, review where you've been and where you're headed.

Where You've Been

The first two chapters dealt with customers. Chapter 1 presented some of the basic facts about customer psychology. When your customers become unhappy, their unhappiness spreads like ripples in a pond. Unfortunately, it often doesn't spread far enough to reach you. They walk out, and you never hear a word.

Chapter 2 showed how customers buy value, not things or services.

Value is the benefit a customer gets for the cost she has to pay. If, after the sale, something happens to increase the customer's cost (in time, money, and effort), the value of her purchase declines. Even more important, the value she expects to get from you in the future also declines.

The third, fourth, and fifth chapters dealt with your frontline people—what they have to do, how to train them to do it, and how to keep them doing it. While the chapters concentrated on the people who deal with dissatisfied customers, much of the information applies to all customer-contact people.

Where You're Going

Now that you've seen how customers react, what they buy, and how your frontline people need to treat them, you're ready to look specifically at what you need to do when they're dissatisfied. Chapter 7 describes what you must do to put the value back in a transaction that has gone bad. Chapter 8 explains how to do this in such a way that you get a second chance.

Then Chapter 9 deals with all of the reasons why "we can't do it here!" Chapter 10 provides suggestions on building a strong customer focus in a public agency. Chapter 11 suggests how to create this focus in your immediate organization even if you don't run the company. The Epilogue summarizes the book for you and provides you with checklists to help you build and maintain a strong customer focus. Finally, the Appendix summarizes the most important points specifically for frontline people.

Where You Are Now—and Why

This transitional chapter is short. It deals with one of the critical problems involved in satisfying customers—finding out what they like and what they don't like about your business. This is obviously important. If you remember Chapter 1 on customer psychology, you know it's also very difficult.

MOUNTAINS OF DATA

In her book *In the Age of the Smart Machine*, Shoshana Zuboff of the Harvard Business School described the impact of automation on businesses. She coined a word, "informate," to describe the tremendous amount of information that automated systems can bring to the firm. As she says, *informating*

> ... provides a deeper level of transparency to activities that had been either partially or completely opaque. ... Activities, events and objects are translated into and made visible by information when a technology *informates* as well as *automates*.

It's easy to read this as no more than a comment on automation. Its real significance, though, is what automation (and its "informating" function) make clear: In every organization, there's a staggering amount of data on the firm's operations. Automated systems don't create this data; they collect a small amount of it and make it visible. Even in the most automated businesses, though, most data remains invisible. This is important no matter what the data is; it's critical, though, if the data concerns your customers and their satisfaction.

A Simple Example

You don't need to look at a giant corporation to see how very much data on customers is out there. Say you operate a 200-bed hotel. Your occupancy rate is about 85 percent, which means that you average 200–250 guests each night. You provide them with a full range of services—cable TV, room service, a lounge and restaurant, and so on.

As a very rough and understated simplified estimate, each guest will have at least 20 contacts with your services and your staff (How comfortable was the bed? Did the drawers open easily? Was the room service courteous? etc.) each night. That's 4,000–5,000 chances *in one night* that guests have to form an opinion about you. Just one or two unfavorable contacts could lose you the customer.

The numbers of people and kinds of contacts are different with each different business, but the principle is the same. There are mountains of data out there on what your customers think about how you're doing your job.

Just how much of this data do you get? When those 250 guests leave in the morning, how much do you know about their reactions to your service? If you're like most hotels—and wholesalers, department stores, auto dealerships, mail-order houses, and so on—not very much.

The Data You Get

You already know the basic reasons for this: Most unhappy customers don't talk to you. Those that do are speaking for themselves. What made them unhappy isn't necessarily the same for other customers. The reverse is also true. People who're satisfied don't often tell you, and when they do, they usually don't tell you *why* they're satisfied.

This is a double whammy. First, you don't hear from most of your customers, so you get only a small bit of information. Second, this information is biased—but you have no idea what the bias is. Briefly, here are some examples:

- "I loved your bed; it was the first good night's sleep I've had on the road in weeks." That's what the comment card said. The individual who wrote it has serious back problems and sleeps on an extra-firm bed at home. Three other guests, who prefer soft foam mattresses, vowed never to darken your door again. But what do you think about your mattresses?

- "Your customer service person was *rude*," according to the card. Actually, Amelia wasn't rude, just a little formal and impatient. She'd just done a brilliant job of satisfying three customers with really serious problems, and this one was raising a ruckus about a problem that he'd actually caused. But what do you think about Amelia?

- "By the way, Mr. Golden, your driver gets here early each morning and gets the stuff on the shelves right away," one of your customers mentioned during a conversation. He didn't mention, because he didn't know, that Mike (your driver) goes to that store first, then has a cup of coffee at a nearby restaurant—so he can work on his relationship with a cute waitress there. This means that three other stores, all bigger, don't get their shelves stocked until well after the business day starts. But what do you think about Mike?

On any business day, you can multiply these examples by thousands of times. Unless you take constant, positive steps otherwise, what you know about your customers is scattered, biased, fragmentary and as apt to be misleading as to be helpful. The information you get is the 1 percent of the iceberg. You don't usually see the other 99 percent, or even have a feel for what it's like.

To switch metaphors, there's a gold mine out there, hidden in the hills. The problem is how you mine the gold.

THE CUSTOMER'S POINT OF VIEW

When you first put out customer response cards, how did you look at them? Did you believe you were doing your customers a favor by giving them an opportunity to provide you with their comments and suggestions? Then were you mystified, like the manager in the vignette at the start of the chapter, because they didn't take advantage of the opportunity?

How do you suppose your customers thought of the cards? "Oh, hot dog, here's a chance to contribute to the excellence of this firm and have my thoughtful views taken into account!" That's possible. It's also possible that you may win your state lottery today. It's more probable that your customers' response was one of these:

- "There's no sense in filling out this—no one ever reads it anyway."
- "There's no sense in filling out this—no one's going to pay attention to just one opinion."
- "I have no intention of filling this out—it's not my job to tell him what's wrong with his business."

The first and second examples reflect the feelings of many people that it doesn't really matter whether they fill out the card. The third example is completely different. I have no statistics on this, but I believe that it's the most common response. It reflects the customer's perception that she's being asked to put forth extra effort (with no payoff in it for her) to do your job for you.

Put this in the context of a dissatisfied customer, and it gets even stronger. "First, you didn't meet my expectations for value. Now, you want to take some of my time to tell you something you already ought to know. Phooey—I can always go somewhere else!"

WHAT YOU CAN DO ABOUT IT

Does this mean you should forget about customer feedback? Never! If getting feedback causes problems, not getting it causes disasters. There are definite steps you can take to increase the amount and value of the feedback you get. Here's an example of how one highly successful firm handles feedback.

CASE STUDY: Looking for Feedback

Micro Center began in May 1980 in a small store in an aging shopping center. Today, it's a major retailer of personal computers and computer supplies, beginning to open computer "department stores" throughout the country.

Micro Center has a fanatical customer focus—and this is nowhere more evident than in their pursuit of customer feedback. Buy something from Micro Center—anything—and you get *three* postage-paid cards. This is what's on each card:

- One is a "Mailing List Request Form." Fill it out, and you receive "catalogs, advance sale notices, and latest product information." You get them, and Micro Center gets your name and address, and the type of personal computer you use, for their mailing list.

- Next is a card headed "Will You Do Us a Favor?" (Micro Center understands how its customers see requests for information.) On it, a customer can identify any new product or service he'd like to see Micro Center carry. The card also repeats the company's "NO QUESTIONS ASKED" 30-day return policy. This guarantee is one of the best in the industry today. When Micro Center began, it was absolutely revolutionary.

- The *pièce de résistance* is the third card. Across the top, in bold letters, is "HELP US GET BETTER FOR YOU!" The card asks, in small letters, for information which store was visited and when. Then, in larger type, it asks "WHY DO YOU SHOP AT MICRO CENTER?" "WHERE DO WE NEED TO IMPROVE?" and "WOULD YOU LIKE TO SHARE YOUR SUGGESTIONS AND COMMENTS IN A GROUP DISCUSSION?" Below that is a place for name and address.

You'll see later that I prefer a slightly different approach. That's virtually irrelevant here, though—because Micro Center does this so much better than any other firm I know. They're sincere about getting feedback from their customers, and they make their sincerity obvious.

If you want comments from your customers, you need to go about it with the same passion that Micro Center has. To be effective, though, you also have to keep some basic goals in mind.

TO GET EFFECTIVE CUSTOMER FEEDBACK, YOU MUST

- Make it easy for the customer to comment.
- Ask for her comments.
- *Never* ignore her comments.

Here each of these are, in more detail.

Make It Easy to Comment

Chapter 1 quoted the notice posted by a convenience store chain that was just going through the motions. It did nothing to make it easier for a customer to complain about bad service. Policy statements like that may make managers feel good—but they don't do much for customers. In fact, they help increase the general cynicism that many customers have about the level of service they can expect.

If you want comments, make it as easy as possible for your customer to give them to you. These are some of the essentials:

- Use a postage-paid card, but provide a box for the cards on the spot as well. You want the customer to make his comments to your local people, if possible. (Remember about supporting your frontline people?)

- Use a heading that grabs the customer's attention. The Papa Gino's fast food chain in the Northeast prints in bold letters at the top of their comment card: **I'd like to know if what you like is what you got.** That's clear and to the point. So are the headings on Micro Center's cards.

- Keep the comment form simple and specific, and ask for enough information to help. One form I've seen asks, "Was the restaurant clean and well managed?" and then allowed only for a Yes or No answer. That's at least two questions, assuming the customer knows what "well-managed" might mean—and they may have quite different answers. Other firms ask "Were you satisfied with our service?" Is it really enough to know only that they were or weren't satisfied?

- A good comment form should have 5–10 relevant, specific questions with four or five alternative levels of response (Poor, Fair, Good, Excellent, etc.) If you ask fewer questions, you'll miss too much information. If you ask more, you'll discourage the customer from answering. The customer should only have to check a box for each response, not write it in—but there should be room below the questions for the customer to elaborate on his check marks if he wishes to do so.

- Don't routinely ask for the customer's signature. Even if you go on to add "You don't have to sign it," the customer may already have backed off when she saw the line for her name. One of the best ways to handle this is to say "If you'd like a response, please give us your name and address," and leave room for them. If the customer doesn't give her name, she doesn't expect a reply. If she does, make absolutely, positively sure you do reply.

Ask for Comments

If possible, have a frontline person hand the customer a card and ask them to fill it out. This reinforces the idea that you really do want the

comments. It also subtly suggests that your frontline people are confident enough to ask for comments.

You'll get more comments this way, but you need to be sure what you're
getting. If your frontline people don't trust you, if they believe the
comments will be used against them, they'll make sure that they're
overwhelmingly favorable. Unhappy customers will somehow be overlooked when the cards are passed out.

If your frontline people do trust you, you'll also get overwhelmingly
positive responses. In part, this will be because they do a good job. In
part, it will be because they will hand them out so graciously that many
customers won't have the heart to say anything unkind.

At the least, include comment cards with their purchases. You may
not want to include them with every purchase (why not?), but at least put
them into a sizeable sample of purchases.

If your contact with customers is primarily by phone or by mail, you
can get comments from a sample (or all) of them in the same way. Mail
a letter requesting comments to everyone who calls your customer
support line during a certain time period on a particular day each week.
Change the day and time regularly. Or mail a card along with the sales
slip for every order that comes in during a certain day or week.

Never Ignore Comments

If you ask for comments, *never* ignore them—particularly if you have a
name on them. Even people who're willing to take the time to comment
will be turned off completely if they think that what they say will be
ignored. Some examples may illustrate this.

CASE STUDY: Using the Feedback You Ask For

When Billy Joe picked up the car from the repair shop, it had a nice, postpaid
evaluation card attached to the bill. The questions were simple, direct, and
relevant. There was room for detailed explanation of the comments.

Billy Joe had taken the car in because it had been running very badly. When
he looked at the bill, he'd been charged for a tune-up *and* for a new spark plug

wire. It sounded very much like they'd fixed the wrong problem, then discovered what was really wrong and fixed it. But they charged for both.

He filled out the card in some detail, explaining that it appeared that the mechanic was either incompetent or dishonest. Then he mailed it in.

That was approximately two and a half years ago. Billy Joe still hasn't heard anything. What do you suppose his opinion of that repair shop is? How many times do you suppose he's been back?

Sondra had finished a decidedly so-so meal and walked to the cash register to pay for it.

"How was everything?"

"Bearable."

"Oh ... um ... oh, my ... " He took Sondra's check and money and gave her change. That ended the transaction.

Would you care to guess how many times Sondra's been back to that restaurant?

Here's an (almost) good example:

Roger had stayed several nights at a hotel in a well-known chain. He had a whole series of dissatisfactions, from an uncomfortable bed to ice machines on three floors that were out of ice. To top it all off, the customer dissatisfaction hot line didn't work.

The company provided a response card, and Roger filled it out in great detail and mailed it. Sure enough, he got prompt replies from both the hotel manager and the president of the chain. Both were very apologetic, assuring him that they didn't intend to give that kind of service and had taken steps to see that the problems were corrected. They also thanked him profusely for calling the situation to their attention.

Though the replies didn't go far enough, they did make it clear that Roger's comments were read, and that the company intended to use them to improve their operations. That would encourage Roger (and other guests) to fill out their comment cards again. (This chapter and the next one show what else is needed.)

The moral here is clear: If you ask for comments, make it clear that you read them. If a customer tells you she was dissatisfied, respond to her dissatisfaction. If you can't respond to all dissatisfied comments, at least respond to the most serious.

IF YOU REALLY WANT THEM, CONSIDER PAYING FOR THEM

Remember, when a customer fills out a response card, he's doing you a favor. He knows that, whether you do or not. Because that's the case, why not pay for his comments?

You may have noticed that this is beginning to happen. When I bought a Toshiba computer, they offered to mail me two disks if I filled out the demographic information and sent it to them. Several firms have mailed me a dollar in the mail in exchange for my filling out an enclosed marketing information form. When I bought a car recently, the salesman promised me a free oil change if I filled out and brought in the evaluation the company planned to mail me.

So why not pay people for giving you the information you want? Here are several examples of what you might do:

- On the table in your restaurant or in your hotel rooms, put a card that says "10 percent off!" The card is a coupon good for 10 percent off at their next visit, and attached to it is a tear-off, postpaid response form.

- Include with a percentage of the (dated) invoices you mail out a form that also says "5 percent off!" It explains that if the customer fills out the (response) form and mails it in with her payment within 5 days, she can deduct 5 percent from what she owes you.

- If you have the right relationship with the frontline people who deal with complaints, arrange for them to hand out gifts-for-comments cards. The customer fills out and seals the card, then takes it to another (convenient) place in the store—where it can be exchanged for a small but meaningful gift. Remember, if your frontline people hand out the cards, it reinforces (even if ever so slightly) the fact that you're treating the customer as a person—which is crucial to a successful transaction.

- The same basic processes work if your dealings are by phone or mail. Mail out a discount coupon good on their next purchase from you, in return for their comments.

A FEW OTHER TIPS

Here are some basics, which you probably already know. If you don't, learn them and use them.

*   Make sure that, at a minimum, you can be reached by phone. Have your phone number on everything, prominently, and encourage customers to use it. If you have many customers outside your metropolitan area, provide an 800 number, if possible.

    Before you decide "I don't need an 800 number," consider this. If you're drinking a diet cola, look closely at the side of it. There's a good chance that you'll find an 800 number on it. The number isn't for information about the cola but about Nu-traSweet, the artificial sweetener in it. If you shop at a Kroger supermarket, you'll find an 800 number printed on the bag your groceries are in. And each pack of Polaroid film has an 800 number you can call for assistance. These are just the tip of the 800-number iceberg.

    One of the neatest ideas I've seen on this is at Ricart Ford. When you pick your car up after it's been repaired, there's a card with phone number on it. If you have questions or complaints, you call that number—which rings in the service bay of the team that repaired your car. You talk directly to the team chief.

*   On all your comment forms, make sure the customer knows that you want information so that you can serve her better. It's not "I'd like your comments so I can do a better job," but "I'd like to know how we can serve you better." Remember Micro Center's heading: "Help Us Get Better for You!" This, like so many other suggestions in this book, is a marginal consideration. As Tom Peters has pointedly remarked, though, competitive advantage is gained and lost at the margins.

*   Respond to individual complaints, but don't stop there. Build a database of complaints. It doesn't have to be on a computer, but that helps. Find a way to categorize the complaints and then review them by category periodically. When you get a series of complaints on one product or service or location or individual or whatever, some action is required.

- If there's not a close relationship between the individual who works the complaints and your frontline people, your frontline people will always have a dozen reasons why what happened wasn't their fault. If they trust you, and you treat complaints as an opportunity to learn, they'll use them to improve.

- Finally, don't ever use highly abstracted data (such as written or checked comments) in place of data obtained directly (remember the OLAF skills?). Comment data can get distorted, and when you're separated from the action, it's easy to start believing that what the comments say is reality. In that lies disaster.

    One simple but useful way to get around the abstractness of comment cards is to have someone you trust come or call in with a problem—particularly to a questionable area. This is very limited information, but it can provide you immediate, relatively objective feedback.

THE REAL THING

You can take everything discussed so far in this chapter and summarize it under the heading: How to do something that's sort of effective very well. Don't let me discourage you from soliciting written comments from your customers; that avenue ought always to be open. But it's not enough, and it's not even the best way to find out how to satisfy your customers. The best way is what this section is about.

What is it? It's simple and straightforward, and it's been mentioned several times already:

> Train *all* of your frontline people to find what customers like and don't like, and then make sure that the information gets where it needs to go.

Your sales force is always your first line of attack in this. They should be interacting constantly with customers, finding out both what they're looking for and what they would look for if you could provide it to them. Remember Ballard Medical Products, mentioned on page 68 in Chapter 3?

Though the sales staff is important, this book is focusing on the other end of the cycle: the people who deal with customers dissatisfied *after* the sale. Their contribution can be almost as great. They *know* what your customers are unhappy about. That information points directly toward changes you need to make in products, service, pricing, delivery, whatever.

Note that this makes the job of frontline people who deal with unhappy customers even more demanding and more responsible. It means more training. It may mean longer time per contact. In other words, it's not free—or even inexpensive.

However, it's *relatively* inexpensive when you compare it to the alternatives. Far more important, it's much, much more effective than the alternatives. You can't sample all of your customers, but your frontline people can sample 100 percent of those who bring you complaints. They won't have the data on the many, many chances for satisfaction or dissatisfaction your business has each day—but they will know about the few people who were dissatisfied enough that they complained.

In case my arguments don't convince you to actively seek information from complainants, you might consider the experience of WordPerfect Corporation. The corporation believes that one of the greatest values of its 800-number customer service (which is an excellent avenue for customer complaints) is that customers will provide input on new features they'd like, as well as the bugs they encounter in the software.

Valued Customers

Remember another benefit that's already been alluded to. When frontline people skillfully ask the customer for more information on her problem, they're reinforcing the customer's perception that she's being treated as a person. In this case, she's being treated as a person whose problem is important enough to be worth this extra time to find out about it.

It may sound as if this point is being overstated. Perhaps it is, but don't forget *why*. Treating a customer as a valued person is an essential of a successful transaction—and successful transactions are what your frontline people are in business to produce.

Going Beyond the Formal Data

If it seems that I'm against formal data gathering and analysis, please understand that I'm not. A variety of formal methods can be helpful, and computers permit much more rapid and complete analysis of the data than anyone can do by hand. However, you need to understand what computers do and do not do well. What they do well is any task that can be reduced to a set of definite steps, particularly if these steps are quantitative.

The problem is that customer behavior can't really be reduced in this way. Human beings generate postures, motions, expressions—a thousand different nuances that can't be captured easily as formal data. Other human beings, given skill and experience, can interpret a wide variety and volume of these subtle signals in seconds. For instance, the Cooker Restaurant Corporation specifically trains its managers to read guests' nonverbal clues.

You should train *your* frontline people to gather information, verbal *and* nonverbal, effectively—and then make sure that your company listens to them. Further, *you* need to listen to them. As long as you talk only to the people who get the information from them—or the people who supervise the people who get the information from them—the part that reaches you is highly filtered. How much? Researchers have estimated that for each level of organization the information must pass through, *40 percent* of it is lost. If you have two intermediaries, you probably lose 64 percent of the valuable information your customers have offered you.

Staying in Touch

Don't let this filtering effect happen to you. Talk periodically with all of your frontline people, particularly the ones who deal with dissatisfied customers. Make sure that their supervisors also stay in close touch with them and with their customers. As Chapter 5 suggested, you might sit in occasionally as one of them, just to see what their work is really like. Or you might meet periodically with a group of them, for an hour or so. Or you might just walk up during a slack time and chat with them. Whatever you do, listen to them, ask questions, get a feel for how things are really going out there. If you've been away from the action for a while, what you find out will probably surprise you!

Talking with your front line serves another, very valuable function. It shows you're concerned about them and care about their working conditions and experiences. Remember

> **Key #9:** Your frontline people won't treat customers any better than you treat your frontline people.

In a fiercely customer-driven business, it's easy to overlook this principle. It's easy to see your frontline people as means to an end, and to forget that they can't do their jobs unless their needs for support are being met.

If you're listening to them and responding to their dissatisfactions, it leaves them free to listen to customers and to solve their problems. If you're not listening, if they believe you don't care about them—they'll spend all too much of their time worrying about themselves and their own problems—not the customers' problems.

You can also use formal means to get feedback from them just as you do from your customers. Linda Goldzimer has sample questions for a frontline questionnaire in her book on customer satisfaction.

The heart of this chapter can be summarized in

> **Key #10:** When a customer provides honest comments, he's doing you a favor—and that's how he looks at it. Give him a reason to do you the favor.

CHECK POINTS

1. My firm has an aggressive program to get formal feedback from our customers.

2. Our comment cards make it easy for customers to give us useful feedback.

3. When we get a signed complaint from a customer, we *always* respond to it, and quickly.

4. We reward customers for giving us their comments.

5. We print our phone number on everything. If we have many out-of-town customers, we use an 800 number.

6. We categorize complaints and analyze them carefully, looking for patterns that need attention.

7. Every frontline person in the organization tries (tactfully) to find out what our customers like and don't like about our products or services and about the way we treat them.

8. We make it easy for our frontline people to get their observations, comments, and suggestions to the people who need them—and then we *use* them to improve our operation.

7 SOLVE THE CUSTOMER'S PROBLEM

On the wall behind the counter is a sign that says "your satisfaction guaranteed." A customer walks up to the counter.

"I need another gallon of wall paint. This one didn't cover with one coat. I think it's the pits to pay $17 for a paint that takes two coats."

"What color did you paint over?"

"A pastel yellow—not even a bright one."

The clerk doesn't reply. He blends the paint then turns the mixer on. While the mixer is going, he takes the customer's money. He rings the sale and hands the customer the change.

The customer sticks the bills in his pocket and picks up the paint. "You know this'll be the last time I'll buy any paint here for a long time."

There's a pause. As the customer turns to go, the clerk says, "Have a nice day."

REPLACING LOST VALUE

In this chapter, you get to the nitty-gritty of the matter: An unhappy customer is eyeball-to-eyeball (or mouthpiece-to-mouthpiece) with one of your frontline people. What happens in the next few minutes will probably determine whether you ever see that customer again.

The dialogue that begins this chapter first appeared on page 1, in "About the Book." There, it was an example of a moment of truth handled poorly. Here, it's an entrée into this chapter's subject matter.

First of all, the clerk's response probably wasn't his fault. He didn't say anything because he didn't know what to say. He wasn't properly trained and/or he didn't know what to do in the situation and/or he was afraid he'd be punished for acting on his own and/or . . . . Because he didn't know how to handle the situation, he did what most people do in the situation—nothing.

No single phrase or principle will make up for poor selection, poor training, and poor support. If the clerk had been told that whenever he wasn't sure what to do, he should follow Key #7, he might have pulled it off. This principle first appeared at the end of Chapter 3. Here it is again:

> **Key #7**: If you intend to deal successfully with dissatisfied customers, focus on saving the customer, *not* on saving the sale.

That's the key as it's stated for you, the manager. As a guideline for frontline people, it can be put much more simply:

Don't save the sale—save the customer!!!

If there were a single sentence I would suggest that you post wherever your frontline people deal with dissatisfied customers, it would be this one. With this in mind, here's what you need to do to turn dissatisfied customers around.

Chapter 2 analyzed why a customer becomes dissatisfied. She made a purchase from you, expecting a certain value from your goods or services. But something has gone wrong. It broke, or it didn't work as she'd expected, or your technician accidentally sprayed weed-killer on her prize tulips. She hasn't gotten the value she expected—and now it's even worse because she's had to take the time and effort to contact you about it.

It isn't just that this particular transaction is in question. Because your product or service hasn't delivered its expected benefit, your customer now expects that she'll be dissatisfied next time. If she's a regular customer, who's been very satisfied over the years, the lowered expectation may be hardly noticeable. If this was her first purchase from you, your failure to deliver is *all* she knows about you—and it's created the very real expectation that she'll be dissatisfied in the future.

Here's how this concept looks as a key:

Key #11: To satisfy an unhappy customer, you must add extra value to make up for the value you promised but failed to provide in the first place.

This key doesn't state some kind of general truth, something to be contemplated at leisure and implemented as you get around to it. Instead, it defines what you must do *now* if you want to keep *this* customer. It defines what The Cooker Restaurant Corporation calls "overcompensation." Because you failed the customer the first time, you go to whatever extremes are necessary to see that he gets satisfied here and now.

When a dissatisfied customer confronts one of your frontline people, the real moment of truth has come. No matter how strong the customer's present dissatisfaction and future expectation are, your frontline person has the opportunity to deal with them and resolve them. But he has only *this* opportunity—your firm has only *this* opportunity to restore the value your customer was expecting and assure him of full value in future transactions. You do it now, or you don't do it.

Reliably Providing Value

Pause a moment to revisit a point that's been made before:

> The best frontline people in the world can only make
> up for so many screw-ups.

At the end of the previous section, I gave a brief example of the value that was lost because your technician sprayed weed-killer on your customer's prize tulips. Just suppose that this did happen to the prize tulips your customer has carefully nursed for the past few years. How can you revalue that transaction? Even if you replace the tulips and provide free lawn-care for a year, the customer is still going to be behind.

This situation may have been a bit extreme, but certainly not unlike foul-ups that really do happen. Remember the situation mentioned in Chapter 4 where the waterbed instructions were confusing? Eddie didn't want to drive to the store, and no one in the store could come to him. No matter how you cut it, there's no easy resolution for that situation. Specifically, poor performance by your firm can hamper—and prevent—you from dealing effectively with dissatisfied customers in any or all of these ways:

- You may create a situation where a good resolution to the problem is *impractical.* Both the waterbed and the tulips are this kind of situation. Short of a miracle, there's just no good solution for the problem.

- The situation may be such that there's no *time* to resolve the problem. If you bought the wrong ticket for a customer and she finds out at the airport that no more first class seats are available and she flies coach or else—well, you and she are stuck.

- In some circumstances, no one may know *how* to resolve the problem. This is what happens, for instance, when you sell software that has a major "bug," or you sell a new machine for which you don't yet have the technical manuals.

- These situations are ones in which you *can't* solve the problem effectively. There's one more kind: those where the solution is prohibitively expensive. Selling a car that turns out to be a lemon may be this kind of situation. Everyone loses, but most companies or dealers aren't willing to replace it.

Far more common, though, are the situations where the sheer *number* of goofs become prohibitively expensive to correct. Hundreds of companies go out of business each year because their product or service or delivery or installation or training or (you name it) is so poor that they can't afford to fix it. As someone so rightly said: It's not the elephants that trample you—it's the mice that nibble you to death.

This is why I've emphasized repeatedly that satisfying your customers is a total process—or else. The kind of positive, decisive action that this chapter and the next recommend are possible *only* when your product or service and its delivery are consistently first-rate. Then you can give the few dissatisfied customers the kind of treatment that brings them back again and again.

Here's what that treatment is.

RESTORING VALUE

If you're going to treat dissatisfied customers effectively, you must remember Key #11. Expanded a little, it says that

> when a customer is dissatisfied, it's because he hasn't gotten the value he paid you for. If all you do is provide him with what he thought he bought in the first place, you're still behind. The fact that he had to take time and effort to complain have diminished the original value of your product or service. To restore the value, you have to provide him with *more* than he initially bought. And you must do it *now*.

That may sound like a tall order, and perhaps a little unrealistic. After all,

- If she bought a hamburger that had too much mustard on it, do you give her *two* hamburgers?
- If you made a mistake drawing up his will, do you throw in free representation the next time he gets a traffic ticket?
- If you did a sloppy job painting his car, do you offer to paint his wife's car for free, too?
- If there's a leak in the new house you built her, do you offer to build her a garage free?

You may; none of these is completely unreasonable. You probably don't have to go to quite such extremes, though. Instead,

- If she bought a hamburger that had too much mustard on it, you might offer her free french fries.

- If you made a mistake drawing up his will, you might offer him an hour of free legal service the next time he has a problem.

- If you did a sloppy job painting his car, it might make sense to put a high-quality paint sealant on it when you redid it.

- If there's a leak in the new house you built her, installing a free garage-door opener might be a sensible way to help restore her sense of value.

In short, there's almost always something you can do to reestablish the value to the transaction.

Making a Point

Perhaps you're not convinced yet. Then look at it from a different point of view. A customer is dissatisfied and complains to you. You correct the problem, no more, no less. What have you communicated to him?

In all probability, you've communicated that it's all right with you if your firm screws up occasionally. It's all right if the boards split sometimes in the fences you build, or the milk you sell him is occasionally old, or a suit doesn't stand up as it should once in a while. In other words,

> You're communicating that your standard is "merely OK," and you're expecting him to settle for that.

In case you don't know it yet, that's a recipe for low profit margins, a diminishing customer base and, quite possibly, failure. In the 1990s, "merely OK" simply isn't enough. There will always be someone who is willing to provide more than that.

On the other hand, when you clearly "go the extra step" to restore value to his purchase, you demonstrate *in action* your commitment to providing first-rate customer service. You show your customers that you care, that you intend to provide them full value—and that they can expect full value from you in the future.

HOW TO DO IT

All right, you're convinced. At least, you agree in principle. How do you actually do it? In terms of one of today's buzzwords, how do you *execute* effectively? Here are some of the hows.

HOW TO ADD VALUE EFFECTIVELY

- See it as an opportunity.
- Respond spontaneously.
- Respond sincerely.
- Focus on the customer.
- Be relevant.
- Be clear.

See It as an Opportunity

It's time to repeat Key #5: Dissatisfied customers aren't problems, they're golden opportunities (and #6: The really picky, demanding customers are *platinum* opportunities).

Did that sound trite when you first read it? Does it sound trite now? Do you have a mental picture of Pollyanna jumping up and down as she exclaims "Here comes another angry customer; isn't this a marvelous opportunity!!" It can be trite, and hypocritical and pure eyewash—but not if you understand that it really is true.

Should there be a lingering doubt in your mind, reread the section entitled "Repentance and Forgiveness" in Chapter 1 (page 30)—to remind yourself how much you accomplish when you restore value for a dissatisfied customer. If a manager at IBM can jump at the chance when he has an unhappy customer on his line, there's probably something to this "opportunity" stuff.

It's not enough, of course, for *you* to understand it. You have to see that your frontline people understand it—down to their bones. And be clear what they're understanding. They're understanding that *you* regard dealing with an unhappy customer as an opportunity, that *you* want them to do what they have to do to restore value to your customers, that *you* really mean to take care of your customers.

And this ties right back into a point that's been made before: you don't ever punish a frontline person for making a mistake that was made *because* she was trying to satisfy a customer. True, there are limits to what you can do to solve problems; they're discussed a little later in this chapter. You have to identify these limits and provide them as policy to your customer-service people. If one of your people goes beyond these limits, you need to counsel her—but if she did it trying to satisfy a difficult customer, you also should applaud what she was trying to do.

If that sounds difficult, and perhaps a little risky, you might keep in mind another point that pops up from time to time in the book. Either you're in business to produce fully satisfied customers, or you're in business to do something else. If it's "something else," you're probably reading the wrong book. If its satisfied customers you're in business for, read on—and be prepared to do *whatever you have to do* to satisfy them.

This is the first point, and the keystone for the rest: A dissatisfied customer is an opportunity, but it's an opportunity you usually get only once.

Respond Spontaneously

I wrote the first part of this chapter in a hotel in a major city. When I checked out, I looked at my statement and saw that I had been charged more for my room than the rate they had quoted me. I brought this to the attention of the desk clerk, who immediately bucked it to the manager. (That was flub number 1; now I'm not just dissatisfied because of the rate but also because I now have to wait for the manager to get free.)

In another minute or so, the manager appeared with the desk clerk in tow. He explained to me that they had quoted a special rate to me and how unhappy the other conference attendees would be if they found out about it. Grudgingly, he told me that they would honor the rate they had quoted me, and that they hoped the others wouldn't find out. I signed my credit card, picked up the statement, and left.

Now, just how happy do you think his response made me? Did it restore the value to my purchase? Did it increase my expectations of value for the next time? Did he communicate to me that I was a valued customer, and that my dissatisfaction was an opportunity for him? Is there really an Easter Bunny?

I got the rate I had bargained for. He did solve my immediate problem. He did it in such a way, though, that he almost completely destroyed its value. He did it because he was pushed into it, not because he wanted to see me satisfied. In other words, there was nothing spontaneous in his attempt to solve my problem. And he won't get another chance to be spontaneous with me.

If your frontline people are to satisfy your customers, their response must be spontaneous. This is part of what's meant by taking on the customer's problem as their own. It's the quick acceptance that the problem is valid, and that they will do what's required to solve it. It's the quality of response that's shown by:

- The waitress who responds to a customer's complaint that there's a rotten piece of fruit in her salad with "I'll replace it right away"—and then adds without a pause, "I want you to have desert on us tonight to make up for it."

- The counter person at the rental car agency who says "I don't know why we don't have the car you reserved, but I'll find you one with another agency and we'll pick up any difference in cost. Let me do one other thing; I'll either give you a free upgrade or take $5.00 a day off the rental. Which would you like?" (He offered the customer a choice because not everyone would prefer the same alternative.)

- The telephone customer-service representative who responds to the customer who was sent a blouse two sizes too large with "I'll have the right size blouse out to you by tomorrow afternoon. When you get it, please use the box it's in and the mailer to return the first one to us. I want to give you a matching scarf for the trouble this has caused you; what color would you like?"

The key point here is the spontaneous response. It communicates that you really *don't* want dissatisfied customers, and that you really *do* want to resolve their dissatisfaction. When a customer sees this kind of reaction to her complaint, she begins to believe that you honestly intend to satisfy her. That perception alone starts to assure her that future transactions with you will be satisfying ones for her.

Respond Sincerely

Spontaneity isn't enough unless the response is clearly sincere. If it's an automatic, routine, "Oh, hell, here we go again" response—well, the spontaneity will be overwhelmed by the impersonality.

Actually, you can't have true spontaneity without sincerity. They go hand in hand. Each requires the other to be effective. A spontaneous but rote response destroys the personal relationship that's so critical to customer satisfaction. A sincere response made after a delay that (to the customer) is unnecessary, dulls the impact of the sincerity.

Each of the examples on spontaneity actually illustrates both spontaneity and sincerity. When they're combined, your customer sees your frontline person responding with immediate, unpremeditated concern. That response seems natural, just the way that people respond who want to see their customers happy. In turn, your customers will respond to them with the kind of positive feelings you want to see.

Focus on the Customer

You've been looking at this since Chapter 3, but it still hasn't all been covered. There's an aspect of focusing on the customer that you may have overlooked, and it's relevant here.

For openers, here are some common responses that *don't* focus on the customer:

- "Gosh, that is terrible. We really screwed up, didn't we?" (This kind of honest response is certainly preferable to any attempt to gloss the problem over or pretend that it doesn't really exist. The customer already knows the mistake's been made, though. What he wants to hear is "I'll take care of that right away for you.")

- "I can't understand how one of our salespeople could have told you that; it doesn't work that way at all." (Just a variant on the previous one, but it's a few degrees worse. The customer is even less concerned to hear *who* made the mistake. If salespeople are creating mistaken expectations, the situation needs to be handled—but not with a customer.)

- "Y'know, it's really funny that it worked that way. We've had trouble with that particular module before, but it's always been . . . " (If you think the customer is uninterested in *who* made the mistake, just check out his reaction to this kind of comparative evaluation of his problem. Again, it focuses on something other than *his* situation.)

- "I'm sorry to hear about your problem and I'm sure we can take care of it. Please tell me what happened again slowly so I can write it down and send it to our technical folks. You know, they plan our improvements based on feedback from customers like you." (Providing feedback from customer service to the people who plan the product or service is an excellent idea—but *after* you've taken care of the customer's problem.)

In each case, the customer-service person focused on something other than the customer and his problem. Some of the responses were truly wrong; others were just inappropriate. The customer is dissatisfied. If you expect to revalue the customer's transaction, your people must focus first on what needs to be done to solve his problem. Everything else comes *after* that.

Remember the discussion earlier in the book about the harm caused by arguing with the customer. In addition to the other problems this causes, it forces the customer to focus on what happened—which you can't change—rather than what you might do to correct it. Doing anything other than focusing on the customer's problem and how to solve it has the same result. It prolongs the time that the customer is focusing on what is *wrong.* Your goal is for both your customer-service person and the customer to focus on what can be done *now* to make things right. This goes hand-in-hand with spontaneity and sincerity. In combination, they refocus the transaction from a disappointing past to a positive future.

Be Relevant

This also picks up on something earlier in the book—in Chapter 3, to be exact. There, I suggested that the solution should always be checked out with the customer. No matter how good you think the solution is, it isn't one unless the *customer* sees it as a solution. You're even further ahead if she sees it as the *best* solution. For example:

- Your service people left Sally's family room carpet spotted when they cleaned it. You think recleaning it is the best solution. Actually, Sally got the stain out with a drug-store spot remover; she'd much rather you stainproofed the carpet for free.

- Your lot personnel left the dome light on when they parked Jerry's car at the airport lot, and his battery was dead when he picked it up. You want to offer him free parking the next time. Actually, he'd rather you washed the car free next time—because his employer pays for the parking.

- Your firm misplaced Derek's tax return down behind a desk and it got mailed two weeks late. You're going to pay the penalty, of course, and intend to offer him a discount on his tax preparation for the coming year. He'd really prefer that you gave him a free hour of your time so he could discuss his wife's IRA with you.

In each case, you miss the best solution if you don't check it with the customer. In the first two cases, you miss any solution at all—because what you propose to do isn't helpful to either individual.

It takes little time to check the proposed solution. If the customer agrees, you're done. If she has another solution, and you can give it to her, you're both ahead.

Be Clear

Now, the final point: Be clear about what you're doing and why. If you're going to add value to the transaction, the customer needs to know that

- You're going beyond simply "making things right"
- You're doing it because you mean it when you say you intend to satisfy him
- You're doing it because you value him and want to keep him as a customer
- Most of all, you're doing it because you care about him.

If any of these are lacking, some of the value you intend to add to the transaction will be lost. If you look at them carefully and think about them, you can see how dependent you are on your frontline people. Not one of these points can be successfully communicated in a mechanical way.

This doesn't mean that there can't be a procedure for touching each of these bases. For instance, your frontline people might use a procedure like this:

1. Identify the problem. (You've looked at how to do this in detail already.)

2. Solve the problem. (You've also looked at this).

3. Tell the customer the extra value you're going to add to make up for her inconvenience. Where it's relevant, let her choose. (Remember the rental car example?)

4. Explain that you want her to be satisfied, and check to see that she really is. (If she's not, find out what will satisfy her, and do it.)

5. End the transaction by assuring her that you want to keep her as a customer, and that she can count on full satisfaction whenever she deals with you. (Just as it's appropriate for a salesperson to ask for the sale, it's appropriate for a customer-service person to ask for future business.)

There's no magic in this particular set of steps. In fact, you don't even have to use a specific procedure. Just make sure that every frontline person who deals with dissatisfied customers understands what needs to be done to revalue the transaction effectively and does it.

WHERE YOU DRAW THE LINE

A positive, proactive customer satisfaction policy is a necessity—but it raises two significant groups of questions.

The first group is concerned with cost. It costs money to hire staff to deal with dissatisfied customers, to solve their problems, and to give them more than they originally bargained for. There's the danger that your customers will take advantage of you, or that you'll be rewarding them for dissatisfaction with your product or service. Chapter 9 deals with these questions.

The second group relates to the limits of your satisfaction policy. Ultimately, this too involves cost. More immediately, it involves the lengths to which your frontline people can go to satisfy your customers. That's what the rest of this chapter is about.

Who Says "No"?

Let me begin by repeating a suggestion made before: your frontline people can tell your customers "yes"; only their supervisors can tell them "no."

This can be done successfully only if you have clear policy. Recall the flight attendant who describes her job as, "listening to the passenger and then doing whatever I have to do to satisfy him." Flowers by Snellings, in Winchester, Virginia, advertises that they are "where satisfaction is *absolutely guaranteed.*"

As a statement of positive determination and a can-do attitude, these are great. As an absolute policy it's also great—if you can afford it. If you can't, and you're going to delegate broad authority to your frontline people, they need to understand clearly where the limits are.

Frontline people, though, ought not be the ones who have to enforce this policy. You've already looked at the all-too-frequent situation where the frontline person "hangs tough" in accordance with the policy, and then his supervisor overrules him and becomes the "good guy." As a way of wrecking the morale of your frontline people, this has few peers. Even more, it encourages them either to stretch policy to the breaking point, so they won't be overruled, or to duck the responsibility and refer everything they can't settle quickly up the line.

If you combine (a) clear policy, (b) frontline authority to settle everything within this policy, and (c) supervisory support for the difficult situations, you'll have the basis for a winning program.

What Are the Limits?

To set policy, you have to decide what the limits are. Chapter 5 described ways to state these, but here's a brief description of the possible range:

- The small bookstore that insists on nonrefundable advance payments for special orders.
- The musical instrument shop that will accept returns within a week for credit but gives no refunds.
- The computer store that offers a "no-questions-asked" refund within 30 days as long as the customer presents the original bill of sale.
- The well-known department store chain that is reputed to have cheerfully refunded the cost of a set of tires—even though the chain has never sold tires.

There are hundreds of permutations, of course. The point is that every business—yours included—has to choose where to set its limits. When the limits are broad, the job of the frontline people is easier, and your guarantee of satisfaction stronger and more believable. When the limits are narrower, your frontline people have to be just that much better, and your ability to satisfy your customers just that much more restricted. The narrower the limits, the more time and effort your frontline people are going to spend dealing with—and trying to satisfy—unhappy buyers.

It would be presumptuous of me to suggest what your policy should be. I can say this: It should never be more restrictive than that of your competition. The stronger your commitment to customer satisfaction compared to your competition, the greater your competitive edge.

This may sound a little gratuitous to you. After all, it's easy for me to say that you should have a strong policy—but you're the one who has to pay for it. True, but remember this. Just as a liberal customer satisfaction policy depends on your ability to deliver what you promise the vast majority of the time, so a sharply limited one may be covering up your inability to deliver this. If you have a restrictive satisfaction policy, you need to ask yourself continually whether it's not the result of flaws in the design or delivery of your product or service.

(By the way, you may be wondering just what "the vast majority of the time" means. I found a definition for you. Motorola Corporation's current quality goal is a 0.0003 percent reject rate by 1992. That's three unsatisfactory products out of every million produced—and Motorola isn't the only American company aiming for quality like this. Think what your guarantee of satisfaction could be if you only goofed three times out of every million!)

How Clear Can You Be?

Chapter 5 looked at how important it is to have clear policies. It's time to revisit the subject again. Here's a look at some examples of the barriers to clarity and their consequences:

- Remember the "assumed benefits" from Chapter 2? Customers *assume* that they'll get a certain payoff from using your product, even though you and they never discuss it. What happens if you have clear restrictions on your satisfaction policy, but they don't read them because they assume that *everyone* in your business has a liberal policy?

- In another, related situation, the customer reads your policy, but assumes that you'll go along with industry policy (which is more liberal). Or assumes that it's only "common sense" to expect more liberal treatment if things go wrong.

- Perhaps you're clear about the restrictions, and the customer accepts them. Then something happens so outrageous that—to the customer—it overrides the restrictions. (For instance, the power drill he bought strips its gears two weeks after the warranty expires.) Or the customer doesn't use an important feature of the product until after the warranty has expired.

- Finally, what happens if the customer simply gets angry at you and/ or your product and refuses to pay you for it? (If she paid with a credit card, your warranty could easily expire before her payment is due.)

These are just a few of the ways that even a "clear" policy can go wrong. Each one of them poses a slightly different problem, but one that sooner or later you'll have to face (perhaps this afternoon). When that occurs, you'll have to decide whether to stick with the letter of your satisfaction policy, or to stretch it to cover the situation in front of you.

It's generally easy in a specific situation to decide to stretch a policy "just this once." Unless the situation is unique, though, the decision to stretch the policy begins to be a precedent. Just a few similar decisions, and the policy has changed. The change may be good or bad, helpful or harmful—but it's genuinely a change.

What should you do? I can tell you with complete certainty that neither I nor anyone else can give you a general answer. You have to make the decision based on your own situation. What's important is that you have a clear view of the consequences each way when you decide whether to make an exception.

Who Do You Want for Customers?

Sooner or later, most of the questions about customer satisfaction policy reduce to this one: Who do you want to have as your customers? How you set and carry out your satisfaction policies will gradually determine who you keep for customers and who you send to your competitors.

There are probably some customers you will do anything to keep, and others that you don't want in the first place. These two groups are the easy ones to deal with. You do literally whatever you must to keep the first. You give the latter whatever he wants—on the condition that he never deals with you again.

What about the 98 percent of customers who fall between these extremes? What about:

- The loyal customer who buys regularly from you but returns 75 percent of what she buys for a refund?

- The customer who shops with you regularly but ties up your sales force with his indecision and continuing need for more and more product information?

- The potential customer who keeps asking for your salesperson to call on him but never buys from you?

- The potential customer who promises to place a large order with you if you'll give her an extra guarantee?

- The high-volume customer who threatens to take his business elsewhere if you don't make an exception to your policy and take back an order?

I could fill another half-dozen pages with examples. If you've been in business for long, you could add at least that many. Each one of them poses the question: Do I do what's necessary to keep his business, or do I decide I no longer need (or don't want to get) him for a customer?

Here's another reason to move the power to say "no" away from your frontline people. As effective as they may be, they're not the ones to be making these sensitive policy decisions. It's all right for them to interpret your policies a little on the liberal side to satisfy their customers. When the big exceptions come along, though, it's time for them to pass the buck to you.

Then what do you do with it? Again, there are no general answers. It really does depend on the kind of customers you want. Here are a few questions to ask yourself as you make these decisions and shape your customer base.

- *"How sophisticated a customer do I want?"* In general, the more sophisticated your customers are the more aggressively they will look out for themselves. In this circumstance, you'll probably need to stick closely to your published satisfaction policies. If you intend to deal with less sophisticated customers, you can be more flexible in how your policies are interpreted.

- *"How wide a variety of customers do I want?"* Is your goal a narrow, tightly defined market segment? If so, you can develop policies targeted to that segment and work within them. If your preferred market is broader, you'll need to have a different set of policies and stretch them further.

- *"How much do I need to depend on repeat customers and word-of-mouth advertising?"* In general, the more you depend on repeat business, the more generous and flexible your satisfaction policies must be. If most of your sales are to one-time customers, your policies can be as rigid as you want—but not if you're depending on loyal customers returning time and time again. The same goes for your need of word-of-mouth advertising; the more you need it, the more flexible you'll have to be.

- *"How much do I want to depend on the honesty and integrity of my customers?"* This certainly isn't a trivial question. If, like L. L. Bean, you guarantee your products for life, you're making a positive commitment to the integrity of your customers. Not all customers meet this standard, and you may not have ready access to those that do. What your policies are and how they're enforced will determine how vulnerable you are to customers who're willing to take advantage of you.

- *"Do I want customers who like a friendly, personalized atmosphere or those who prefer a formal, business-like one?"* This relates to several of the preceding questions, but it also stands on its own. The more business-like your dealings are with your customers, the more fixed your policies can be. Conversely, if you want customers who prefer a friendly firm, you'll have to practice the kind of flexibility that goes with this.

- *"Do I want customers who work closely with me to improve and develop products, or are they simply customers?"* At first glance, this may sound like a strange question. It's not. Many firms, especially those that sell to a relatively small, identifiable group of customers, expect customers to work closely with them in designing and testing their products or services. Others get feedback through more formal methods, and customers are involved only by filling out an occasional marketing questionnaire (if at all). Rigid satisfaction policies are much harder to enforce in the former situation than the latter.

Like many other lists in this book, this one could be expanded at length. Whenever you set a satisfaction policy, and whenever you decide whether to abide by it strictly, to interpret it loosely, or to make exceptions to it—you're making a decision that moves you toward

certain types of customers and away from others. In the long run, what
the policy is and how it's enforced may not be as important as the subtle
pressure it exerts to attract certain kinds of customers and shunt others
away.

HOW DO YOU DRAW THE LINE?

You've covered all of the generalities. Now you get to the nitty-gritty—
that moment of truth when a dissatisfied customer walks up and
demands what you aren't willing to give. How do you handle it?

My first answer is the one I gave before: Give your frontline people
the power to say "yes," but never "no." If the customer wants more than
your policy will permit, it's time for her to be referred either to a senior
customer-service person or to a supervisor.

This shouldn't be done in frustration or hostility. Your frontline
person should be able to say, and mean, "I can't help this person; would
you see if you can." No matter how irrational the customer seems, there
may be an undiscovered rational reason for it. It's up to the senior
representative or the supervisor to find that reason or to close the
transaction.

Second, you use *great* tact (did I really need to say that?). If "no" must
be said, it must be said as objectively and courteously as possible. The
customer may seem furious, irrational, completely unforgiving. It may
seem pointless to treat him with consideration. At the moment that's
true—but how will he be in an hour, or a day?

- Will he have gotten over his emotions and realized that your
  response to him was reasonable?
- Will he have gotten partly over his emotions, so that because you
  were courteous to him he feels that he ought to give you another
  chance?
- Will he still be angry but realize that you treated him as fairly as
  anyone would have?
- Will he perhaps smile wryly to himself that his negotiating ploy

didn't work and decide that he can take your word on what your
warranty is?

You don't know—and neither does anyone else. I can't tell you what
percentage of angry customers relent and return if they're treated
well—but you and I both have a pretty good idea what percentage never
return when they're treated poorly.

Finally—and this should be obvious, too—*explain* why you can't give
him what he wants. If possible, combine this with the best offer you can
make to satisfy him.

An old joke says, "There's no reason for it—it's policy." Unfortunately, it's not very funny when that's the answer *you* get to your
problem. There should be a reason for every limitation on your ability
to satisfy customers. It should be logical, and your frontline people (and
their supervisors) should know it and be able to explain it.

If possible, though, don't end it there. If there's anything reasonable (and relevant) you can do to try to satisfy the customer, offer it then.
There's a lot of difference between saying,

> "We can't do that."

and

> "We can't do *that* because . . . , but we would be
> happy to do *this*, if it's acceptable to you."

While the customer may turn the offer down, you haven't ended on
a negative note. You have given it "your best shot." And in a certain
number of cases (I don't know how many), the customer will change her
mind and take you up on your offer. You certainly can't say she's
satisfied in this situation—but she's going to be more satisfied than if
she got nothing.

Here's a summary of much of what this chapter said:

> **Key #12**: Always treat a customer as if he will remain a
> customer. Never treat him as though this is the last time you'll
> see him.

CHECK POINTS

1. When my frontline people face a dissatisfied customer, they always focus on saving the customer, not the sale.

2. My frontline people understand the importance of overcompensating—adding extra value to make up for the value the customer didn't get in the first place.

3. My firm has a liberal policy for dealing with dissatisfied customers because we almost always satisfy the customer from the beginning.

4. My frontline people approach a dissatisfied customer as a challenge and an opportunity—not a problem.

5. I and my frontline people respond spontaneously and sincerely to dissatisfied customers, we focus on them, and we solve their problems.

6. My firm has a very clear idea of where the limits are on complete customer satisfaction, and I understand the consequences of these limits.

7. I really believe in satisfying customers; only a manager can say "no" to a customer.

8. Neither I nor my frontline people ever give up on a customer!

8 GET THE CUSTOMER BACK

John has been dealing with Pat Wheeler's Garage for the past 15 years. Other places have opened up, several of them even closer to John's home. They've offered him discounts and deals, but he still takes his car back to Pat. He doesn't think much about why, except that he likes the service there. If you ask him why and press him, though, he can remember the exact incident.

It happened just a few weeks after he first stopped at Pat's. He took his car in for a lube and oil change. He picked it up on his way to the ball game, but before he got to the game his "oil low" light came on. He pulled into a convenient station, and found that the oil filter hadn't been tightened properly. The oil had run out around it. There wasn't anything he could do but pay for another five quarts of oil.

He was hopping mad when he went back to Pat's and demanded his money back. Pat apologized and handed him his money. Then he did something more:

"Look, there's no way I can prove to you that this isn't how I do business," Pat said, "unless you come back. You bring this in with you"—he handed John a small piece of paper marked IOU—"and we'll change the oil in that car for free as long as you own it."

That was three cars ago, but John wouldn't think of dealing with another garage. When he thinks of it, he has to grin at the return on Pat's investment. Those free oil changes probably cost Pat $50 in lost profits— but John figured that in just one year he spends just under $1000 with Pat. Not bad!

In the Prologue, I described four situations where a firm had to deal with a dissatisfied customer: "The Unsuited Traveler," "The Unsuitable Room," "The Mangled Computer," and "The Air Unconditioner." Each of these is a fairly typical example of the things that can go wrong when trying to satisfying customers. (And each one of them actually happened.)

These incidents offer a way of looking at the issues this chapter raises. You might want to go back and review them—perhaps even make notes on what you'd do—before you continue with the chapter.

THE REAL CHALLENGE

Your journey in this book started with a general understanding of customer psychology and the meaning of "value." You toured the specifics of what your frontline people must do and how you need to train them and keep them doing it. You made a quick sortie into the ways to get customer feedback.

The previous chapter was your first destination. In it, you put your frontline people eyeball-to-eyeball with a customer who hadn't gotten the value she'd paid for, and asked what they needed to do to satisfy her. Then the chapter suggested a variety of methods to solve her problem and to resolve her dissatisfaction.

You may think that your trip is done. After all, you've resolved the problem. You've sent the customer away happy, with the value she wanted from you. You were responsive, concerned, focused on her. What more could she ask from you?

To answer that, turn the situation around and look at it through the customer's eyes. She needed a particular benefit (like Rosalind Jones needed a way to get supper over with quickly). She selected you instead of a competitor because she thought she could get this benefit from you at the best value. She didn't get the value, though, because she didn't get the benefit. She had to get back in touch with you (which cost her time, effort, and perhaps even money). She may have had to come to your store or wait on your service technician. Then, finally, she got the value she paid for in the first place.

Now that you see it the way she sees it, ask yourself this: Why should she deal with you again?" Using the realistic definition of cost from Chapter 2, what she bought from you cost her more than she'd expected. She got less value than she'd expected. The commonsense course of action is to buy from a competitor next time.

It's not enough that you solved her problem. You must take one more step. This is it:

Key #13: Always provide a dissatisfied customer a positive reason for dealing with you again.

Are you surprised at this? From my observation, most firms probably would be. But why? You failed the customer the first time around. Sure, when you found out she was dissatisfied, you took prompt, effective action. But that may not be enough—you can't count on its being enough. You have to give her a solid, tangible reason for dealing with you again.

The present chapter is about just this—how to make sure that dissatisfied customers give you a second chance to satisfy them. Before getting to the nitty-gritty, though, look at three related issues. Two of them are cautions, the third is a word of encouragement.

THREE POINTS TO CONSIDER

You're Not Just Giving Something Away

This is an easy mistake to make. On a casual reading of the story at the start of this chapter, you might think that the key was that Pat *gave* John something. Not at all. Pat did indeed give John something of worth: free oil changes for the length of time he owned his car. But that's not the point. Pat gave him something that was only of value *if he dealt with Pat again.*

This is the key. It's not the value of what you give that counts. It might be worth a few cents or hundreds of dollars—but that's irrelevant for your purposes here. What's relevant is that you give something that only has value to the customer if he deals with you again. Its purpose isn't to placate him or make him feel good about you in general; it's to get him to come back so you can show him that you really can satisfy him "the first time" around.

It's important to get this distinction, if only for the cost implications of it. Look at it from a strict cost viewpoint. If you give a customer a gift, it's an out-of-pocket cost when you give it to him. When you give him something that has value (i.e., costs you something) only if he deals with you again, it's not a cost but—literally—an investment. You don't pay unless the investment works.

You see, satisfying customers *doesn't* mean throwing money at them. Most of the points I've emphasized in the book require time, money, and effort by the firm. Not one of them is strictly a cost. Every one of them is an investment—money spent up front in expectation of a greater return downstream.

That's the case here. Your goal is to get the customer back. You don't spend one cent less than is required to accomplish that goal—but you don't spend one cent more, either. You design the situation so that what you offer (a) has maximum impact, (b) only has value if he deals with you again, and (c) costs no more than is necessary to achieve those two goals.

You're Not Playing a Game

What a strange heading. Of course you're not playing a game. No? Look just a little more closely:

"Hey, Tom, want to pick up lunch at Henry's Quick-Serve."

"Not really. They never serve it as fast as they say."

"I know—but now they have a guarantee. If it's not ready in 10 minutes they give you a free meal. I've gotten two free meals already this week.

"Hey, I don't mind waiting a few extra minutes for that!"

This is a game. In effect, Henry's customers are betting he can't deliver on his promise—so they'll get an extra benefit. The cost of a meal is the cost of playing. It's really not a bad deal at all for his customers if they have the time to spare.

This is really another variation of a theme that's run through the book, surfacing again and again. You don't dare adopt the strategies this book presents for dealing with dissatisfied customers unless you are very good at everything else you do. Every word, every tactic assumes that your firm is competent at everything else.

Here's a good example of what this means. As I began writing this chapter, a major car manufacturer began offering their "QuickLube Plus" service locally. The advertisement reads: "An oil change, lube and more in 29 minutes or less, or the next one's free!" On the face of it, it's just the kind of inducement that this chapter is about.

In fact, though, it might not be. Read these two statements and notice the subtle difference between them:

> "An oil change, lube and more in 29 minutes or less, or the next one's free!"

> "An oil change, lube and more in 29 minutes or less, absolutely guaranteed!"

To me, the first form implies that they may miss their deadline, so they're preparing themselves and their customers for it. The second says that they'll do what they say, period. The factual warranty—a free oil change—may be the same in both cases. The first one, though, creates just a tinge of doubt about whether they'll deliver.

That's almost (but not quite) a minor quibble. The decisive factor is whether the company actually, consistently delivers an oil change and lube in 29 minutes or less. If they do, customers who need a quick oil change and lube will come to them because they're delivering value. If they don't, these customers will go elsewhere. The customers they'll get are the ones who can spare the extra time and are willing to bet the cost of the service that the company won't deliver on their promise.

If you intend to stay in business, there's only one reason for wanting a dissatisfied customer to deal with you again. *You want the chance to prove that his dissatisfaction was an isolated case—and that your normal performance is full value the first time around.* If he doesn't come back, you can't prove that to him. On the other hand, if you don't consistently do it right the first time, having a second chance does you no good. Save your money.

The Future Value of Solved Problems

Those were negative examples; here's a positive one. While you can't count on it being enough, prompt and effective resolution of customer complaints is itself a motivator for the customer to return. In a world where so much customer service is perfunctory, effective service stands out like a beacon. Somewhere in his books or tapes, Tom Peters quotes the auto salesman who says: "I want to sell you a lemon so you can see just how good our service department is." You probably wouldn't want to go that far, and I doubt that he really does—but his intent is clear.

Recall two points from earlier in this book. When a customer doesn't receive the value she counted on, her *expectation* of getting future value drops. When your frontline people respond with concern and skill to her dissatisfaction, they raise this same expectation of future value.

Your frontline people should understand this, and they should be broadcasting this message in every transaction with a dissatisfied customer. Oh, I don't mean that they need to use the words. It's often better if they don't. But their actions should be shouting to the customer,

> "We don't make very many mistakes, and when we do make one, we jump through hoops to correct it. You can absolutely count on that!"

This is a powerful motivator. Everyone in your firm who deals with dissatisfied customers should be aware of it, should think it, and should act it. Even this is still not enough, though, and that returns you to the chapter's main theme.

COME BACK, COME BACK!!

I'm not suggesting that you broadcast your message to dissatisfied customers with this much passion and pleading. But this is exactly the message you need to broadcast. The way to do it is to provide her a meaningful value that she can only get by dealing with you again.

Now, revisit the examples from the Prologue again. I hope that you did reread each one and think about what you'd do to get the customer back again. That way, you can compare your answer with the answer(s) given here. (After all, yours may be better!)

The Unsuited Traveler

Remember, you're alone at Reliable Cleaners, it's 6:30 A.M., and you've gotten a note that Mr. Wentz's suit wasn't cleaned as promised yesterday. Because he'll be leaving on his trip within an hour, you either do something now or let the situation ride. What do you do?

This is a serious situation. No matter what you do, a good customer is going to be seriously inconvenienced. If you do nothing, he leaves without the suit. If you run it by, he may have left or it may otherwise be inconvenient. If you call, you may disturb his family (or even him, if he isn't leaving early). As so often happens, there are no really good solutions.

Still, you can't afford not to act. You've dissatisfied a good customer, and you have to get rid of that dissatisfaction *now*. You might just run the suit by and hope that he's home. I'd probably call first. Either is okay.

Even when you do that, you've given him far less value than he was expecting. What do you do to restore the value—and to get him back so you have another chance to satisfy him?

Your first reaction may be to give him a book of discount coupons. That seems to be a fairly popular practice. However, this has two (closely related) drawbacks:

1. Discount coupons are very common. If you're the manager of Reliable Cleaners you probably issue them and may even accept

those of other cleaners. Mr. Wentz will probably see this as a "ho-hum" response. If he's unhappy enough, he'll try to find another cleaners who'll take the coupons—and defeat the purpose of the whole endeavor.

2. Discount coupons aren't enough to make up for your failure, and probably not enough to get him back. Not having his suit ready when he emphasized that he needed it for a trip was a major boo-boo. It takes a step on your part that's just as major to resolve the situation.

In other words, you need to make a dramatic response. It has to convey clearly and emphatically your understanding that you let him down. So what do you do?

It should have struck you how similar this situation is to the story that introduced this chapter—and I'd take the same basic step here that Pat did. I'd call Mr. Wentz to make sure you caught him in time (that's slightly less intrusive than showing up unexpectedly). I'd give him the cleaned suit, with appropriate apologies. Then I'd give him a small card, good for free cleaning of that suit for as long as he owns it. (Actually, I'd like to pin a permanent label in the coat that said the same thing, but I'm not sure that's practical.)

This is the kind of forthright statement the situation demands. Taking the suit to him helps, of course—but all you're doing is delivering him what you promised a day late. It needs something more. Free cleaning for the suit for as long as he owns it is that something more. Telling him to bring you everything that he has that needs cleaning and that you'll clean it for free (one time) is another.

Isn't this a little much? After all, if he gets the suit cleaned every month or so for the next five years, that's a lot of free cleaning. What about offering to clean it for the next year, or to clean it forever at half price?

The free cleaning for a year would be a possibility, but it doesn't make quite as strong a statement. You'd just have to make a judgment call. Cleaning at half price probably won't work; there are too many "half-price" offers in the world for that to stand out.

If you're still troubled by the cost of the remedy, this is a good point to reevaluate your priorities. Which comes first, cost or customers? If you put customer satisfaction first, if you truly want to save the customer and not the sale—then you've got to make a strong statement and accept the cost. If cost comes first, you'll probably opt for another solution—but it may lose you the customer.

If you believe that this solution may be too expensive, you may be confessing to another shortcoming. You may not have confidence in the ability of Reliable Cleaners to deliver as promised, when promised, time after time. This takes us back to the point that's made over and over in this book: a commitment to complete customer satisfaction is the icing on the cake of an effective business. If you're afraid you may set a costly precedent by making a strong reaction here, is it because you're afraid the situation will occur again and again? If so, it's probably your delivery processes that need changing, not what you do to get the customer back.

It might be interesting, by the way, to compare this solution, or the one you'd try, with what actually happened. The cleaner called Mr. Wentz and told him that if he would come by they'd have the suit for him. When he did, they charged him for the cleaning. What do you suppose his reaction was? How many times do you suppose he's been back? What do you suppose "customer satisfaction" really means for Reliable Cleaners?

The Unsuitable Room

Now you're the manager of the local Hospitality Hotel, and the President of the chain just sent you a letter he received from a couple who stayed with you. Their room wasn't ready, and the TV didn't work. Room service was slow and billed them for the wrong meals. The ice machine on their floor was out. The maid ignored the "Do Not Disturb" sign. When they left, valet parking brought them the wrong car.

This is a particularly sticky one. Your first response may be to refund the couple's money, with your apologies. (This is what the hotel actually did.) This makes their stay free, but it doesn't give them any reason to think you'll do better next time. And it doesn't get them back—unless they decide it's worth betting the cost of the room that you'll screw up again and their stay will be free. (Remember the game?)

Frankly, my first reaction was to offer them a free stay any time they wanted to return. This isn't very good, either. You've done nothing to satisfy them, nor to create any belief that the next stay will be satisfying. In fact, such an offer might even be insulting: "We want you to come back and enjoy our truly lousy service again."

So what do you do? What would you do?

Here's what I think I'd do.

- I'd call the couple if I had their number or could get it. If not, I'd write them and ask them to call me. I'd invite them to be my guest for lunch or dinner (their choice—remember the advice earlier in the book to let the customer choose whenever possible).

- If they accepted, I'd see that they got first-rate meals with all the trimmings and I'd apologize profusely. I'd offer to refund their money from their previous stay completely; if possible, I think I'd have it in an envelope I could lay on the table in front of them. I'd also have a personal IOU for a 100 percent free weekend. I'd ask them to accept this instead—if they were completely willing—so that I could prove how much of an aberration their experience was.

- If they were really angry and refused the invitation, the wicket gets stickier. If possible, I'd drive to their home and then make them the same offer (their previous stay free or a future stay free). Whatever they chose, I'd leave my IOU for a completely free meal with them.

What if they were from out of town? I'd call and ask if they were going to be back in town any time soon. If the answer was "yes," I'd ask for them to stay as my guest and then give them a full refund for their past stay. If it was "no," I'd mail them the full refund and my personal IOU for a completely free stay whenever they wished to use it.

Expensive? Yes. Time-consuming? Yes. How else are you going to make the point that their experience was a terrible, terrible exception to your commonly superb service? If the expense and the time are still bothering you, remember (1) none of this works unless the lousy service really was a rare exception; (2) your goal is to save the customer, not the sale; and (3) if you don't do something, one bad experience may cause you to lose as many as 15 or 20 actual or potential customers.

The Mangled Computer

Now, with a puff of magic dust, you've become the president of a small mail-order computer company. Andy, your customer-service rep, has just brought you a note about a customer who received a computer after the promised delivery date and with several major problems. Andy's told her that you will replace everything and asked if you want him to do anything else. Do you?

This situation brings up a common problem that mail-order firms face. A product that is in excellent shape when it leaves the warehouse may be unacceptable when it reaches the customer. Boxes may have sides kicked in, sensitive parts may have been vibrated until they give up—any number of things could have happened in transit. If you did a sloppy job packing your product, it's your fault. Or it may be the carrier that fouled you up.

Question: Does the customer care who caused the problem? Answer: Of course not. You committed yourself to deliver her a working product. You didn't. If the carrier was at fault, you and the carrier need to have what diplomatic dispatches call "an open and frank discussion." But that can happen later. In the meantime, you have a dissatisfied customer to take care of.

Look at the situation from her point of view. She selected you as a vendor, probably because you were less expensive than her local computer store. She ordered from you because you guaranteed your product and offered a 30-day return period. These calmed her anxiety enough that she was willing to deal with you.

Now she's looking at an unusable computer. She knows you'll replace the nonfunctioning parts; she may know that you'll have it done quickly. She hopes you'll do things right this time, but that's up for grabs. The extra $100 or so that her computer store wanted suddenly doesn't seem so high. After all, she could dump the offending machine on their counter and insist that they replace it on the spot. (This may be unrealistic, but there's no requirement that she be realistic.)

You can't call on her in person to reassure her. You can call her on the phone—and you should. The question is, What are you going to say when you call?

As you know by now, just replacing the defective equipment isn't enough. What are some of your options? You might offer to:

- Add another floppy disk drive at no cost.
- Increase the amount of internal memory.
- Upgrade the video card and/or monitor (so the screen has higher resolution).
- Upgrade the computer itself to a faster one.
- Provide a free extended warranty.

None of these alternatives are tremendously expensive, and any of them is possible. There are others; if you're in the computer business, you can probably think of several. So, which do you do?

This is what I'd do. I'd call the customer, if possible. I'd apologize and promise her that the new parts (with someone to install them) would be there the next day. I'd talk with her a bit, to find out what she's going to use the computer for. Then I'd offer her choice of one of the two or three most relevant options. I'd let her make a choice, but I'd also make the choice as relevant for her as possible.

As good as this offer might be, you've done nothing to get the customer back to deal with you again. This is unique neither to mail order nor to computer firms. Like automobiles, homes, and clothes dryers, people normally buy computers only once every few years (at most).

Again, this is what I'd do. First, I'd wait a month—until she's been using the computer and decided she's gotten the value she bargained for. Then I'd call her, to make sure this actually is the case. I'd try to get a feel for how she's using the computer and, if possible, what her next logical addition to it would be. If I sold that peripheral, at the close of the call, I'd tell her I'm sending my personal IOU for a 50 percent discount on it. If not, I'd still send her the best 50 percent discount I could.

(If you had sold her a car, your first offer might be an upgraded radio-cassette player—followed after a month by a 50 percent discount on rustproofing. That gets her back in twice. If it was a dryer, delivering her six months of free detergent and then, a month later, offering her any hamper she chose from your store would be a possibility. I'm sure you can think of better ones; the point is that there's always something you can do not only to restore value but also to get the customer dealing with you again.)

Please notice several aspects of this transaction:

- You should try to identify what will be most useful to the customer, and then offer her that (with a choice if possible). If she bought a monochrome monitor because color is hard on her eyes, and you automatically offer to give her a color monitor—well, you won't make many points. Finding how she's going to use your product and making her an offer with that in mind is far more effective. It earns you double points: for listening, and for increasing the benefit of the product.

- It doesn't have to be the president who does this—though there's no substitute for that. Whoever contacts the customer should clearly be speaking for the firm and expressing the policy of the firm. In other words, the customer should be confident that she'll receive the same response no matter when she contacts you or whom she deals with.

- You may have wondered why, in this and the previous example, I talked about using an IOU. Why not just a voucher? You use an IOU to *personalize* the transaction (remember Chapter 4?). It doesn't matter whether the IOU is signed by the president—what matters is that it's signed by a *person* and that it expresses the concern not only of your firm but of *that person* as well. It says "Somebody, some real, live human being, cares."

The Air Unconditioner

In the final example, you're the manager of a heating and air conditioning firm. You've overheard Marguerite, your customer-service rep, dealing with Mr. Olson—a customer whose "repaired" air conditioner still isn't working. You're short of technicians, and all of the ones who are at work are fully scheduled for the day. What do you do?

This adds another dimension to the problems posed by each of the previous situations. The customer is dissatisfied. He's also *hot*, and that's going to increase his dissatisfaction by the hour. On the other hand, you've made commitments to other customers, who'll be dissatisfied if you don't keep those commitments. What do you do?

First, you check to see if there's any slack. Is one of your service calls routine maintenance or repair at a vacant house that could slide a day without harm? Or do you have someone installing a unit in a new house who has enough time to take care of Mr. Olson's air conditioning? Or is there another situation where someone can be diverted to take care of him? If there is, the first step of your problem is solved.

What if there's not? Well, you do whatever you have to so that Mr. Olson gets taken care of as quickly as possible. If feasible, have someone work overtime to solve his problem (and be sure he knows that you scheduled the overtime just to take care of him). You'd know what your other options were; pick the most responsive one and do it. *Don't* be casual about it and get to Mr. Olson when you can—or delay promised service to someone else to take care of him. Does this pose a problem? The solution isn't in dissatisfying your customers, but in getting it done right the first time.

Now, how do you get him back? In this kind of situation, that's the easy part. You offer him free service—say a free checkup at the start of heating season in the fall. Then *you* take care of managing that. You call him, remind him of the offer, and ask if he'd like to take you up on it. Perhaps he'd prefer you came by in the spring; reschedule and call him again then. (One more note on this. If you do the checkup and find something wrong—fix it free if at all feasible. Most of us—probably including you—have a deep suspicion of someone who promises us a free inspection that turns out to cost us.)

WOW—DO I HAVE TO DO ALL THAT?

The answer is "Yes"—and "No."

"Yes"—when your firm's failure to deliver value is as serious as the failure was in each of these examples. If you think about them, these weren't your routine goofs; in each case, the firm failed to provide the basic product or service that the customer had purchased. When the failure is this serious, it takes strong measure to counteract it. Without prompt response and a clear reason to return, the customer will most likely conclude you don't know how to do your basic business very well. That's when your competitors get their chance.

What if the failing wasn't so pronounced? You still need to be just as responsive, but you find less costly ways to bring the person back again. Here's how each situation might have been less serious, and how you might have handled it:

- The customer left a routine cleaning order and your frontline person promised it for Thursday at 2:00 P.M. When she came by at 2:30, it wasn't ready. She dropped back at 4:00 and picked it up. Just a minor goof, right? Right—but you don't overlook it. Your frontline person hands the customer a note good for 50 percent off her next cleaning order, or one good for one garment cleaned free. Then he tells the customer, "I'm doing this so I can prove we'll get it done on time next time." (Suppose this customer has been coming by every week for five years, and this is the first time it happened. Great—the frontline person says, "Gee, we let you down this time, and we want to make up for it.")

- Your guests enjoyed their weekend at the hotel, except that they couldn't get the HBO channel on their set. This wasn't a big deal; they mention it as they're leaving so you can have it fixed. Your frontline person says, "Our rate is for perfect rooms. Will it feel right to you if I take $5 off the rate? And please take our IOU for 50 percent off any meal the next time you stay with us."

- The computer arrived on time, in working condition—but the "B" drive isn't working right. Of course, you take care of that problem promptly. Then you write him a short note of apology, enclosing a coupon for a free mouse, or perhaps one that's good for 50 percent off on a grammar checker you sell. As always, the note explains that you expect to give flawless service, and you want him to order from you again so he can see how well you do at it.

- The customer's air conditioner is working all right, but your service technician left tracks on her carpet. You send someone by to clean the carpet right away, of course. Then, the day after he cleans it, you send the customer a note of apology that contains (perhaps) a note offering her your $35 checkup for $10 at any time during the next year.

In each case, you took positive steps to satisfy the customer and get him back again, but none of them were costly or complicated. The key is simply to do something that clearly restores the value of your product or service in the customer's eyes—and then get him back where you can do it right the next time.

The Orvis Company believes strongly in this policy. When they've dissatisfied a customer, they resolve his problem. If the firm's error caused the problem (and sometimes even if it didn't), their frontline people issue the customer a gift certificate. Simple. Straightforward. Clear. They're not locked into this approach. When a Christmas present for her boyfriend's dog didn't arrive on time, they airmailed the present and included a free bone!

Is it really worth all this trouble over such small failings? Yes! Tom Peters has made the point repeatedly that competitive advantage is created day after day *at the margins.* It's the little things, the everyday courtesy, concern, and responsiveness of your firm that distinguish you from your competitors. And they're what creates and keeps the loyalty of your customers.

Peters particularly emphasizes everyday courtesy. I certainly agree— but I'd add another factor. It's come up before, but it's worth repeating—especially when you're dealing with a customer who's already dissatisfied. It's this: do *what* you say you'll do, *when* you say you'll do it, *every time.* Your customers should be able to rely unhesitantly on your simple statement. "I'll be there Friday by 2:00" should mean exactly that.

What if you can't be sure you'll make it by 2:00? Then don't promise it. It's tempting sometimes to make a commitment and hope you can keep it to get a troublesome customer taken care of. Don't! **Don't!!** Don't ever promise anything you can't deliver.

Then what happens when something changes and you can't deliver what you promised? Depending on the circumstances, you write or phone or telegraph or fax or Fedex the change to the customer. Plans never go perfectly. Even the most conscientiously made commitments sometimes can't be fulfilled. Most people—including most customers—are prepared to accept this, *if* they're told promptly and the reason explained to them. When the customer calls asking where his order is, though, and your answer is that you ran into a problem a couple of days ago and it won't be ready for another three days—you're in trouble.

Hire, develop, and reward frontline people who are courteous, all the time. Who are responsive, all the time. Who do what they say they'll do, all the time. And then support them. Don't you promise what you can't deliver, so they end up holding the bag.

WHAT IF THEY JUST WANT TO RETURN IT?

You may have been asking this question as you went through the first part of the chapter. What if the way the customer wants her problem solved is for you to give her money back? What do you do then?

For openers, you apply all the basics. You treat her as a person, respond promptly and courteously to her problem, and solve it for her. Here are some of the other key points.

Accept the Return Graciously

If you have a guaranteed return policy, that's what your frontline people should practice. When a customer shows up and says "I want my money back," the appropriate response is "Certainly." There are some other steps that an experienced frontline person can take, but they never come first. First, you accept the return, without reservation.

Think about your own experience as a customer. How many times have you returned something and been made to feel that it was really wrong to do so? The frontline person then inspected it closely, to make sure you hadn't harmed it or asked you pointed questions about how you'd used it or just what was wrong, or the person didn't say anything but treated you with cold formality. When that happened, what did you think about the firm at that moment?

Don't do this to your customers. When they want to return a product, take it back with the same courtesy and friendliness that they experienced when you sold it to them.

This brings up a touchy point regarding how you organize and reward sales staff. In many firms, salespeople are paid partially or totally on a commission basis. When what they sell is returned, they lose the commission. The question is, do they handle the returns, or does someone else? There are advantages and disadvantages both ways.

- If someone else handles the returns, that person doesn't have a personal stake in it. No income is leaving his pocket because of it. He can afford to be friendly and courteous.

- On the other hand, if the customer sees the same person who sold her a product taking it back with the same concern for her, she'll be more apt to believe that you mean to satisfy her. If you have salespersons who press too hard, or sell the wrong thing, this is pointed, useful feedback—if they're able to accept it.

I doubt that there's a final answer. The more mature and effective your salespeople are, the more of the total transaction they should handle. Then they can focus on the overall satisfaction of the customer, not just the specific sale.

Find the Reason, Tactfully

Remember, this comes second—if at all. Once the customer can see that she's not going to be hassled about the return, your frontline person can try to find why she was dissatisfied. This is important information. The product may have been defective, or wasn't the correct one for the customer's need. It may not have been the product; the customer may not have known how to use it properly. It doesn't matter. Whatever the reason, your firm needs to know it. And, as earlier chapters emphasized, the information needs to get to the appropriate point in the organization.

Your frontline people should know, however, that this is strictly secondary to being responsive to the customer. If the customer is upset, angry, hurried, expecting a hassle—let the information go.

Find Another Way to Satisfy Her

This is the third step. Your frontline person has accepted the return graciously and tactfully found out the reason. Is there another product you carry that would meet the customer's need? Or if the customer used the product just a little differently would she be satisfied?

On the one hand, this requires great skill and delicacy on the part of the frontline person. On the other, many of them have abilities in this area that far exceed yours and mine. If their response is made from genuine concern for the customer, most customers will respond to it. Even if the customers' answer to all of the suggestions is "sorry!" they'll appreciate the try. (Just as she'll be offended if the suggestions are just a veiled attempt to switch her to another product.)

The goal of your frontline person is to satisfy the customer. If you don't have what she needs, but some other firm does—that means telling her about the other firm. This isn't where you start, of course. The frontline person doesn't start off with, "Gee, I'm sorry this didn't work. You know you can probably get just what you want at Acme, just up the street." But that may be exactly the right thing to say at the end of the transaction.

Isn't there a risk in this? You bet there is. Acme may treat her better than you do, so she starts dealing with them. They may have a product line (or a set of services) that are more what she needs. In other words, you may lose her.

On the other hand, none of this may occur. They may not have what she needs, or they may be much less customer focused than you are. Whether true or not, the customer knows that you cared enough about her and her satisfaction to refer her to a competitor. That's apt to make a pretty strong impression on her. It also influences how she looks at her next purchase from you. After all, if you were willing to refer her to a competitor, you must be willing to take the time to sell her just what she needs.

There's no pat answer, of course. Your frontline person takes the return graciously, then lets the transaction happen as it needs to—which suggests a final point.

THE JOY OF EFFECTIVE FRONTLINE PEOPLE

The point's been made before that when you become a manager, you begin to lose your touch for the intricacies and niceties of what's really happening "on the floor." This is particularly true when the work is customer service. Well, it's time to look at this again, in a slightly different context.

It's easy to start thinking about satisfying customers in the abstract—particularly when you have a book like this to stimulate your ideas. Then you can fall into the trap of believing you know better than they do what frontline people should do to handle specific situations.

That may be true. If it is, either you're particularly intelligent or your frontline people aren't. Whichever the explanation, it's a poor situation. If you're that intelligent, you should probably be using it somewhere else. If they're not, how come they're representing you to your customers?

That's oversimplified and flip, of course. It's also true. If you have an experienced and effective cadre of frontline people, they'll think of ways to deal with, satisfy, and keep customers that will often astound you. Remember that one of the reasons for delegating so much freedom and authority to them is that they develop pride and confidence in their skills. When this happens, you get a rising spiral of effectiveness. The main thing you need to do is stay out of their way.

Such a competent frontline staff doesn't happen automatically, or overnight. It takes all the steps the book has identified: being clear about their role; selecting the right people, and training them well and rewarding them properly; having responsive, clear policies; and supporting your people. When you take these steps, consistently and effectively, you build up a core of expertise in your front line that seldom needs intervention from you.

Why do I mention this now? You've just looked at what generally needs to be done to satisfy customers and bring them back. But this is abstract. Every situation is a little bit different, and what works in one may be just a little awkward in another. The solution for this is an effective front line. They'll come up with the appropriate responses, tailored to the situation in front of them.

If they can't, nothing else will substitute. If they can, nothing else is required.

CHECK POINTS

1. Getting a customer back so we get a second chance to do it right the first time is standard practice at my firm.

2. My firm understands clearly the difference between doing what we must to get a customer back again and just give him something "to make him happy."

3. We also understand the difference between getting her back and playing a game where she wins if we don't deliver.

4. My frontline people all understand how important solving a customer's problem is to his expectation that we'll satisfy him in the future.

5. Every frontline person understands and communicates to a dissatisfied customer that we want her back again so we can prove that her dissatisfying experience won't ever happen again.

6. My firm's policy and its actual practice tailor what we do to get a customer to return in relation to the magnitude of our goof. We take small steps if the goof was small—and extreme measures if it was serious.

7. Our frontline people are just as friendly and courteous when a customer wants to return a product as when he bought it. (Then, when they can, they try to find out as exactly as possible why he was dissatisfied with it.)

8. When it's appropriate, our frontline people will suggest a substitute product or service to a dissatisfied customer. If necessary, we'll recommend another vendor.

9. Thank heavens for the expertise of my frontline people!

9 FORGET THE EXCUSES

"Oh, I can't possibly do all those customer-satisfaction things. I'm going broke as it is."
"Do you think there might be a message there . . . ?"

TOO LIBERAL—OR TOO CONSERVATIVE?

I really thought, as I began this book, that I might be going a bit overboard. After all, I'm suggesting that you organize your whole business around a passionate emphasis on customer satisfaction. I'm suggesting that you go to extreme lengths to satisfy unhappy customers and get them back again. I'm suggesting that cost control, return on investment (ROI), and value to your stockholders comes in second. While I believed this, I was afraid when I started that I might be overstating it a little.

Forget it!!! After talking to frontline people, managers, and CEOs in some exceptional companies, I found I was really a little timid. They don't just *say* "customer," they shout it. They go to truly extreme lengths to see that their customers are satisfied and happy. Customers come first; everything else—profits, ROI, cost control, whatever—comes, well . . . later.

In other words, their customer focus and dedication to customer satisfaction approach the fanatical. *And they're all extremely successful!!* In fact, they're each among the most successful firms in their field.

I realize that these may sound like so many words to you. You may have serious doubts about the practicality of what I've said up to this point. If so, this chapter is for you. It talks very specifically about the benefits and costs (i.e., the value) of organizing your business to create and increase value for your customers. I can say, with no hesitation at all, that

> If you think there's some other basis for business success than a fanatic customer orientation, you're creating a gold mine—for your competitors.

Still don't believe me? Read on.

TWO RELEVANT QUOTES

I've deliberately avoided a lot of quotations in this book because you didn't buy it to find out what other people have said. On this point, though, you might like to read what two writers say about concentrating on customer satisfaction, based on real-world research. Here they are.

Milind M. Lele:

The basic dichotomy still holds: You can maximize customer satisfaction while keeping costs below a specified level, or you can minimize costs while maintaining a parity level of customer satisfaction. You can't do both.
. . . Products that provide parity levels of satisfaction become commodities; customers don't have a reason to stay with a particular brand or manufacturer. Mistakes in judging what constitutes an acceptable level of customer satisfaction create a pool of discontent that rivals can exploit.

Linda Silverman Goldzimer:

Satisfying customers is not just another platitude. Increasing a customer's level of satisfaction pays off by building loyalty and increasing the likelihood that a customer will repurchase a company's products.

For example, the Ford Motor Company reports a 23 percentage point difference in the level of repurchases between its customers who are very satisfied with their dealers' service and those who are very dissatisfied with their dealers.

Another large manufacturer of consumer durable goods found that among its retailers that failed to satisfy their customers' service requirements, product-repurchase loyalty was only 20 to 25 percent. By contrast, those retailers that generated high levels of customer satisfaction had a repurchase loyalty that averaged more than 50 percent.

FIVE STAR FIRMS

Perhaps you're uncomfortable taking the word of people who only write about devotion to customer satisfaction. What about the people who practice it? That's a reasonable question, and this is where you get down to the proverbial brass tacks.

Here's a brief description of five firms who're absolutely devoted to satisfying the customer—and who're making a lot of money doing it. Almost every one of them has been mentioned before, but here they are in more detail. They're Ricart Motors, Micro Center, WordPerfect Corporation, The Orvis Company, and The Cooker Restaurant Corporation. They're located as far apart as New England, the Midwest, and the Rocky Mountain west. They're superb representatives of the hundreds of firms across the country who are doing well for themselves by doing extremely well for their customers.

THE WORLD'S LARGEST CAR DEALER

When I first got the idea for this book, Ricart Motors operated one of the largest Ford dealerships in the country. By the time I started writing the book itself, Ricart was the largest Ford dealer in the world. As I write these words, they're the world's largest volume automobile dealer, period.

If that rate of growth doesn't make you sit up and say "WOW!", you're probably asleep.

Rhett Ricart, president of the firm, discussed its success with me. He didn't talk to me about their marketing initiatives; his brother, Fred, handles them. He didn't talk much about Ricart's profits (except to say that "they're good"), or the firm's ROI, or even its sales figures.

Ninety-five percent of what he said concerned one aspect of his business: his customers. He really believes (as the quotation at the beginning of the epilogue says) that customers *are* his long-term investment. Here's some of what he means by that:

- The concern for the customer starts at the very top. "If there's a problem that comes into this dealership, I keep track of it."

- Ricart's service department is open 24 hours a day on weekdays. And the firm guarantees that their service charges will be at least as low as a customer can find elsewhere. If not, they refund the difference.

- Chapter 6 looked at one of their innovations—their direct phone lines to their service bays. But they don't wait for service customers to call; *they* call to find out if the customer is satisfied with the service.

- Ricart's sales personnel are paid on a commission basis—hardly news for an auto dealership. They *also* get (or don't get) a significant bonus based on customer satisfaction. (When's the last time you heard of that in a car dealership?)

- The firm has a Quality Control (QC) Coordinator—an ombudsman that a customer can call if he has a problem with his new car. The QC Coordinator has $500 *carte blanche* per customer to see that the customer is satisfied.

A FORTRESS FOR CUSTOMERS IN A DANGEROUS WORLD

Could you claim that your customer-service policies make your firm a "fortress,"—protecting your customers from an industry whose products often don't live up to their billing? Micro Center, which sees itself as a computer "department store," can, and the firm's policies back up the claim.

- Micro Center's prices are almost as low as those of computer mail-order houses—but they will take back any product they sell if it's returned within 30 days. They've been doing this since their beginning just under a decade ago. It's still an unusually responsive policy; when they started, it was revolutionary.

- Micro Center is expanding rapidly. The company's philosophy is that with customers, they can do everything. When they opened their Atlanta store, they already had 8,000 customers in the area.

- Chapter 6 described the tremendous amount of time, effort, and money they spend getting formal feedback from their customers. Nobody does that better then they do.

- What limitation do they put on the authority of their frontline people to satisfy customers? Well, all of the customer-service people know that if they don't give the customer what she wants, the boss will. So what do you think the frontline people do?

With all of this customer orientation, how are they doing? They're already a leading retailer nationally. Their goal is $1 billion a year in sales by 1995—with no drop in quality—in one of the most competitive fields in the country. Does that tell you enough?

THE WORLD'S BEST-SELLING WORD PROCESSOR

In the highly unlikely town of Orem, Utah, is WordPerfect Corporation. In case you aren't familiar with them (and even if you are), I'll give you some basic information on the corporation in a later section. First, though, look at their frontline emphasis:

- Between 50 and 80 percent of all employees hired each month at WordPerfect work in Customer Support. Other departments select their employees largely from the Customer Support Department.

- WordPerfect interviews about 20 percent of their applicants for customer-support positions. About 25 percent of these are interviewed a second time, and about half of those invited for the second interview are hired. Granted they're in a relatively good job market—but that's one customer-service person hired out of each 40 applications they receive. That's picky!

- Each customer-support person gets eight hours of training in problem-solving, attitude development, and creativity skills. For the next *three weeks*, they're carefully tutored while they field actual calls. Then, they're integrated into a customer-service team.

- You think you get calls? WordPerfect answers an average of 10,000-plus customer-support calls a day—every one of them free to the customer. The company doesn't see this as a drain on their resources—they believe it makes them *more* profitable.

OK, this is what they do for customer support. How well do they do as a company? They've gone from five end-users in 1979 to 2.6 *million* customers by the end of 1988. Their sales have doubled almost every year for a decade. Put another way, from 1980 to 1988, their sales increased by just under 40,000 percent.

THE CUSTOMER IS ALWAYS RIGHT, EVEN IF . . .

The Orvis Company bills itself as "America's Oldest Mail Order Company," which makes it by far the graybeard of our five exemplary companies. There's nothing gray about its performance, though. It's present owner, Leigh Perkins, took over in 1965—beginning its dramatic growth. Just to give you an idea of his success, in 1988, they mailed some 23 million catalogs, supporting sales of $73 million.

All through the book, I've wanted to quote Leigh's clear policy on customer satisfaction, but instead I saved it for this chapter:

> The customer is always right, even if you know damn well he is wrong. Replace, repair, or adjust his product according to his wishes.

That's just what Orvis does. Their frontline people have broad authority to do whatever's necessary to resolve customer dissatisfaction—including issuing gift certificates. Orvis's instructions to its frontline people are short and to the point:

> Ask the customer, "How may I help you?" and take immediate action to see that their needs are met.

Unlike many mail-order companies, they maintain an 800 number for sales *and another* for customer service. They recognize the importance of their customer's time and try to resolve any problem during the first contact. The customer-service specialists know not only the policies and procedures but also the whole order flow through the organization.

Not surprisingly, despite its small size, The Orvis Company has a staff position devoted to training both new and experienced employees. The company also maintains three full-time technical consultants to answer customer questions on hunting and fishing items.

They offer a 25-year guarantee on their fly rods. Do they mean it? Well, they replaced a three-ounce fly rod for a customer that he broke when he tried to kill a snake with it. Yeah, they mean it.

"IF YOU'RE NOT PROUD OF IT, DON'T SERVE IT"

Like the other exemplary firms, The Cooker Restaurant Corporation is still growing rapidly. In fact, it's the newest one of the five—opening its first restaurant in April 1984. Since then, it's grown to nine restaurants in Tennessee, Ohio, and Indiana. The 10th opens shortly in Michigan.

You think your frontline people have authority? The quotation at the start of this section is written on the front of the area where the servers pick up their orders—and they take it seriously. If a server doesn't believe that he can be proud of an order, it's redone. It's redone *even if the general manager of the restaurant disagrees.* The server, who has to actually put the food in front of the customer, is the final authority on whether it's good enough to serve. Period.

You might expect this in a restaurant where the average tab is $100 to $500. In fact, you read all the time about the excellent service offered in expensive clubs and restaurants like this. Well, Cooker's goal is to provide this same level of satisfaction in a $7 or $8 meal—and they sure are trying.

You read Cooker's 100 percent satisfaction guarantee in the prologue. Arthur Seelbinder, president of the firm, believes that the guarantee was instrumental to the success of the firm. It makes it clear to the customer what Cooker's policy is—and everyone in the firm knows that their job is to live up to it. If a customer isn't completely happy, the server, the manager—everyone—knows that their job is to change the situation *NOW*. (If you reread the guarantee, you'll see that it commits *everyone*, not just the boss or the firm in the abstract. This is rare—and a superb idea.)

Chapter 3 looked at "friendliness" as a prerequisite for effective frontline people. Cooker's version of this is "woo"—the desire to have people like you. If you want to be a manager at a Cooker restaurant, woo is an essential.

One last point. Like Micro Center and so many other firms, Cooker's supervisory style is incredibly hands on. Managers visit every table. The visits aren't perfunctory, either; they're trained to read body language and to respond to the whole situation, not just the words the guest says. If they detect something wrong, they *act*.

IF YOU'RE STILL NOT CONVINCED . . .

If the book up to now hasn't convinced you to worship customer satisfaction, I doubt that what I say for the rest of this chapter will. Let me take a few pages, though, to talk about some of the major objections to a strong focus on customer satisfaction. Then I'll end this chapter with a few implications of a customer-focused operation for accounting and management action.

WE'D LIKE TO GUARANTEE SATISFACTION, BUT . . .

- Buyer remorse will kill us!
- They'll take advantage of us!
- We don't sell little things!
- We can't hire the people to do it with!
- We can't afford it!

Here's a closer look at each one.

Buyer Remorse Will Kill Us!

All salespeople know about buyer remorse. It's the bane of their existence. They talk the customer into the product or service, the company delivers, and then the buyer has sober second thoughts. It's bad enough that you have to deal with buyer remorse, right? It's murder if you have to let her bring back what you sold her.

Buyer remorse *is* a fact of life. The more expensive the product or service is, the more a fact of life buyer remorse is. There are perhaps some businesses where the reality of buyer remorse prevents a complete customer satisfaction policy. It's hard for a realtor to offer your money back if you don't like your new house, or a car dealer to give you a complete refund if you're not satisfied. (Some car dealerships have offered to exchange a new car if the customer isn't satisfied with it, as long as he buys another that's at least as expensive. Unfortunately, I don't know how successful this has been.)

You need to be careful, though, before you jump to the conclusion that buyer remorse makes a complete satisfaction policy impossible. After all, General Electric has offered a 90-day money-back guarantee on their major appliances. Because these appliances can easily run into hundreds and thousands of dollars, that's not chicken feed.

Even if you can't offer a money-back guarantee, you can offer to do everything reasonable, and a little bit more, to see that the customer is satisfied with what you sold him. Look at the policies of Ricart Motors again. You probably don't sell anything more expensive than a Ford Taurus SHO, so can you afford a less extensive customer satisfaction policy than theirs?

You still feel that buyer remorse makes it impossible for you to allow your customers to return what you sell them for a refund? Okay—I believe you, almost. Let me say what I repeat often in this chapter: If you haven't tried it, you don't *know.* You may be cutting yourself off from a powerful competitive weapon.

So, do you forget your best judgment and offer the refund anyway? Not necessarily. You can pick one (or a small group) of your products or services and test a full-refund guarantee with them. Obviously, you pick the product(s) that you expect the least dissatisfaction with. Then you try the guarantee and see what happens. The down side is limited; the up side could be dynamite.

They'll Take Advantage of Us!

This is very different, but very real. There are people out there who will take advantage of your customer satisfaction policy. One major retail TV and appliance chain used to offer an unconditional three-day return on any purchase from them. After a few months, they had to stop the guarantee on their VCRs. It was remarkable how many people bought VCRs on Friday, got dissatisfied over the weekend, and returned them on Monday!

Don't miss the larger lesson in this, though. The firm competes as the low-cost provider in a highly competitive market—but it still offers a 10-day exchange on many of its products if the customer is dissatisfied.

The simple fact is that you weigh the cost of customers who take advantage of you against the benefit of those who're genuinely grateful for your dedication to their satisfaction. In most circumstances, the benefits will outweigh the costs. When it won't, you make your best guess of how far you can go to guarantee satisfaction.

Remember, however, that unless you've tested, you don't really know the answer. Try a full guarantee with the highest probability of success. Do it long enough to have valid results—then make up your mind how strong your satisfaction guarantee should be.

We Don't Sell Little Things!

This is an important concern. If your company stays in business by selling a half dozen of something in a year's time, giving a full satisfaction guarantee is scary. And it may not be realistic.

There is an alternative. You ought to be able to give a strong "We can't take it back but we'll do everything we can to make it work for you" guarantee—and stand fully behind it. Your customer deserves to know that you're fully committed to his success with your product. It may well make the difference between a sale and no sale—and if you only sell a half dozen of them a year, that's a *big* difference.

There's a principle here. You may not be able to offer a full money-back guarantee, but if you're not willing to offer to do everything possible short of that—well, you need to stop and ask what your expectations are of your company and its products or services. If you're offering products or services for which you can't offer this guarantee, the problem probably isn't with the guarantee. On a purely financial level, firms that offer so-so products at so-so prices make the least money of any firms. Certainly your profit goals are a bit higher than that!

We Can't Hire the People to Do It With!

This is a real problem in many areas, and it's getting worse all the time. Not only are businesses running short of skilled people, they're running short of any kind of people. Then the skills shortages are often made worse by poor work habits and attitudes. How in the world can people like this satisfy your customers? And—perish the thought—how can you delegate to them the broad authority they need to solve customer problems?

The first question you have to answer, of course, is what you're willing to pay to get effective frontline people. That's not a trivial question. If you increase what you're paying them, you may get your pay scale out of balance. A higher scale for them could lead to higher pay all up the line. You'll be paying out more salary dollars, regardless of whether the high pay spreads through the organization.

That's how it looks when you look at frontline people as a cost. What happens if you look at them as an investment? The whole point of an investment is to get the greatest return for your money. You have to ask which gives you the greatest return: partly skilled and motivated front-line people at minimum wage, or more skilled and motivated people at a higher wage. There's no pat answer to the question, though the profit consequences of poorly skilled and poorly motivated frontline people can be severe indeed.

Actually, another approach is usually more effective. This is a compensation plan that pays real dollars to frontline people who really satisfy customers. This was covered in detail in Chapter 5, and there's no point in repeating that here. Hiring customer-service people at an average wage but paying top dollar in bonuses and increases gives you the best chance of attracting and holding the kind of people you want on your front line.

We Can't Afford It!

This objection may have been running through your mind from the first page or so of the book. It does take money to produce a fully customer-focused business. The question comes down to whether you can afford to do otherwise.

Because I'm not in the business of trying to sell you on maximum customer satisfaction, I've tried to identify the situations in which a firm can aim for less than 100 percent satisfaction and survive (and perhaps even prosper). You'd be surprised how many situations seemed to be this way on first look, but then evaporated on a closer analysis. My final conclusion is that there are a maximum of two situations in which you can afford less than full customer satisfaction:

1. Having little or no competition.
2. Having repeated contacts with your customers.

Little or No Competition

I don't like the policies of my local cable TV company—but they have a monopoly and don't have to be that concerned about their policies. If I want cable TV, I get it from them, period. If you have that kind of situation, you can get by with less than a full commitment to customer satisfaction.

But be warned: you have competition you may not recognize. I can only get cable TV from one local firm—but I can rent movies on videotape from a half-dozen places. I've cancelled the movie service on cable and I rent movies instead. The same thing can happen to you, no matter how secure your monopoly seems to be. No matter what your product or service is, there are always what the economists call "substitute goods and services" out there.

Remember, customers buy benefits—not goods and services. It's very rare that several different firms, in very different lines of business, can't provide that benefit. To continue the example of cable TV, they're really in competition not only with regular TV and rental videos but also with game manufacturers, local theater groups, and even movie theaters. Before you decide that you can provide merely adequate customer satisfaction, be sure you know what goods or services your customers can substitute for yours. You may reach a different conclusion once you have this knowledge.

Many, Many Contacts with Your Customers

There's one other situation where you may get by with less than 100 percent satisfaction: if you have repeated satisfactory contacts with your customers. (I'd want to ask, though: If you can satisfy them 95 or 99 percent of the time, why not go ahead and satisfy them 100 percent?)

My observation is that many, many firms try to get by on this basis. They hope that contacts are frequent enough and mistakes rare enough that customers will put up with the infrequent dissatisfactions. Even this has a serious downside. Say you have 10,000 transactions with customers a month (not difficult at all). You get 98 percent of these right. That's 200 that will be done wrong. Some of these customers will forgive you and keep dealing with you. To be wildly optimistic, you could say that 90 percent of them do that. This means that 20 dissatisfied customers will leave you—and tell about 200 other people how dissatisfied they are. Two hundred lost (actual or potential) customers a month times 12 months in a year begins to add up to a lot of customers. . . .

Nonetheless, you can probably get by—if all your competitors are settling for less than 100 percent satisfaction along with you. Let just one of them decide that his standard is 100 percent, and you're in trouble. (For years, Columbus, Ohio has had only one department store. They used to make a fetish of customer satisfaction. Because they were bought by a large chain and their headquarters moved away, customer service has suffered. At the same time, two other department stores are moving into their competitive area. In the name (I'm sure) of cost containment, the local department store has handed its competitors an opportunity most marketing people only dream about.)

I hope you see how chancy it is to opt for less than complete customer satisfaction. At the very best, your customers will carry around enough dissatisfaction to provide a ready customer base for any competitor who's truly customer focused. At worst, they'll find other ways to get the benefits you so unreliably provide them.

COSTS VERSUS INVESTMENTS

Because costs are so important to any firm (and to any public agency), this section is specifically about costs. If you have a strong accounting background, I want to warn you that you may be upset about what I say. It won't square with customary accounting procedures. Realize, though, that I'm not writing for accountants. I'm writing for managers—and they need to understand just where their competitive bread is buttered.

This section covers three points: (1) realistically assessing the impact of customer satisfaction on costs (and vice versa); (2) the real meaning of "investment" where customer satisfaction is concerned; and (3) the way that managers who care about customer satisfaction need to set priorities.

The Impact of Customer Satisfaction on Costs

This is the traditional way to evaluate the problem: what will a given customer satisfaction policy cost? Figure out the costs of returns and exchanges together with warranty costs, and then determine if you can afford it. In other words, costs drive customer satisfaction.

This gets back to an issue that's surfaced before. Which is primary, cost control or customer satisfaction? If you try to make both first, you'll end up with a compromise that everyone—including your customers—will be dissatisfied with. If cost containment is primary, you don't have a customer-focused firm; this is a perfectly defensible business decision, but please don't delude yourself that you're customer focused if costs come first. (If you want to try to delude your customers on this point, that's your business.)

The simple fact of the matter is that in most firms most of the time, and in every firm some of the time, *nothing* can compete with cost control. It has a countable immediacy to it that simply wipes out alternatives. "Mailing expenses are too high—cut them 10 percent by the end of the month!" has a virtually unstoppable force to it. Besides, managers like to feel that they're in charge, and cutting costs is a way to demonstrate that they are. (If you feel insulted, I'm sorry. The only excuse I can give for saying this is that I've been a manager for two decades.)

If you want to state the problem as costs versus satisfaction, I'd suggest you phrase it this way:

> Given that we're going to provide 100 percent customer satisfaction, how can we do this at the lowest cost?

That keeps everyone focused on customers, where they need to be, and it keeps cost control on their minds, too.

I don't think this is the most useful (or profitable) way to look at it. If you want to really deal with the question of costs versus customer satisfaction, I think the next two points are far more relevant.

Overlooked Investments

What's the difference between a cost and an investment? An accountant could put it much more elegantly, but this is my definition:

> A *cost* is an expenditure you want to keep as low as possible.
>
> An *investment* is an expenditure on which you want to get the greatest possible return.

Cars burn gas, and gas is a cost. You want a car that burns the least gas possible, consistent with your other goals in owning a car. A CD (certificate of deposit) is an investment. You put money into it so you'll earn interest (get more money back). If a CD that requires a greater investment pays a higher return, and you can afford the extra money, you'll make the greater investment.

Firms, of course, make investments. Your tools, land, and buildings are investments. Business consultants and advisors (including me) have argued for years that people are an investment; but this reasoning is a bit fuzzier.

Firms also have costs. Salaries, raw materials, consumable supplies, and so on are all costs. They get taken off the bottom line before it becomes a bottom line.

Now, here's where my heresy comes in:

> Every expenditure that leads directly to customer satis-
> faction and increased value to the customer is an
> investment. Everything else is a cost.

Now I realize that you can't reorganize your formal accounting system to reflect this. But it's how you should look at your business. Here are a few examples:

- Salary costs of frontline people are typically carried as costs. Phooey! If you believe what you've been reading in this book, you *know* that this is an investment. So is every dollar you spend for training. You don't try to minimize either one—you work to get the maximum return on investment for what you spend.

- Envelopes, printing costs, and stamps are usually treated as costs. If they're used to contact customers, they're *investments*. You don't try to minimize them—you work to get the biggest bang for your buck from them.

- Managers normally talk as though the raw materials for their products are costs, to be kept as low as possible. That's 90 degrees out of true. Your customers are going to be looking for a benefit from what you make from your raw materials. If you skimp on the materials, you're jeopardizing customer satisfaction at the very beginning of the cycle.

- On the other hand, the new building you buy because it has more spacious offices for the staff and a health club—it's a cost. What direct benefit does it offer to customers? (You may decide it's a reasonable cost, but at least call it a cost.)

- If you purchase another firm because it has a good cash flow, or its assets are undervalued—that's probably a cost. Integrating the firm is going to take time and attention away from satisfying your customers and making yourself more valuable to your market—and that's as costly as anything can be. (Buying another firm because its products are synergistic with your own and beef up customer satisfaction, however, is a definite investment.)

This was a very short list, but I hope it suggested a way of looking at your expenditures in light of your customer-satisfaction goals. You minimize every cost you can—but before you do that you filter out everything that directly supports customer satisfaction and label it as an investment. This is strange in conventional accounting terms, but it certainly puts your focus where it needs to be.

Setting Priorities

You've probably read some books on managing, and perhaps taken a course or two on it. You've probably heard that a manager's job is something like planning, organizing, directing, and controlling. You have my sympathies; unlearning is harder than learning—and you need to unlearn this.

A manager's basic job is setting priorities. That's right—setting priorities, for yourself and for the organization. The most precious commodity you and your firm have is time. Your basic job is to see that it's used in the right way. Everything else—*everything*—is secondary to this.

Now that that's settled, you can get down to the proverbial brass tacks. If you intend to run a customer-focused firm, this is your job:

> Give first priority to everything that will directly
> maintain or increase your value to your market, second
> priority to those things that will indirectly maintain
> or increase it, and last priority to everything else. Period.

This job has two goals. The first is long-range—the actions you take to identify and segment your market, create the products for it, and build your market position. The second is short-range—the actions your frontline people take here, today to satisfy *this* customer, and the next one, and the next one . . .

This, as they say, is where the rubber meets the road. It's the real purpose behind the distinction between costs and investments. You don't have to implement my definition of *investments*—though it might be interesting if you did. You do have to get your priorities straight.

In case you're used to such terms, this is saying that *effectiveness* always takes priority over *efficiency*. You're *effective* when your actions achieve your goals—when you provide customer satisfaction. You're *efficient* when you do this at low cost.

If you're wondering why I'm worrying with this, I can tell you in a nutshell: left to themselves, organizations give priority to efficiency over effectiveness. Here are some examples:

- Most automation projects are sold on the basis that they'll save money, either directly or by reducing salary costs. That's fine, and useful—but it doesn't increase customer satisfaction one whit. If you pass the savings on to your customer or use them for R&D, it indirectly increases your value to your customers. Suppose, though, you changed your system so that your customers could call in and find the exact status of their shipments in 30 seconds, 24 hours a day. That's a direct benefit.

- Revising the management compensation plan to pay a bonus for short-run profitability may make your managers more efficient in the short run, but it probably won't pay off for customers. Paying the bonus, at least in part, based on customer satisfaction won't directly help your customers—but it will encourage the kind of management action that will.

- Paying your sales personnel commissions based entirely on sales may produce apparent effectiveness. If 15–20 percent of those sales become returns because they don't fit a real need, it's neither effective nor efficient. Paying a hefty commission and then subtracting returns from it will produce a much sharper customer focus in that part of your front line.

- Increasing the number of calls a customer-service person handles an hour by 15 percent sounds like real efficiency—but the predictable result (other than fudging the figures) will be a lower level of customer satisfaction. Spending the time and effort with your customer-service people so they become more skilled and can provide the same level of service in 15 percent less time is both efficient and effective.

Like everything else in the book, this is a very brief sample, intended to point to the kinds of priorities you need to set. If you truly believe in a customer-focused business, that becomes the priority. Every action, every expenditure, every change in emphasis must be judged by its contribution to this priority. You might want to put a little reminder on your desk that goes something like this:

- Will it directly benefit our customers? Why shouldn't we do it?
- Will it indirectly benefit our customers? Should we do it?
- Is it of no benefit to our customers? Why should we do it?

This seems like just the place to introduce the next-to-last key, which has been stated in one form or another throughout the book:

> **Key #14**: The whole process by which you create and deliver your product or service must support the creation of customer satisfaction and loyalty.

A FEW FINAL BENEFITS—AND A CAUTION

There are a few other reasons why your firm should be strongly customer focused. They're important, but there just didn't seem to be a logical place for them in other chapters. So, here they are.

Benefit #1: Protecting Your Markets

In cold, hard economic terms, a high level of customer satisfaction is the greatest barrier to entry into your market that you could build.

There are various steps you can take to make it harder for competitors to raid your market—but this one is the closest at hand and the easiest. Everything considered, it's also the cheapest. To successfully enter a new market, a firm must offer a clearly greater value than the firms already in the market. If you practice 100 percent satisfaction, nothing short of a major innovation will be an effective entry wedge.

This relates closely to a point made earlier: High customer satisfaction gives you time to recover and recoup when a competitor springs a hot new product or service on your market. If your customers have confidence that their satisfaction is important to you, they'll be willing to wait a little until you can come up with a competitive offering. Conversely, if you've been practicing a so-so satisfaction policy, you'll probably get a good look at the backs of their coats as they leave you for your competitor.

The value of high customer satisfaction for protecting your market is a great deal like the seat belt in your family car. Wearing it day in and day out is a nuisance, just as maximum customer satisfaction may seem to be a strain on your budget. Let an accident happen, though, and the belt is worth every moment of discomfort it caused you. Let a new competitor try to gain entry into your market, and you'll suddenly discover just how important this focus on your customers has been.

Benefit #2: Anticipating the Market

Remember the story of WordPerfect Corporation at the beginning of this chapter? Their customer service is exceptional—and they believe it makes them *more* profitable. Their customers are an endless source of new ideas for their products, as well as providers of quick feedback on any bugs in their software. A potential competitor would have trouble getting in a year the information about customer wants that WordPerfect gets in a week or two.

When your customers know you care about them and their satisfaction, they talk to you. They tell you about the small dissatisfactions—the points they'd never mention to a company with a lesser commitment. They tell you what they'd like to see you offer and give you reliable feedback when you ask them about the benefit of potential new products or services. The benefits of this are almost literally incalculable.

If I may repeat myself, the time, money, and effort you devote to satisfying customers isn't a cost—it's an investment.

Benefit #3: Getting Priceless Advertising

Americans are so used to high-powered (and expensive) advertising campaigns that we forget that word-of-mouth is the most effective form of advertising there is—and it's free. This was mentioned at the beginning of this book, and it's worth repeating here.

The statistics in Chapter 1 showed the number of people with whom satisfied and dissatisfied customers talk. When you're devoted to their satisfaction, your customers tell their friends. Often, it's more than a casual mention. TV ads sometimes show one woman enthusiastically telling another about a particular product. Though it may seem silly, that's the way that satisfied customers act. If you're really good, they're not just advertisers for you but missionaries as well.

Caution: The Danger in Automated Efficiencies

This is so important that I want to repeat it briefly here because it's relevant to the preceding points:

> Be very careful about the machinery—particularly the automated machinery—you buy to make your firm efficient and cut costs. Make sure that, at the very least, it doesn't hinder your ability to deliver satisfaction.

That certainly sounds negative, doesn't it? Well, unfortunately much automation has a negative impact. You may have an automatic telephone routing system, the kind where the customer presses a number key (sometimes several times) to get to the department she wants. I have yet to find one of these systems that is as effective for customers as a human being would be. In other words, every firm I deal with that uses such a system has increased their efficiency and simultaneously lowered my satisfaction as a customer.

It's not just answering systems. People are so used to the small inconveniences in computerized billing systems that they no longer notice them—but the systems are still there. Automated tellers in banks are helpful, but they've also helped produce a situation where the branch manager is effectively a message carrier between downtown specialists and customers. Automated check-out systems at hotels are really great—but they prevent front-desk personnel from getting feedback on customer satisfaction.

I could go on and on, but I won't. I know of no other facet of organizations that has so fallen prey to efficiency at the expense of effectiveness as automation. If you take everything else in this chapter with a boulder of salt, I beseech you to insist that your computers serve your customers first and your internal processes second. For many companies, just doing that would amount to a major revolution in customer service.

AND IN CONCLUSION . . .

Why should you run a customer-focused company? Perhaps Harry Lamm, president of Subaru of America, Inc., answered this question as succinctly as anyone:

> To satisfy the customer, it means that everybody in the company has to understand that the total existence of a company depends upon the

customer, so if the customer is not satisfied, he is not going to be a customer tomorrow, and if he is not a customer tomorrow, we don't have a business tomorrow.

CHECK POINTS

1. If I'm not practicing a fanatical customer focus, at least I understand the competitive risks I'm running.

2. My company's customer focus, level of customer satisfaction, and growth are at least as great as that of any of the five exemplary firms.

3. I don't use any of the excuses (buyer remorse, being taken advantage of, not selling little things, can't hire the people, can't afford it) unless I've carefully tested to see that they're unavoidably true.

4. I understand how to control costs aggressively *within* an overall customer focus.

5. I understand that everything I spend money on that's used in, for, or to make my product or service is really an investment.

6. I know how to set my priorities as a manager: Direct benefits to customers come first; indirect benefits come next; all else comes last.

7. I understand the value of a strong customer focus in protecting my market, anticipating the market, and getting word-of-mouth advertising.

8. I never adopt automated systems unless they directly or indirectly benefit customers—or, at the very least, don't have a negative impact on them.

10 DO IT IN A PUBLIC ORGANIZATION

Rod sold his car to Paul, his neighbor down the street. There was an irregularity in the title, so Rod had to go to the Division of Motor Vehicles (DMV) to straighten it out.

Two days later, Paul called him. "I'm sorry, buddy, but there's still a hitch of some kind. You'll have to go back to the DMV and try again."

"No way! You can try and get it taken care of. You can bring me back the car and I'll give your money back. But there's no way I'm going to go back to that place!"

This was an actual incident, one I heard as I was finishing this book. Does it sound familiar? Is Rod echoing your reaction to all too many of the public agencies you have to deal with? More important, are you a manager in a public agency—and Rod sounds like some of your clients?

This chapter deals specifically with public organizations. Every day, thousands of individuals who work for federal, state, and local governments—and for public hospitals, health clinics, universities, and a myriad of other public facilities—work hard to satisfy their clients. I want to do everything I can to help them, and to encourage thousands of others to do the same.

Many books that concern customer service and customer satisfaction make only a ritual nod toward the public sector. They often display little

knowledge of the significant differences between public organizations and private ones. As a result, their suggestions are well
intentioned but hard (sometimes *very* hard) to apply in a public
organization.

I want to do more than that. Almost every idea in this book can be
applied in the public sector as well as the private—but not necessarily
in the same way. There are special problems—not excuses, just *problems*—in public organizations. This chapter deals with some of these
problems and how to overcome them.

If you're in a profit-making firm, you may be interested in some of
the reasons why so many public agencies so often aren't customer
focused—and in how you, as a citizen, can encourage them to change.
If you're a manager in a public agency, the information in this chapter
will help you satisfy your clients—and give you reasons why you should
concentrate on doing so.

In any case, let me state this as unequivocally as I can:

> The fundamental objective of increasing its value to
> its market is as absolutely necessary for a public
> organization as it is for one that hopes to make a profit.
> It's also based on the same first step: increasing the
> organization's value to individual customers.

The first draft of this chapter was headed "Do It in a Nonprofit
Organization." When I thought of the variety of nonprofit organizations, though, I paused. They run the gamut from nonprofit hospitals
who must compete for customers just as though they were profit-making
firms, to endowed foundations that have no visible customers at all. It
seemed almost impossible to lump them into one pile. So, I decided to
concentrate on public organizations—most of which have certain
characteristics in common.

If you want to apply the principles in this book to a nonprofit
organization, don't despair. Between the first nine chapters and this
one, you're almost certain to find something that fits your situation. For
the moment, though, look at some reasons why public agencies are as
they are.

GENERAL PROBLEMS OF ORGANIZATIONS

Not all of the problems that public organizations have are unique to them. In fact, many of their problems are ones that afflict organizations in general—including those that (want to) make a profit. However, certain characteristics of public organizations make it easier for them to fall victim to these problems. Here are the most common problems.

GENERAL PROBLEMS THAT PUBLIC ORGANIZATIONS SHARE

- They operate with limited competition.
- They're control oriented.
- They're heavy with staff.
- They're averse to risk.
- They provide reverse incentives.

Why are public organizations especially prone to these problems? Read on.

Limited Competition

You may think that this belongs in the list of characteristics that separate public organizations from private ones. Wrong! While the absolute amount of competition in American business and industry has been increasing for the past number of years, many companies operate with little or no effective competition. What matters here is not whether a company is public or private, but whether it exists in a market-driven part of the economy.

First, note that I labeled this section "*Limited* Competition." While many private and public organizations have seeming monopolies (the gas company, the Department of Defense), even the strongest monopoly has some limits. There is almost no product or service for which there is no substitute. The gas company may have a monopoly on gas, but customers can substitute electric heat, even wood-burning fireplace stoves. Congress can increase the funding of the Department of State or the Agency for International Development as a partial alternative to dependence on the Department of Defense.

Given this caveat, many private firms exist with very limited competition. Before the advent of Japanese steel and autos, competition among American steel and auto companies existed—but it was very, very limited. The previous chapter showed that when a firm has limited competition, it can be a bit more cavalier about satisfying its customers. In fact, many firms in a situation where there is limited competition focus much more heavily on customer service (courtesy, etc.) than on providing value as such.

Some public organizations exist in situations where there is significant competition. Public colleges must compete with other public colleges, as well as with private ones. Public hospitals compete with both nonprofit ones and privately operated ones.

Despite this, public organizations tend to have fewer competitors than private ones. It's hard to think of a really effective competitor to your state welfare department or department of motor vehicles. This leads them to react as any organization does when it has limited competition: direct its attention to goals other than customer satisfaction and value. This combines with other significant characteristics of public organizations (described later in this chapter) to sabotage effective customer satisfaction as an objective.

Control-Oriented

This is most commonly what's meant when people speak of an organization as being "bureaucratic." In these organizations, the focus is on following the rules, making and adhering to plans, predictability, administrative tidiness. Control-oriented organizations normally generate great amounts of internal paperwork and expend great amounts of energy to see that everyone does everything "by the book."

Control-oriented organizations are almost always poor at satisfying customers. There's no particular mystery to this. By the very definition, an organization that concentrates on controls is focusing its attention inward. It's oriented toward itself, not toward its customers.

In a control-oriented organization, the basic job of frontline people is to follow the rules. The organization carefully decides what a customer has a right to expect and then sees that she gets it. If she's not satisfied, if she wants more—well, that's a shame (or a crisis). If it's not spelled out in the policy or the procedure, she's not entitled to it.

Don't think that public organizations have a monopoly on control orientation. *Any* organization can become focused on controls. It's extraordinarily difficult for a large one *not* to do so, but a small one can fall into the same trap. This is one reason why American corporations have gone through such gut-wrenching change in the past eight years—they've had to recover from the inward-looking, control-oriented encrustations of the previous two decades.

Nonetheless, public organizations are *typically* control-oriented. This may result from sheer size and dispersion (the Department of Defense, state welfare agencies). It may be encouraged because the organization's mission is control (the Internal Revenue Service, state and local occupational health agencies). Or it may stem from the constant oversight of the organization by government bodies and the media.

Whatever the reason, public organizations tend to be control oriented—and this is a major obstacle to a strong customer focus.

Heavy with Staff

As any organization grows, the trend is for a higher percentage of its resources to move into staff units. This is a very general principle: the larger and more complex any system gets, the more of its resources are devoted to maintaining itself rather than to accomplishing its objectives.

These staff units do planning, human resources analyses, curriculum development, affirmative action, quality control, and so on. Nothing is intrinsically wrong with any of these activities; they're all important. Unfortunately, each staff organization gains a vested interest in

seeing its program succeed; it's just a small step from there to the point
of view that the success of the program is an intrinsic part of the mission
of the organization. In the eyes of the staff, the effectiveness of the
people who do the work of the organization is measured by their success
in carrying out these programs.

This takes authority away from the frontline people; they become
messengers instead of players. Worse, staff positions get the prestige
and the salaries, so that the best people are drawn from direct customer
contact to jobs progressively further removed from customer satisfaction. The process feeds on itself; as the staff gets stronger, it becomes
more imperious, more disdainful of the people on the line, who either
lose their motivation or direct their energies toward getting away from
these lowly jobs.

Again, the public sector has no monopoly on this. As recent history
has testified all too vividly, corporations can become just as staff heavy—
and suffer just as badly from it. Shedding staff has been an intrinsic part
of the downsizing in corporations. On the other hand, public organizations, in part because of their control orientation, still tend to have
layers of staff overseeing everything that happens. Unfortunately, this
is often aided and abetted by their pay plans—which put the people
who plan, analyze, and evaluate higher on the scale than those who
merely *do.*

In these organizations, in addition to generalized over-control,
frontline people have to contend with the incessant direction from staff
departments, which reduces their authority to act even further. This is
yet another significant obstacle to customer satisfaction.

Aversion to Risk

What happens to the willingness of the front line to take risks to satisfy
the customer in this situation? It vanishes. If a frontline person
bends a rule to really satisfy a customer, he risks a low appraisal,
lessened chances of promotion, perhaps even a formal reprimand. On
the other hand, if he can show that he did just what the policy required,
he's home free. That the customer wasn't satisfied becomes almost
irrelevant.

An environment that forces frontline people to operate without taking risks is the very opposite of what an effective customer focus requires. Customer-service people get frustrated and cynical because they're forced to carry out policies that override their common sense. Their initiative and their imagination are stifled. This virtually guarantees that the good ones will get frustrated and leave.

All too many private organizations are burdened by this kind of safe, by-the-numbers approach to customers. These are the ones whose customer-service people cheerlessly follow the procedures, mumbling woodenly "May I help you" and "Have a good day," as they sneak a glance at the clock.

Unfortunately, such an attitude is often endemic in public organizations. While thousands of individual workers are exceptions, this is still the common picture of frontline people in public service. Even the truly customer-focused ones among them must often cloak their effectiveness in the jargon of the rules.

Control orientation, a bloated staff, and now risk aversion—three potent enemies of a strong customer focus: Taken together, they add up to one more.

Reverse Incentives

In the kind of public organization you're looking at, what kind of action pays off? Creative problem-solving for customers? "Going the extra mile" to resolve a complaint? Taking extra time to work with a customer whose problem is unique? Yeah—sure. If you believe this, I have some really fine waterfront property in central New Mexico I'd like to sell you at a bargain price.

Of course this isn't what happens. What pays off is just the reverse: following procedure and policy, not making waves, not identifying with the customer or client. Giving them exactly what they're due—no less, but certainly no more. Going through all the necessary motions, with none of the redeeming emotion that's required for successfully dealing with customers.

Does this sound all too much like some of the firms and agencies you deal with?

PROBLEMS UNIQUE TO PUBLIC ORGANIZATIONS

This certainly wasn't a complete list of the characteristics of organizations that often get in the way of their satisfying their customers—though it touched on the most common ones. Now it's time to look at the characteristics specific to public organizations that frequently keep them from focusing on customers. While there are more than just three of these characteristics, these three are the most important.

SPECIFIC PROBLEMS OF PUBLIC ORGANIZATIONS

- Control/apportionment function.
- Ambivalence toward "clients."
- Separation of customer from consumer.

As you look more closely at these, you may see that each one significantly affects a public organization's ability to focus on its customers. However, the third characteristic—the separation of customers from consumers—represents the basic difference between public and for-profit organizations. First, take a closer look at the first two characteristics.

Control/Apportionment Function

This language may sound a little strange to you, but it represents a major functional difference between public and private organizations. The difference is in the way that these organizations answer a basic economic question: Who gets what, and how do we decide that?

In the private sector, prices set by a market economy allocate goods and services. What you can pay for, you can buy. If people want more of something than is available, someone will start creating it to make a profit. If there is too much of something, someone will stop making it and begin making something else. Except for products or services that may be illegal, you don't worry about whether you have a right to buy what you want. If you have the money, and it's available, it's yours. (You can agree here that this is a wildly simplified but basically true analysis, can't you?)

In most public organizations, who gets what is decided on a very different basis. It's not a question of who has the money for something, but who has the *right* to it. Goods and services are allocated not by price or by value to the customer, but by a set of rules. Who can get treated at this clinic, and how much will they be charged? Who must go to school, and what school must they attend? Who's eligible for Aid to Dependent Children or unemployment insurance? These are allocation decisions made in accordance with specific (and often detailed) sets of rules. (When this involves a payment of some kind, as in unemployment or Social Security benefits, economists call it a "transfer" payment—just in case you wanted to know.)

Not all public organizations allocate goods and services. Many of them exist to exercise control in a particular area. How is this lot to be zoned? Did this firm commit mail fraud? Who gets this liquor or radio station license? These decisions, too, are made in accordance with sets of rules. In this case, the benefit is a public good, and the agency controls who uses it and/or how it may be used.

This is a very different world from the world of a private firm. This grounding in rules creates at least two attitudes that are inimical to a customer focus:

- The organization tends to focus on the rules, rather than on those to whom the rules are applied. The applicant isn't Joe Jones, but case #4431.

- The organization's basic defense against attack is to show that it was acting strictly in accordance with the rules. It might be easy to justify an exception for *this* situation—but a dozen other clients will be asking for the same exception by Friday. So stick to the letter of the rules.

It's very difficult to focus on individuals as customers in these circumstances.

Ambivalence Toward Clients

When the individuals who benefit from a public organization's products or services pay little if any of the cost, a shift in attitude often occurs in the organization. The shift may be subtle or blatant. The people who use the products or services are no longer customers, but now become clients. Instead of trying to satisfy them, the organization concentrates on seeing that they get their due—and that they don't get away with anything.

If the organization is the Internal Revenue Service, this is easy to understand. After all, the majority of contacts between the IRS and its clients are adversarial. The client wants to keep more of his money; the IRS wants to take more of it. We, the taxpayers, don't want people to get away with paying less tax then they rightfully owe.

The same attitude can come to characterize organizations who are "serving" their clientele. Because clients don't pay full value for what they get, dealing with them can become a continuing process of ensuring that they don't get more than they're entitled to. For their part, clients may believe that if they don't ask for *everything* they won't get *anything*.

Thus, a curious ambivalence can develop. On the one hand, the organization exists to serve the client; even the IRS proclaims (I think sincerely) that it wants to be of service to the taxpayer. On the other, it covertly and even overtly distrusts him and tries to control him. Then the client responds with distrust and attempts to get his fair share. Everyone knows that the IRS is unreasonable, so it's OK to try to slip one by them, right?

It should be clear how this increases the difficulty of being customer focused. But, important as these characteristics are in their own right, the control/allocation function and the ambivalence are just prologue. What really separates public agencies from profit-making organizations is the separation of customer from consumer.

"What?" you ask. "What's so important about separating customers from clients? And why is it *the* most important characteristic?"

Those are good questions, because most of us aren't used to looking at public agencies in this way. Read on to find the answers.

Customers Versus Consumers

So far, this book has assumed that the customer is the consumer of the good or service. Surprisingly enough, that's not true where most public organizations are concerned. Start by looking at what each word means:

- A *customer* is the person who selects and pays for a product or service. In Chapter 2, Rosalind Jones was Handi Dandi's customer. She decided what she wanted from them, and paid them for it. When the wrapper was cut, she was the one who was dissatisfied.

- A *consumer*, on the other hand, is the person who actually uses the product or service. Rosalind was a consumer of the loaf of bread, but so was each member of her family. The difference is that her family neither selected nor paid for the loaf of bread.

This may seem like an overdrawn distinction. Rosalind bought the bread she did because she knew her family would like it. Besides, people are always buying products and services that others use; husbands buy perfume for their wives, mothers buy clothes for their kids, and so on.

That's true, but in most transactions with profit-making corporations, the customer and the consumer, if not the same, are in a close relationship. Rosalind knew what bread her family liked, and that guided her purchase. If her son had asked her to pick up a package of crackers for him, she would have—and she would have picked crackers that he would eat. When a husband notices that his wife doesn't wear the perfume he got her, he doesn't get the same brand again.

This close relationship of customer with consumer generally doesn't hold in public organizations. In fact, there's generally no relationship at all. Here are some examples:

- The first example is simple and close to home: public schools and colleges. On first glance, students would appear to be the customers. They're the consumers, and to some extent the customers. The real customers, though, are usually parents and one or more legislative committees or school boards.

- Another prevalent example is a state welfare agency. The consumers of the agency's services are clear: the people who get assistance from them. However, they aren't the people who pay. Again, the true customers—the ones who select and pay for the services—are legislative committees and, perhaps, one or two other state agencies.

- Moving further afield, look at the Federal Food and Drug Agency. At least in theory, the American people are the customers. In fact, they neither select nor directly pay for any activities of the agency. The agency's customers are, again, legislative committees. Here, though, there's an interesting and common extension. Because the agency spends most of its existence dealing with drug companies, they tend to become its customers, too.

- Finally, look at an agency such as the Department of Defense. Who are its customers? To make matters worse, it's difficult even to identify its clients. What, if anything, does it mean for the Department of Defense to have "satisfied customers"?

This, then, is the difference between profit-making and public organizations:

A *profit-making firm* deals day-to-day with its customers, the people who determine its mix of products or services and whose purchases keep it in business. The firm satisfies them so that they'll continue to purchase from it—thus providing a continuing income stream and feedback on the suitability of its products to its market.

A *public organization* deals day-in-and-day-out with "clients"—a fancy name for consumers who neither determine the products or services to be offered nor provide the money that enables the organization to keep offering them. The interests of these clients may be significantly different from those of the real customers—the groups who decide what products or services the organization will offer and how much income it will have. If not taken to extremes, the way that a public organization treats its clients may be almost irrelevant to either its product mix or its future budget.

That, my friends, is heady stuff!!

WHAT ALL THIS MEANS

To repeat quickly, public organizations are often characterized by

- A rule-based mission.
- Ambivalence toward clients.
- (Most of all) "clients" who aren't really "customers."

Why have I taken the time to describe this?

- It's certainly not to excuse public organizations that aren't client focused. Whether you're in the private or the public sector, though, it may have helped you understand why so many public organizations don't seem to care about satisfying their clients.
- If you're a manager in a public organization, this may help you understand your situation a little more clearly. You may have been trying to do an effective job, without realizing the difference between your organization and one that at least aims to make a profit.
- It may also help you understand why your frontline people aren't as responsive to your clients as you'd like them to be.

This was a short analysis of the way that public organizations work. Now you get to the critical question: What can a manager in a public organization do to become customer focused? How can she motivate her frontline people to concentrate on satisfying their clients? Here are some ideas.

TAKE THE LONG VIEW

In private industry, satisfying customers is how you stay in business. While that's not true in just the same way in a public organization, there are similarities. Part of the reason why public agencies survive and prosper—when they do—is that the people who deal with them are satisfied with their transactions. Politicians, by the nature of their job, pick up on "the popular will." When the popular will happens to be dissatisfied with your agency, guess what politicians will tend to do. Conversely, if they get positive feedback on the way you're treating your clients, they'll consider that, too.

That may be a difficult idea to get across to your frontline people. I'm not sure, though, that's it's that much more difficult than the problem a public utility or a local bank has. Part of the answer is seeing that your frontline people stay informed. When the paper carries a complimentary article, or a representative makes a positive statement— make sure your frontline people know about it. If there's negative information, see that they know that too.

It always helps, of course, if you can find or invent a competitor. There may be real competitors. For example, if you're a public college or junior college, you really do have competitors. They may be private colleges, private or public technical schools, or other public colleges— but they're *bona fide* competitors. See that your frontline people stay aware of them. Whenever possible, provide them information on how you're doing compared with them.

What if you don't have any real competitors? You might want to consider developing a "friendly" competition with a similar agency. Try to pick one whose relationship to its clients is similar to yours (i.e., both allocate benefits or both are control agencies). If you're just one unit within the agency, find another unit to compete with for customer satisfaction. (The material in Chapter 11 about satisfying internal customers is just as relevant for you as for a unit in a private firm.)

In short, do whatever you have to, as often as you have to do it, to keep your frontline people focused on the payoff your organization gets by satisfying your clients.

This leads neatly to the next point. . . .

REWARD CLIENT SATISFACTION

Most public pay systems are flexible enough to allow some sort of incentive pay. Many are quite flexible in this regard. Often, rewards go to individuals who are efficient or satisfy other internal needs: "Mrs.

Renati completed the study a full two weeks before it was due." That's fine, but that ought to be a secondary focus.

If you want an organization that's focused on customers, your reward system must be focused on satisfying them. A great deal of what was said in Chapters 5 and 6 is relevant here; in fact, most of it is just as applicable to public as to private organizations. Organize systematic ways to get feedback and then use it as a basis for rewarding frontline people. Make it part of everyone's performance plan.

TRAIN A CLIENT-FOCUSED ORGANIZATIONAL CULTURE

Here again, most public agencies can develop and use client-focused training, just as private firms develop and use customer-focused training. Most of the skills and ideas presented in Chapter 4 apply here. If you think your training budget isn't large enough to properly train your frontline people, you may be right. There are thousands of private firms where the same constraints exist; it's largely a case of deciding that training is a priority and then finding a way to do it. Again, job aids are a marvelous tool—particularly if the training budget is limited.

The training you give will be reinforced by the culture of the organization. If your agency has ingrained an ambivalence toward its clients, your new frontline people will pick it up. That makes your training problem much, much harder; now you have managers and experienced workers to train and probably to retrain. Be realistic, make it clear you mean to be client focused, and persist.

BE RESPONSIVE AND FAIR

Chapter 7 emphasized solving the customer's problem, no matter what. Chapter 8 followed up on this, pointing out how essential it is to give your customer a positive reason for dealing with you again. Satisfying the customer and getting him back are sometimes difficult in a private firm, but almost always doable. In a public organization, the situation is often different.

In a for-profit company, it's easy to bend the rules to satisfy a customer. In fact, the rules should just be guidelines and should never substitute for good judgment by frontline people. In a public agency, however, the rules have stronger force—particularly because many of them may be based on law.

In other words, a public organization has to satisfy its clients *within* its rules and regulations. It can't normally offer them something extra to make up for lost value or to get them back again; if it's doing its job right, it gives each client what he's entitled to up front. As satisfying as it might be to get a special discount from the IRS because they gave you misleading information, it won't happen. Nor will the workman's compensation agency give you a little something extra because your payment was delayed last month.

Added to this is the fact that public organizations have to tell a client "no" more often than a private firm has to. Face it—it's difficult to tell a client "no" in a satisfying way. If the organization is a control agency, the problem is multiplied manyfold. If you give your "client" a parking ticket or deny him a building permit, it's hard to make him feel good about it.

That doesn't mean, though, that there's nothing you can do. Your frontline people can do a great deal. They can make a considerable difference in how the client reacts and what she thinks of your agency. The key is two words: *responsive* and *fair.*

Being Responsive

Most people don't like to tell someone else "no," especially when it's a client who doesn't want to take "no" for an answer. To avoid the emotional strain of this, frontline people in public agencies often put up a protective facade of impersonality. "Sorry, that's the way it is—who's next?" This may indeed protect them from strain—but it goes over with clients as well as the proverbial lead balloon.

The cure for this is remaining responsive to the client's situation. It takes skill and concern to do this, but it can be done. Chapter 3 discussed the importance of creating successful transactions by personalizing them, then described the steps in a successful customer-focused interaction. All of this applies directly to transactions with clients in a public agency. Your frontline people establish the relationship, focus on the client's problem and then end the transaction gracefully.

Keeping focused on the client's problem is the key to real responsiveness. There may be nothing your agency can do for a client, but if your frontline person is focused on the client she may be able to suggest other possibilities. Over time, your frontline people build up an understanding of most problems they'll confront and the alternatives that exist for the ones you can't solve. You need to make sure that this knowledge is widely shared and constantly used.

In this and other ways, you can establish your organization as *responsive* to the needs of its clients. Then you go on to ensure that it's *fair* in all its dealings. The order is important: Responsiveness comes first. Fairness without responsiveness degenerates into cold, impersonal rule-following. (Just as responsiveness without fairness degenerates into a chaotic attempt to satisfy everybody.)

Being Fair

Fairness, in the context of responsiveness, communicates a different message. It tells your client that she's important to you—important enough that you won't make an exception for someone else you wouldn't make for her. That's the key to fairness.

If a client believes that you've given him what anyone else would have gotten—even if it's nothing—his disappointment and anger will be toned down somewhat. Let him believe that you gave someone else something you won't give him, though, and it's a different ball game. That's when he digs in his heels and becomes blatantly dissatisfied.

So the way the rules are administered becomes a critical factor. They need to be interpreted consistently and applied consistently. The interpretation needs to be true to the spirit and intent of the rules, not just the letter. This intent to be consistent and fair needs to be communicated, over and over again—within an atmosphere of genuine responsiveness.

It's not just public organizations that need to be fair; private firms have to worry about it, too. However, there's a special reason why it's important in public agencies: Most of the time, their clients must deal with them, or with no one. If you need a check to tide you over to your next job or a replacement for the car title you lost—there's only one place you can go to get them. Most agencies are monopolies; their clients have no one else to turn to.

If clients believe they're being treated unfairly, the whole relationship is poisoned. Look at it from their point of view—you force them to deal with you, and then you mistreat them. They're trapped. They get angry and resentful—as you would—and this drives up the stress level among your frontline people. The whole relationship disintegrates into a painful series of thinly disguised confrontations.

As long as your clients are dependent on you, there's no final cure for this. However, clear and responsive fairness will help, and help immensely. If clients believe that you will do your best to give them what you can, and that you won't deprive them of something you'll give another—they can accept the dependence more easily. They may not learn to love you, but they'll deal with you more openly and receptively.

Supporting Your Frontline People

The challenge that frontline people face in public organizations means that the manager's function of supporting and protecting them becomes doubly important. They need to be protected against abuse from clients; in this, they're no different from their counterparts in the private sector. They also need to be protected against political pressure to make exceptions for certain people, or to oil a squeaking wheel. It's often difficult for a manager to protect against this, but the cost of not doing it is high.

One final point on this is really an aspect of training. Fairness is a characteristic not only of what you do but also of what people *believe* that you do. So you carefully and continually train your clients to understand both that you intend to be fair, and what fairness means to them. You communicate, as much and as often as you need to, what the basic rules are, how you intend to follow them—and that you don't make exceptions based on pressure or threat. This will probably be neither quick nor easy, but it will be an effective source of support for your frontline people.

THE REAL BENEFIT OF BEING CUSTOMER FOCUSED

Chapters 1 through 9 presented a variety of reasons why private firms need to be focused intensely on satisfying their customers. This chapter has looked at several reasons why a public organization should focus just as intently on satisfying its clients. There's one more reason, applicable in private firms, but just as applicable in public agencies:

> Your frontline people are going to be happier, more highly motivated and less stressed if they and the organization are consistently and honestly focused on satisfying its customers or clients.

Think back to Chapter 3 (which probably seems part of the distant past by now). It described what your frontline people have to do if you're to be successful. After describing several characteristics, the chapter suggested that they should do it "so well that the process is satisfying to your frontline people as well as to their customers." Doing it, and doing it well is truly the key to having satisfied frontline people.

Cynicism

Your first reaction may be to scoff at this. Customers can be surly, unreasonable, even impossible. (During my annual physical, I told my doctor I was writing a book on dealing with dissatisfied customers, with a section on handling those you couldn't satisfy. His response, without a moment's hesitation, was "Let me write that for you!" Even doctors have problems with unreasonable "customers.") Isn't it foolishness to suggest that frontline folks are going to feel better if they try to satisfy people like this? Won't they be less emotionally drained if they adopt a by-the-rules approach and don't waste energy?

That sounds seductively logical, but it's not how human nature operates. When customer-service people—private or public—take a minimum-service approach, they suffer even more than the customers or clients do. Their suffering shows up in various ways, but most of all in *cynicism*—the inability to believe in or care about what they're doing.

If you've never worked in an organization where people are just going through the motions, where no one believes in the formal objectives, where everyone's motives are questioned—then you don't know what bone-deep cynicism can do to people. And to good people! Scratch the surface of a cynic and you'll find a deeply disappointed and disillusioned person. A *cynic* is someone who really cares but can't express his caring in what he's doing. It's the occupational disease of bureaucracies, but you don't have to have a bureaucracy to catch it.

(By the way, don't be too sure it hasn't been caught by your organization, or at least by parts of it. Unless you keep in close contact with your frontline people and really listen to them, your organization may have the disease and you may not even know it. Don't worry, though, you'll find out sooner or later—when your customers start disappearing. Cynicism is contagious.)

Why does this happen? Why does not caring about customers and their problems lead to cynicism and generally low morale?

- There probably are a few people in the world who don't care whether they add anything to it or not—but there aren't very many. It's very corrosive to a person's self-image to have a job where she has no feeling of accomplishment, where what she does doesn't seem to make a difference. When you're just going through the motions of helping people—customers or clients—you don't get much satisfaction.

- There's something else you don't get—strokes from customers or clients. Very few people are going to give frontline people their heartfelt thanks for dealing with them perfunctorily. "Oh, thank you so very much for condescending to deal with me today!" isn't in most of our verbal repertoires. Real gratitude from a client or customer can brighten a whole day; it's lack for days on end is enervating.

- When a frontline person solves a customer's problem, the gratitude of the customer isn't his only reward. He also gets a kick from being good at what he does, from being the kind of person who can solve problems. This feeling of competence is important to his self-esteem. Its absence is frustrating and depressing. When frontline people just go through the motions, they're deprived of this sense of mastery, of being good at what they do.

- In short, when a customer-service person doesn't provide real customer service, she has nothing positive to take home at the end of the day and nothing to look forward to when the next day begins. If you've been around this kind of negativity, you know that it's highly contagious. It creates a vicious spiral, pulling people further and further down. (If this seems overblown, congratulations— you've never worked in a really negative environment. If it sounds familiar, you have my sympathy.)

Preventing and Curing Cynicism

This cynicism and negativity, like most diseases, is easier to prevent than to cure. By now, it should be crystal clear how to prevent it: Stay focused on the customer, his needs, his problems, his satisfaction. If no other argument existed for creating a customer-focused organization, doing it just to avoid cynicism would still be compelling.

How do you do it? Well, the book up to this point has almost every idea I could think up, beg, borrow, or modify. Find the ones that seem most realistic for your situation, and try them.

The critical point, though, is to make your intentions clear to your frontline people. If you intend for them to be customer focused, let them know it—not once, but over and over and over again. If they've just been going through the motions, just giving customers or clients what they "deserve" they have to understand that the situation has changed.

If you can change it gradually but forcefully, by gently leading them to a customer focus, so much the better. That takes tremendous skill, and you may not have time to do it right. If you have to, decide to make the change, plan how to do it—and then just *do* it. You'll meet walls of resistance. Your people will have endless ideas on why you don't really mean it, why it won't work, why it's foolish even to try.

But do it. Reward your frontline people who become customer focused, correct those who don't. Be consistent, be firm, be clear. When they begin to decide you mean it and they'd better fall in line, something will start to happen. They'll begin to have the experience of helping people, of feeling people's gratitude, of their own sense of competence. Then the change will snowball. Just as negativity is contagious, so are feelings of self-worth, self-esteem, and genuine helpfulness.

This seems like a good place to end the chapter, with this key:

> **Key #15**: Every organization has customers—every one. The organizations that thrive and prosper and *feel good about what they do* are those that consistently satisfy their customers.

CHECK POINTS

1. I understand the debilitating effects of being control oriented, staff heavy, and risk averse, and of providing reverse incentives for frontline people in both private and public organizations.
2. As a public manager, I understand both what having a control or an apportionment mission means and how it affects my ability to satisfy clients.
3. As a public manager, I've gone out of my way to see that my frontline people aren't ambivalent toward our organization's clients.
4. As a public manager, I understand what it means to my organization to say that our consumers aren't usually our customers.
5. As a public manager, I understand how important it is to increase my organization's value to our market by consistently satisfying its clients.
6. As a public manager, I make sure that frontline people are rewarded for satisfying clients, and *never* rewarded for just playing it safe.

7. As a public manager, I see that my frontline people are always responsive to our clients, even when we can't give them what they want.

8. As a public manager, I protect my frontline people from pressures to make exceptions inappropriately—so that they can treat all of our clients fairly.

9. Because our organization is so strongly oriented toward our customers or clients, our frontline people are tremendously satisfied with their jobs. In turn, they do a great job for us.

11 DO IT EVEN IF YOU DON'T RUN THE SHOW

"Charlie, this firm just doesn't treat our customers the way we should. If I only ran the show, things would be different."
"Yeah—I know what you mean . . ."

You've almost reached the end of this book. You've looked at all the things you can do to develop a customer-focused organization. You've examined all of the factors involved in turning an unhappy buyer into a loyal customer. You've considered everything—with one very important exception:

How do you apply all this if you don't run the show?

Suppose you're a unit supervisor or a section chief? Perhaps even head of a department. You want your operation to be customer focused, but you can't make some of the crucial decisions. You know what you'd do if you ran the company or agency, but you don't. How do you apply what's in this book?

There are two slightly different answers to that question, depending on your situation. You may manage a unit that deals directly with the customers of the firm, or you may deal only with internal "customers." This chapter looks at each situation in turn. (It talks in terms of a private firm, but most of the material applies equally to a public organization.)

BEING THE FIRM TO ITS CUSTOMERS

You may be responsible for part of the firm's contact with its customers. Perhaps you manage salespeople, or service technicians, or the people who deal with complaints. No matter what your people do, though, they deal with dissatisfied customers. Because dealing with dissatisfied customers is what this book focuses on, this chapter concentrates on that. As always, much of what's said applies to dealing with customers in general.

If you manage frontline people and your firm isn't following the principles in this book, it probably shows up in one or more of the following ways.

HOW YOUR FIRM MAY FALL SHORT OF A STRONG CUSTOMER FOCUS

- Frontline people aren't given the authority they need to solve customers' problems.
- The company isn't hiring the kinds of people it must have to deal successfully with dissatisfied customers.
- You can't give the training that your frontline people need in order to do the job right.
- The compensation plan doesn't reward good customer service.
- The policies and procedures for satisfying your customers aren't clear or are unduly restrictive.

There may be more, but these are the most common roadblocks. They're what you'd expect from reading the first part of the book. Examine each one in turn, and consider what you can do to make up for the lack.

Lack of Authority

Chapter 3 looked at how important it is that frontline people have the authority to do what must be done to satisfy customers. This is never absolute; Chapter 5 discussed some necessary limitations and how they should be stated. Even so, if frontline people can't responsively solve problems for the customers they encounter, they won't be able to satisfy them.

Your company may put tight limits on what your people can do. There may be rigid policies that they can't break. Situations that are just slightly unusual may have to be referred to you or to another manager. They may be expected to "go by the book" no matter what. In other words, they may have little chance to develop and to use good judgment in dealing with customers.

How do you deal with this? The answer to this question requires the answer to another question: How much risk are you willing to take? That question is relevant to each of the problems in this section; it's particularly relevant to this one. If your unit is going to be effectively customer focused, it's going to have to have some authority to solve customer problems. You're the only person who can get it for them.

The first course of action when it's feasible is to try to persuade your boss (and his boss and . . .) to let you delegate more authority to your people. Point out how important that is, how that's the way many successful firms do it.

You might want to suggest a limited test. Identify some increased delegation that would make a difference. Be as specific as possible. Arrange for your people to have this authority for a definite period of time—one that is long enough for you to really see the results. Be clear about what you expect these results to be, the payoff the company can expect from the test. Then keep your boss informed as the test progresses. Be honest if there are problems, but don't let the problems stop you. When (not if) the test succeeds, be ready with the next step.

I hope you can change things that way. But what if you can't? What if the company isn't willing to make any changes, even on a trial basis? As I said, how much risk are you willing to run? If you're willing to take the risks, you can make some changes—and hope that they'll be so successful that the company will come around.

Here's an example. Suppose one of the requirements is that every situation not specifically covered by policy has to be brought to you as the supervisor for a decision. Pick one or two of your best people and agree that they can make the exception without asking you—as long as they inform you immediately what they did and give you a chance to discuss it with them. This is a low-risk strategy, and one that moves your people in the right direction.

There are other steps you can take, other risks you can accept—but I'm not going to pursue them here. You know your situation. You know how much initiative on your part your firm is willing to tolerate, and how much risk you're willing to take. Just remember that you can't avoid some risk. Trying to be customer focused in a company that doesn't focus on the customer as its first priority is neither safe nor easy, but it is important. You just might come out a hero.

Wrong Kind of People

You may work in an organization where a central personnel office makes selections for all of the "routine, noncritical" jobs—like most of the frontline jobs. Or they may apply a quick clerical test that doesn't measure the friendliness or people orientation of the few people they send you to pick from. Or perhaps your firm has been using an employment agency or ads in the paper and you can only make selections from whomever they send you.

Your people are an investment. If any of the situations described in the preceding paragraph are true of your unit, you're investing in trouble. The time has come to stop—*now*. You can't afford another person like this on your work force. (Go back to the very first of the book and reread the story of Saba Zegeye. Now compare what your most customer-focused person does to what she did. Convinced?)

How do you stop it? The easiest situation to correct is the one you cause by giving too low a priority to selecting your work force. All you have to do to change this is to—change it. If there's other, more pressing work, find a way to get it done or postponed. Decide that making high-quality selections is a high-priority responsibility for you.

"Oh, sure," you say—"he doesn't know all the pressures I'm under." That's true. I don't. If you've been making mediocre selections, your selectees are producing part of the pressure. By stealing time now to select well, you'll relieve some of the pressure downstream. Is that difficult? Of course it is—but it can be done.

The next easiest problem to solve, most of the time, is the one caused when the personnel office makes your selections or sends you candidates who aren't the kind you need for your job. Go talk with the personnel office. Explain to them just why the current practice isn't working and what you need in order to do an effective job. See if they won't let you either make the selections or at least screen the applicants for the characteristics you need in your job.

Most personnel offices will try to accommodate managers, particularly if it doesn't involve much of an added work load for them. Yours probably won't. If it will, it may be time to talk to your boss and perhaps even on up the line. You can't do your job properly if you can't get the right people for it. Your management should be able to understand that—particularly if you have a hip pocket full of horrible examples.

Correcting referrals from a private employment agency should be almost as easy. They get business because they deliver the people you want. Unless they're the only one in town, they know as well as you do that you can go to other agencies. You may need to work with them until they understand just the kind of person you're looking for. After that, they should deliver without much further attention from you.

This all takes effort, up-front effort. If you're successful and the quality of your new employees rises, it may take weeks or even months before the results show up. I'm sorry, but you'll just have to live with that. You didn't get a poor-quality work force overnight, and you can't correct it overnight. Make it a priority, then spend the time and effort you need. It's the right kind of investment, and it will pay you continuing dividends.

Lack of Training

No matter how good your people are when you hire them, they still need training. Unfortunately, many companies still look at training simply as a cost. It's hard to put the difference between a trained and an untrained person in an accounting system as an investment. Many companies don't even try. They treat training as a cost, and they try to minimize it.

Perhaps you have a short training videotape. Perhaps new employees are expected to learn by getting on-the-job training from an already overworked senior employee. Perhaps—perish the thought!—your company thinks that frontline jobs are too menial and unskilled to be worth a training investment. Whatever the reason, your people aren't getting the training they need.

Your problem probably boils down to lack of time, lack of money, or both. No one has the time to train new employees. There's no company training for them, and you can't afford the time or the money to send them to an outside course. Your people are held to strict performance standards, and a new employee has to start working full-time the hour he reports for duty. Or the problem is one of another hundred variations on these same themes.

This is a solvable problem. Here are a few ideas that require little time and no money, but that can pay off in big improvements:

- Find an employee who's both very effective and has the temperament to help others. Arrange with her for a set time each day or week. It would be nice if it could be an hour a day, but even an hour a week is better than nothing. For that period of time, her primary responsibility is to work with another frontline person and train him. If you have new employees, let her start with them. If not, let her begin with an employee who's not doing well. You and she both have to agree that the time is sacred—she's to use it for training, and you'll protect her however you need to. Then do it, and keep doing it.

- If you don't have a senior worker who can do it, you do it. If you've delegated responsibility appropriately, you should be able to find the time more easily than any of your employees.

- If you live in a city of any size, the central library probably has videotapes—or at least audiotapes—that will help. There might be one or two on dealing with customers; obviously, they'd be the most valuable. If there aren't any of those, you're still not out of luck. See if you can find ones on dealing skillfully with people, or any specific person-to-person skill that your people need.

  When you find a tape, preview it yourself. Take notes on it. Then, if possible, have your entire work group watch it together with you and use your notes to focus discussion after the tape is over. *Don't* treat training as a one-way process; people don't learn well just by being passive observers. Use the tape as a way to stimulate your people, and give them plenty of opportunities to contribute their own ideas.

• Don't forget books! Books, even this book, aren't substitutes for training and experience. They can be a good place to start, though, and they beat heck out of doing nothing.

You could begin with the appendix to this book. It's intended to summarize everything you've been reading here in a way that's most helpful for frontline people. Another approach is to find a good book on customer service in your local library, read it, then ask your people to read the portions of it that directly relate to their jobs. (This has three purposes. First, it takes a minimum amount of time on your people's part. Second, it shows them that you want them to make wise use of their time. Third, it demonstrates that you've actually read the book.) Try to get the group, or at least several employees, together to discuss the book. If you can't, take a little time to discuss it with each one of them individually. These discussions help them get the main points in mind—and they're a not-very-subtle way of seeing that people really do read the book.

There are more solutions, of course. These are meant just as idea starters. The message is that there are *always* ways to train. Find and use them.

Wrong Compensation System

If you have the other bases all covered, but nothing in your company's compensation plan rewards good customer service—well, you're still in trouble. Your people may get their rewards by playing it safe or putting in their time or not making anyone mad or keeping costs (especially returns) low, or any of a dozen other, non-customer-focused ways. If that's where your company provides a payoff for them, that's what they'll do.

Unfortunately, changing the system is very difficult. That doesn't mean it shouldn't be done, or that you shouldn't try. You should. Marshal your best arguments, show the company how they can make money by changing the compensation plan to reward customer service. They may not listen the first time, or the second, or the third. But keep at it, and develop as keen a sense of timing as you can. If you succeed, the payoff will be worth it for you and the company both.

What do you do until then? The answer is short and simple: Use every way of recognizing your people you can find, and use every bit of flexibility that the compensation plan permits you. Here are some ideas:

- If you go back and look at Chapter 5, you'll see that many of the ideas there for rewarding employees are under your control. Many of them don't even require money. For instance, having a customer give your frontline person a star when she does a particularly responsive job is something you can initiate anywhere, anytime.

- I'm not much on pep talks and other motivational speeches, but they do have their places. You may be able to improve the level of customer service if your people see that you're really committed to it and want them to be. (Remember, though—this means being committed to it day-in-and-day-out, not just when you're making a speech, or once a month.)

- See if you can get accounts of your unit's exceptional service in your company newsletter, if it has one. The editors of in-house organs particularly like this kind of material. Your public relations folks may even be willing to issue a press release to local newspapers if the service was particularly noteworthy.

- Finally, you might steal an idea from the previous chapter. Can you arrange a good-natured competition with another customer-service unit? Of course, there has to be enough similarity that the competition is meaningful. If you can arrange it, and if the competition is on realistic measures, it will make a difference in how your people treat customers. It's amazing how many people will respond to a competitive situation, particularly if they can have fun at it.

There's one final point to be made on motivating your people. Many kinds of recognition "wear out" in a few months or weeks (or even days). Employees who struggle hard to be "#1" today may be bored with the whole program in a couple of months. A worker who's gotten 112 service stars probably won't care a lot about getting a few more.

In other words, if your firm's compensation system isn't firmly anchored in customer service, you'll have to find substitutes for it over and over again.

Restrictive or Unclear Policies

This is another serious matter. Properly done, your company's policies and procedures are the expression of how it intends to operate. Practices and habits may grow up without anyone really noticing, but policy is supposed to be done on purpose. If the policy is restrictive, it puts a damper on the best efforts you can muster.

The first requirement here, of course, is to interpret policy as much toward satisfying customers as you possibly can. This needs to be consistent; you don't want to be liberal one day and tight the next. You should make sure that all your people *understand* it the same way, and *practice* it that way.

Closely tied to this is a point made earlier in the book: Be sure your customers understand the company's policies. This is always important, but doubly important when the policies are restrictive. One of the worst situations you can get into is a sales department that conveniently overlooks the restrictions when they make the sale—and then leaves it to the service technicians and complaint desk to break the bad news.

Over and over, this book has emphasized that customer service, and particularly service once the customer has been dissatisfied, won't make up for sloppy performance in other parts of the process. If you have to enforce restrictive policies, do everything you can to see that the company publicizes these policies. You're doing not only yourself but also the firm a big favor.

Your constant goal should be to persuade the company to loosen its restrictive policies. There's one *caveat* on this: Be sure that the restrictions aren't a business necessity. Most of the time, they're not—but sometimes they are. Check this out carefully first. Then, if there's no compelling business need, go full steam ahead—and keep steaming ahead until the policies change.

Unclear policy can produce almost the same result. Frontline people may be so confused that they're forced to take the safe route—

which usually means providing less effective customer service than they could. This is particularly true if a frontline person went out on a limb to satisfy a customer and then was severely criticized for it.

This is shaky ground. See that your people give the customer the benefit of every possible doubt. Have periodic sessions to discuss both the policy and how your unit interprets it. (One of the biggest dangers of unclear policy is that different people and/or units will apply it in very different ways.) Resign yourself to spending more time than you'd like to interpreting the policy and helping your people be consistent.

Spend the rest of your time lobbying for a more consistent, customer-focused policy. Here, again, there's a caveat: Sometimes policy is murky because it was a compromise; if so, there's the danger that a firmer policy may be a more restrictive one. Evaluate this situation carefully. You may be best off by accepting the frustrations of an unclear policy, but applying it in the way that will most satisfy customers.

If there's not a specific reason to stick with a restrictive policy, keep working to get clearer, more customer-focused policy. If you've read this book carefully, you know how great the payback from it is.

FOCUSING ON YOUR IN-HOUSE CUSTOMERS

Every unit has customers, but not all of them are the firm's customers. In many companies (and public organizations as well), much of the work force never comes into contact with an outside customer. The personnel department fills jobs and provides training; accounting keeps the books and makes reports; manufacturing builds the products; but none of the people in these departments regularly deals with the firm's customers. What do you do if you manage a department like this, where all of your "customers" are internal to the firm?

Adopting the standard that you will do everything possible to satisfy your customers will seldom get you in trouble. In fact, it is the single most effective step you can take to provide job security for you and your people.

In the short run, organizations that provide a product or service only to other organizations within the company are much like a public agency. Every organization that depends on you is a captive consumer. If managers want a new automated report or an engineering fix to a problem, they have to come to you. For this reason, it would be tempting to use the term *consumer* for your internal relationships. You can, of course, if you want. But it seems more realistic, and more in keeping with the language of today, to call them "customers."

In the short run, your customers are locked into the products or services you provide. But that's *only* in the short run. No company is static, and many are dynamic indeed. As situations change, some organizations within the firm grow and prosper, others wither and fade. Instead of using the Personnel Department to find candidates for management jobs, the company turns to an outside "headhunter." On the other hand, the Director of Management Information Systems is given control of all new personal computers. The breaks? Possibly—but more likely a reflection of the firm's idea of the service it's been getting from the two organizations.

Even at the level of a unit within an organization, constantly increasing value to customers is a survival imperative.

HOW TO DO IT

You can adapt the ideas throughout this book to satisfy your internal customers. Everything that's said about being responsive, solving their problems, and creating the expectation of satisfaction in their minds is just as true of internal customers as of external ones.

You may have problems if your firm doesn't see internal relations as supplier–customer transactions. The culture of the company may encourage a more formal, "go by what the organization chart says" kind of approach. Your people may not feel that there's any point in trying to provide superior customer service.

If this is the case, all of the ideas in the first part of this chapter could be useful to you. You need to do whatever you can to see that your people (a) have the authority needed to satisfy your customers; (b) are properly selected, trained, and rewarded; and (c) have clear, positive policy to guide them.

In addition to these generalities, here are some specifics:

- It's always important to be dependable in your dealings with customers. When you've promised something, it should be delivered when promised, as promised. This is just as true of internal customers as external ones. Because they depend on you, it's critical to them that you meet your commitments. If they've called a meeting for Monday to discuss a competitive analysis your folks are producing, and you don't get the analysis done until Tuesday— you've fouled up their plans. Meet your commitments, period. Every customer of yours should be able to take your word without a second thought.

- Be sure that you and your people talk regularly to your internal customers. You need accurate feedback from them just as surely as your firm needs accurate feedback from its customers. You might even want to use questionnaires, in special situations or as a regular practice.

- Help your people see and practice the idea that your fundamental job is to help your customers to be successful. You don't just refer people to them for their jobs—you refer them people who will do the job they need effectively. You don't just design packages—you design packages that will help your sales force sell effectively. If your people believe and practice this, much of the rest will fall into place.

- Let me end this list on a very pragmatic note. When you're dealing with real live customers, they need to know that you want to satisfy them. It doesn't really matter whether anyone else in the world knows it or not. That's not quite true, though, when your customers are within the organization. There's one other person who needs to know you're busting your gut to satisfy them: your boss. I'm not talking about creating some kind of image that your unit runs around trying to live up to. I simply mean that your boss needs to know your real orientation and accomplishments in this area. If you're lucky, your customers will tell him and you won't have to. If you're not so lucky, you tell him—unobtrusively, but clearly.

There are no new keys to end this chapter. All of those that have gone before apply here. Perhaps, though, it's worth repeating the key introduced at the end of the preceding chapter:

> **Key #15**: Every organization has customers—every one. The organizations that thrive and prosper *and feel good about what they do* are those that consistently satisfy their customers.

The ball is in your court.

CHECK POINTS

1. Even though I don't run the show, I take steps whenever necessary to see that my people have the authority they need to deal with customers.
2. I also take the necessary steps to get the kinds of people I need.
3. I see that my people are properly trained and compensated.
4. I make sure they have clear, customer-focused policies to work under.
5. My unit takes our in-house customers seriously and treats them as customers.
6. Most of all, I and my people have a clear idea of the benefits we provide our customers, and we work at providing more and more value to them.

EPILOGUE: NOW MAKE THE TACTICS WORK FOR YOU

The Customer is the long-term investment.

—Rhett Ricart

I hope that you've found some interesting ideas in the chapters you've just finished. Remember, though, that interesting ideas by themselves don't put bread on the table or money in the bank. To work, they have to be applied. This epilogue summarizes the ideas in this book—to help you focus them on your situation in the here and now.

You don't have to go through the sections systematically or all at once. You might want to skip to the appendix, where the key ideas are summarized for your frontline people—and come back here later. Or you might want to concentrate on one or two areas at the moment, then look at the others as the need and/or time arises. In other words, I've tried to arrange this so that you can find and use what's valuable to you right now. If I'm successful, this chapter can be a continuing resource for you.

THE 15 KEYS

The ideas in this book were built on 15 keys of successful customer satisfaction. They were summarized in "About the Book," and they've been restated throughout the book. Here they are again:

1. From the point of view of your customers (potential, actual, or former), your only excuse for being in business is to satisfy them.

2. You don't sell products or service or even benefits. You sell value— or you don't sell anything at all!

3. Customers define value in their own terms. If you want to satisfy them, you have to look at your products or services through their eyes—always!

4. If anything happens after the sale to prevent the customer from getting at least the value he expected, he hasn't gotten the value he paid for—and the customer knows it! In short, you've created a dissatisfied customer.

5. Dissatisfied customers aren't problems; they're golden opportunities.

6. The really picky, demanding customers are *platinum* opportunities. Keep satisfying them, and you're in business for life.

7. If you intend to deal successfully with dissatisfied customers, focus on saving the customer, not on saving the sale.

8. Either customer satisfaction and loyalty are primary, or something else is. No compromise is possible.

9. Your frontline people won't treat your customers any better than you treat your frontline people.

10. When a customer provides honest comments, he's doing you a favor—and that's how he looks at it. Give him a reason to do you the favor.

11. To satisfy an unhappy customer, you must add extra value to make up for the value you promised but failed to provide in the first place.

12. Always treat a customer as if he will remain a customer. Never treat him as though this is the last time you'll see him.

13. Always provide a dissatisfied customer a positive reason for dealing with you again.

14. The whole process by which you create and deliver your product or service must support the creation of customer satisfaction and loyalty.

15. Every organization has customers—every one. The organizations

that thrive and prosper and *feel good about what they do* are those that consistently satisfy their customers.

If you really believe, with Rhett Ricart, that "the customer is the long-term investment," these are the basic guidelines you need to create that investment.

APPLYING THE KEYS

To help you turn the keys into dynamic realities in your firm, here are a series of checklists. They're intended to guide you through the steps you must take to build a truly customer-focused business.

Organizing an Effective Front Line

Select, train and reward frontline people to do everything necessary to satisfy customers.

Delegate full authority to frontline people to resolve all customer dissatisfactions possible within the firm's policy.

Define the jobs of all supervisors and managers so that their first responsibility is to support frontline people.

Define the jobs of all supervisors and managers so that they regularly come into contact both with customers and with frontline people.

Create the procedures necessary to get information on the reasons for customer dissatisfaction to sales, manufacturing, and wherever else it needs to go.

Continually monitor the performance and morale of frontline people to ensure that they understand and perform their job and that the job is satisfying to them.

Continually monitor the performance of frontline people and their supervisors to ensure that almost all customer dissatisfactions are being resolved by the frontline people, not the supervisors or higher management.

Selecting an Effective Front Line

Delegate decision-making authority to frontline people, and train and reward them so that the type of people you need to select for your front line will find the work satisfying and rewarding.

Identify the basic qualities (friendliness, good host, "woo") that your frontline people must have to succeed at the job.

Identify the (nonstereotyped) personal characteristics that your frontline people must have to succeed in your organization.

Ensure that your personnel department, employment agency, or other source of candidates screens applicants for these qualities and characteristics and refers to you only those who possess them.

Spend however much time it takes to properly interview those referred, and select only the best.

If feasible, have one or two of your best frontline people interview applicants as well.

Ensure that all applicants selected understand your specific customers so that they're able to deal effectively with them.

Training an Effective Front Line

Select and reward frontline people and organize their jobs so that they will learn from and use the best training you can give them.

Train frontline people carefully, and ensure that what they get in the training is completely consistent with the way that your firm actually operates.

Train your managers and supervisors first to delegate full authority and responsibility to frontline people to resolve customer complaints and then to support them fully.

Train frontline people that the customer is *never* the problem and that their goal is to save the customer, not the sale.

Train frontline people to never argue with the customer and to focus on the solvable present, not the disappointing past.

Train frontline people to create a successful (personalized) transaction with the customer every time they interact..

Train frontline people in a simple, very effective problem-solving method.

Train frontline people in the OLAF (Observe, Listen, Ask, and Feel) skills.

Use job aids (such as checklists, diagrams, even small "expert systems") whenever possible to replace or enhance formal training.

Provide refresher and update training regularly.

Provide corrective training whenever necessary.

Motivating an Effective Front Line

Select and train frontline people and organize their jobs so that they will respond to your customer-focused compensation system and effectively carry out your customer-focused policies.

Create clear policies that support your frontline people's ability to satisfy customers.

Ensure that customer satisfaction takes precedence over every other consideration in your policies.

Summarize your policies into short, customer-focused statements that you can post in your store, print on your catalogues, mail with your bills, and otherwise communicate to your customers in every possible way.

Create a different summary of your policies for your frontline people, focus on their roles in meeting those policies, and make clear what you expect them to do to satisfy customers.

Support these policies; don't just give them lip service.

Support your policies with whatever procedures are necessary to help your frontline people carry them out.

Establish a simple but effective system for protecting your frontline people from abuse without depriving them of the chance to deal with challenging customers.

Establish a variety of small rewards and recognitions for frontline people when they effectively resolve customer dissatisfactions.

See that the only way for a frontline person to make a really high salary is to be superb at dealing with customers.

Expose every supervisor and manager directly to dissatisfied customers on a regular basis.

Develop (with frontline assistance) a measurement system that focuses on customer satisfaction and that does not sacrifice quality to quantity.

To the maximum extent possible, include customer satisfaction in the compensation plan of every employee and manager in your organization.

Getting Valid Feedback

Remain aware of the limitations of even the best feedback system, and keep looking for new sources of valid feedback.

Understand that there's no intrinsic reason why most customers would want to provide you with feedback. Offer them something of value to provide it to you.

Develop a clear, simple feedback form, focused on the customer.

Ask 5–10 questions that will give you specific, useful feedback.

Provide a place for the customer to sign *if she wants a response from you.* If she signs, be sure that she gets a quick, relevant response.

Ensure both that your frontline people get constant feedback from the customers they deal with and that this feedback gets to the right places in the organization.

Evaluate feedback religiously and systematically. Use it regularly to improve your ability to satisfy customers.

Replacing Lost Value

See that every frontline person knows that his primary responsibility is to save the customer, not the sale.

Make sure that every frontline person understands the concept of value and how he must overcompensate to make up for the value the customer expected but didn't get in the first transaction.

Besides good training and job aids, establish simple, effective procedures for frontline people to follow to satisfy unhappy customers.

When frontline people confront a dissatisfied customer, ensure that they see the encounter as an opportunity, respond spontaneously and sincerely, focus on the customer, provide a relevant solution, and are clear about what they're doing.

Be sure that every frontline person knows whether there are any limits on what he can do to satisfy a customer, and what these limits are.

Give frontline people the authority to say "yes," but limit to supervisors the authority to say "no."

Be sure that your policies will attract the kinds of people as customers that your firm wants.

Constantly review all of your operations to see that errors early in the process aren't causing unnecessary dissatisfactions for your customers and thus unnecessary problems for your frontline people.

Getting the Customer Back

Adopt a policy for dissatisfied customers to do whatever is necessary to satisfy them, and then give them a reason to do business with you again.

Ensure that you and your frontline people clearly understand the difference between doing something to get the customer back and just giving her something.

Make sure that you understand the difference between getting the customer back and playing a game where the customer wins if you screw up. Your message should always be, "come back so we can show you how superbly we ordinarily do business."

Ensure that your frontline people understand that resolving the customer's current dissatisfaction completely is a major step toward getting him back again.

Establish a policy that when the firm has failed significantly to deliver what it promised, it will go to almost any lengths to get the customer back.

Develop a keen sense in your frontline people of how big a gesture to make to get the customer back. Don't make a dramatic gesture to correct a small error, and vice versa.

See that your frontline people accept returns graciously and without question—but that they find out why the product was unacceptable if they can tactfully do so.

When a customer has returned a product and still has the same need, train your frontline people to suggest another product of yours—if there is an appropriate one—or to recommend another source to the customer.

Building a Customer-Focused Public Organization

Ensure that *everyone* in your organization understands that the organization's long-term survival and growth depends on its ability to increase its value to its clients and customers.

Identify the ways in which your organization is control oriented, staff heavy, and risk averse. Develop a realistic plan to correct these wherever possible.

Identify the ways that your organization provides reverse incentives (for safety, passing the buck, etc.) where customer satisfaction is concerned. Begin to change these immediately.

Make sure that everyone in your organization understands that even though you have a control or apportionment function you still need to focus on client satisfaction.

Eliminate any ambivalence toward clients that your frontline people may feel. Replace it with a genuine client satisfaction orientation.

Establish a strong commitment to responsiveness as your ordinary way of doing business.

When responsiveness is firmly established, establish and maintain a strong commitment to fairness to all clients.

Protect your frontline people from having to make exceptions based on political pressure, favoritism, or other criteria that sabotage your overall responsiveness and fairness.

If you detect cynicism among your frontline people, redouble your efforts to establish a strong, honest client focus in your organization.

Building A Customer Focus When You're Not the Boss

Decide what level of risk you'll accept to develop a customer focus that's stronger than that of the organization as a whole— because you may have to take risks to do it.

Get all of the authority you can for your frontline people. Nothing else is apt to succeed unless it's built on that.

Try to see that you're furnished with the right kind of people to select for your frontline positions.

In one way or another, provide your frontline people the training they need to be effective.

If your organization's compensation plan isn't focused on customer satisfaction, try to change it if you can. In the meantime, use whatever means of recognition and reward you can for your frontline people who effectively satisfy customers.

Unless there are specific reasons for keeping them somewhat vague, work to get your organization's customer satisfaction policies as clear and as strong as possible.

If your customers are internal to the organization you work for, use all of the ideas and techniques in this book to move your unit to a strong focus on these internal customers.

No matter what your situation is, train your frontline people to always deliver what they say, when they say. Make sure you do the same.

AND NOW TO THE FRONT LINE

This ends the part of the book that's addressed to you, the manager. The appendix, which follows immediately, is designed specifically for your frontline people and is written directly to them.

APPENDIX: JUST FOR FRONTLINE PEOPLE

You have a position that requires you to deal directly with customers. That means you're a frontline person—and the success of your organization depends directly on how well you do your job. Here are some ideas, skills, and procedures to help you to be as effective as possible at dealing with customers—particularly dissatisfied customers.

THE FIRST COMMANDMENT OF CUSTOMER SERVICE

The first rule at Eckerd Drug Stores is the one that needs to be your first rule, too:

1. Helping a customer will always take priority over any other task.

THE OTHER NINE COMMANDMENTS

2. You're here to satisfy customers. The other reasons for your presence are secondary.
3. A customer is satisfied when he gets value for his money. Because he's the only one who knows when he's satisfied, he's always right.

4. When a dissatisfied customer shows up (or calls up), she's telling you that your firm didn't give her the value she expected.

5. She's not a problem—she's an opportunity. Instead of walking away and griping to other people about you, she's giving you the chance to make it right.

6. To satisfy her, look at the situation through her eyes. Then do what you'd want done if you were in her situation.

7. If a customer is dissatisfied, it's not enough just to give him what you should have provided him in the first place. Provide him something extra.

8. This "something extra" should always include a positive reason for him to deal with you again.

9. When you deal with a dissatisfied customer, concentrate on saving the customer, not the sale.

10. Always treat a customer as if he will remain a customer. Never treat him as though this is the last time you'll see him.

BE GRATEFUL FOR DISSATISFIED CUSTOMERS

You may think that a customer who complains to you is an exception. He is, but perhaps not the way you think. For everyone who complains to you, 19 other customers are probably unhappy but won't say anything. These 19 will tell as many as 60 other people how unhappy they are with you. Of that 19, 18 won't be back.

A dissatisfied customer who tells you he's dissatisfied really *is* an opportunity.

CREATE A SUCCESSFUL TRANSACTION

You may think that a transaction with a customer only happens when she buys something. That's not so. Whenever you deal with a customer, for whatever reason, a transaction occurs. Your job is to make sure that it's a successful transaction. If the customer you're dealing with is dissatisfied, this is how you create a successful transaction:

- Relate personally to her

    To solve her immediate problem and

    Increase the value she expects to get if she deals with you again.
- Use your own common sense and a practical understanding of company policy.

How do you do this? You personalize her contact with you—and this is how you do it:

1. Recognize the customer as a person:
   - Establish eye contact.
   - Clearly give her your whole attention.
   - Shake hands, smile, do whatever is an appropriate greeting.
2. Focus on the customer:
   - Forget any other concern, and just deal with the customer.
   - See her problem through her eyes.
   - Listen actively for as long as it takes to understand her.
   - Clearly attempt to resolve her problem.
   - Either resolve the problem then or agree how it will be resolved as quickly as possible.
3. End the contact gracefully:
   - Check to ensure that the problem is solved or that you both agree on the way it will be solved.
   - Check to ensure that the customer feels good about the contact.
   - Assure the customer that you're available if she has any further problem.
   - Close with an appropriate phrase and/or gesture (such as "have a good day" or a short handshake).
   - Make a final eye contact as you close the transaction.

SOLVE THE CUSTOMER'S PROBLEM

If you're going to satisfy a dissatisfied customer, you have to begin by solving his problem. There are three steps to this:

1. *Define the problem.* You do this by letting the customer define it for you.

2. *Identify the alternative solutions.* This is very important. You should try to think of several ways the problem can be solved before you jump on just one. If you can, ask the customer for suggested alternatives.

3. *Select the right solution.* If you can, give the customer several possible solutions and let him select the one he wants.

AVOID "KILLER" REACTIONS

These reactions are very common, but they'll kill you with the customer.

* "I didn't cause the problem, so I shouldn't have to deal with it!"
* "The situation is uncomfortable—what's the quickest way I can get rid of him?!"
* "The customer is wrong, or unfair, or trying to take advantage of me!"
* "The customer is rude and doesn't deserve for me to be polite to him!"
* "If he's gonna yell, I can too!"

Those are bad enough, but the next two are the worst. Don't ever, ever:

* *Argue* with a customer.
* Treat the *customer* as the problem.

LEARN AND USE THE OLAF SKILLS

If you want to deal successfully with people, you need to master the skills of observing, listening, asking, and feeling (OLAF).

- *Observe* the customer. How agitated is she? Does she seem angry or disappointed? Is she hesitant about complaining? You can learn a lot about her in the second or two it takes for her to get to you.
- *Listen* to the customer. Focus on her problem, as *she* sees it.
- *Ask* the customer for more information about the problem, if you need it. This helps you understand the customer—and communicates that you *want* to understand her. It's usually best to ask open-ended questions ("what went wrong with the product?") rather than ones that can be answered with a simple "yes" or "no."
- *Feel* the customer's situation. This is what's called "intuition"—and men can develop it, just as women can. It comes from reacting sensitively to experience. Having a "feel" for the customer's problem will often help you get to the heart of it quickly.

MOVE TO THE PRESENT

Problems can only be solved in the present.

Customers sometimes want to dwell on the past, on what happened to them. This may have been very painful and dissatisfying, but no one can change the past. Listen, then gently move them to the present and what you can do to solve their problem *now*.

This is another reason never to argue with a customer. Arguing with him keeps you both focused on the past—and it escalates his dissatisfaction.

USE FEEDBACK

Always be grateful for feedback from customers. Be happy with the ones who are satisfied, and remember that the ones who complain are just a small percentage of all the ones who're unhappy.

Use the customers' feedback to improve your skills. Look on it as free training. Not *comfortable* training, but free.

If your firm's products or services are causing dissatisfaction, see that the people who can improve them know exactly what the dissatisfactions are.

HANDLE RETURNS GRACIOUSLY

If your firm accepts returns, this is how you handle them:

1. Accept the return graciously and sincerely. Treat the customer just as warmly as you would if he were buying it instead of returning it.
2. If the customer is willing, find out *why* he was dissatisfied with the purchase. Explain to him that you'll use the information to keep other people from being dissatisfied in the future.
3. If it's appropriate, suggest another of your firm's products that may satisfy the customer's need.

What if you don't accept returns?

1. Explain what the policy is and what you *can* do for him instead.
2. Do your very best to satisfy him within the policy guidelines.

REMEMBER THE VERY BOTTOM BOTTOM LINE

What keeps most companies in business is repeat business. Customers who are satisfied become return customers. Customers who are dissatisfied can also become return customers—but only when the firm's frontline people respond quickly and resolve their dissatisfaction *completely* and *sincerely*.

Whenever you solve a problem for an unhappy customer, you not only remove that dissatisfaction, but you also help persuade the customer that your company will satisfy him again in the future.

NOTES

About the Book

Jan Carlzon coined (p. 2): From Jan Carlzon, *Moments of Truth* (Cambridge, MA: Perennial Library (Harper & Row, 1989), p. 68.

His biggest single change (p. 13): Carlzon, *Moments of Truth*, p. 26.

Chapter 1

This is a book about (p. 19): You can find the statistics in this chapter in a number of places. Three books contain them, which are also well worth reading on their own merits:

Desatnick, Robert L., *Managing to Keep the Customer* (San Francisco: Jossey-Bass, 1987), pp. 4ff.

LeBoeuf, Michael, *How to Win Customers and Keep Them for Life* (New York: Putnam's, 1987), pp. 13–14.

Peters, Tom, *Thriving on Chaos: Handbook for a Management Revolution* (New York: Knopf, 1987) p. 91.

Chapter 2

Studies have shown (p. 38): For instance, see Tom Peters, *Thriving on Chaos* (New York: Knopf, 1987), pp. 67-68.

The assumed benefits (p. 39): John Guaspari calls the overt and assumed benefits "macroexpectations" and "microexpectations). See his *The Customer Connection: Quality for the Rest of Us* (New York: AMACOM, 1988), pp. 52–53.

Significant cuts (p. 45): See Carlzon's brief account of this in *Moments of Truth*, pp. 10-19). In this context, it's quite significant that fare cuts *did not* play a significant role in his turnaround at SAS.

Or, in the words (p. 50): Leonard Schlesinger, quoted in *Inc.,* April 1989, p. 45.

Chapter 3

For instance, Nordstrom's (p. 61): See Linda Silverman Goldzimer, *I'm First: Your Customer's Message to You* (New York: Rawson Associates, 1989), p. 65. This is part of a more complete discussion of Nordstrom's legendary treatment of its customers, which begins on p. 64 of the book.

If you want to see (p. 68): Tom Richman, "Seducing the Customer," *Inc.,* April 1988, pp. 96-104.

By giving more responsibility (p. 70): Carlzon, *Moments of Truth*, p. 63.

It became clear that the shops (p. 70): Shoshana Zuboff, "Smart Machines, Smart People." Interview in *Inc.,* January 1989, p. 33. The emphasis is the author's.

The fundamental principle (p. 71): Kaoru Ishikawa, *What Is Total Quality Control? The Japanese Way* (tr. David J. Lu) (Englewood Cliffs, NJ: Prentice-Hall, 1985) p. 112.

But one of the most basic (p. 71): David Lu, in Ishikawa, *Total Quality Control*, p. vii. Dr. Ishikawa echoes the same sentiments. This book probably emphasizes the complete customer orientation of the Total Quality Management process less than most newer works.

Companies that had nearly given up (p. 71): James B. Treece and John Hoerr, "Shaking Up Detroit," *Business Week*, August 14, 1989, p. 76.

According to Daniel Finkelman (p. 71): Daniel Finkelman, "If the Customer Has an Itch, Scratch It," *New York Times*, May 14, 1989. (Mr. Finkelman is a principal in the Cleveland office of McKinsey & Co.)

Their customer service representatives (p. 71): This and all other material on the Orvis Company is based on personal communications from the firm.

We try not to limit (p. 72): This and all other information on WordPerfect is based either on personal experience or on personal communications from the company.

In an age (p. 79): Bruce G. Posner, "My Favorite Company," *Inc.*, April 1989, p. 99)

Chapter 4

According to Carlzon (p. 90): Carlzon, *Moments of Truth*, p. 68.

Zuboff, speaking of the kind (p. 90): Zuboff, *Inc.*, Jan. 1989, p. 36.

Jan Carlzon said (p. 93): Carlzon, *Moments of Truth*, p. 6.

Carlzon also points out (p. 93): Carlzon, *Moments of Truth*, p. 26.

Unlike many traditional plants (p. 94): *Family*, Mazda Motors of America, V.3, I.3, n.d., p. 6.

As John Guaspari has said (p. 94): John Guaspari, *The Customer Connection* (New York: AMACOM, 1988), p. 44.

Chapter 5

In a customer-driven company (p. 129): Carlzon, *Moments of Truth*, pp. 108-109.

Chapter 6

As she says (p. 133): Shoshana Zuboff, *In the Age of the Smart Machine* (New York: Basic Books, 1988), pp. 9-10.

Linda Goldzimer (p. 146): Goldzimer, *I'm First: Your Customer's Message to You*, pp. 46-47 and Appendix 2.

Chapter 7

If a manager at IBM (p. 155): Tom Peters and Nancy Austin, *A Passion for Excellence: Lessons from America's Best-Run Companies* (New York: Random House, 1985), p. 83.

Chapter 8

Tom Peters has made the point (p. 186): Peters and Austin, *A Passion for Excellence*, pp. 45 ff.

Chapter 9

The basic dichotomy (p. 194): Milind M. Lele with Jagdish N. Sheth, *The Customer Is Key: Gaining an Unbeatable Advantage Through Customer Satisfaction* (New York: Wiley, 1987) pp. 18, 21.

Satisfying customers (p. 194): Daniel Finkelman, "If the Customer Has an Itch, Scratch It," *New York Times*, May 14, 1989.

They're Ricart Motors (p. 195): All information that follows, as well as that on any of these companies anywhere else in the book, is based on material furnished directly by the companies. In some cases, it is augmented by my personal experience.

To satisfy the customer (p. 213): Quoted in Lele, *The Customer Is Key*, p. 75.

BIBLIOGRAPHY

Albrecht, Karl, *At America's Service: How Corporations Can Revolutionize the Way They Treat Their Customers.* Homewood, IL: Dow Jones–Irwin, 1988.

————and Ron Zemke, *Service America! Doing Business in the New Economy.* Homewood, IL: Dow Jones–Irwin, 1985.

Carlzon, Jan, *Moments of Truth.* Cambridge, MA: Harper & Row (Perennial Library), 1989.

Desatnick, Robert L., *Managing to Keep the Customer.* San Francisco: Jossey-Bass, 1987.

Family, V.3, I.3., n.d., Mazda Motors of America.

Goldzimer, Linda Silverman with Gregory L. Beckman, *I'm First: Your Customer's Message to You.* New York: Rawson Associates, 1989.

Guaspari, John, *The Customer Connection: Quality for the Rest of Us.* New York: AMACOM, 1988.

Hanan, Mack, and Peter Karp, *Customer Satisfaction: How to Maximize, Measure and Market Your Company's "Ultimate Product."* New York: AMACOM, 1989.

Ishikawa, Kaoru (tr. David J. Lu), *What Is Total Quality Control? The Japanese Way.* Englewood Cliffs, NJ: Prentice-Hall, 1985.

Katz, Bernard, *How to Turn Customer Service into Customer Sales.* Lincolnwood, IL: NTC Business Books, 1988.

Lash, Linda, *The Complete Guide to Customer Service.* New York: Wiley, 1989.

LeBoeuf, Michael, *How to Win Customers and Keep Them for Life.* New York: Putnam's, 1987.

Lele, Milind M. with Jagdish N. Sheth, *The Customer Is Key: Gaining an Unbeatable Advantage Through Customer Satisfaction.* New York: Wiley, 1987.

Norman, Richard, *Service Management: Strategy and Leadership in Service Businesses.* New York: Wiley, 1984.

Ohmae, Kenichi, *The Mind of the Strategist: Business Planning for Competitive Advantage.* New York: Penguin Books, 1983.

Peters, Tom, *Thriving on Chaos: Handbook for a Management Revolution.* New York: Knopf, 1987.

————and Nancy Austin, *A Passion for Excellence: The Leadership Difference.* New York: Random House, 1985.

————and Robert Waterman, *In Search of Excellence: Lessons from America's Best-Run Companies.* New York: Warner Books, 1982.

Zemke, Ron with Dick Schaaf, *The Service Edge: 101 Companies That Profit from Customer Care.* New York: NAL Books, 1989.

Zuboff, Shoshana, *In the Age of the Smart Machine.* New York: Basic Books, 1988.

INDEX